ARE WE
SPECIAL?

ARE WE
SPECIAL?

THE TRUTH
AND THE LIE
ABOUT GOD'S
CHOSEN PEOPLE

JEFFREY S. REBER, PHD
STEVEN P. MOODY, MSW

DESERET
BOOK

SALT LAKE CITY, UTAH

Library of Congress Cataloging-in-Publication Data

Reber, Jeffrey S., author.
  Are we special? : the truth and the lie about God's chosen people / Jeffrey S. Reber, PhD, LPC, and Steven P. Moody, MSW.
    pages cm
  Includes bibliographical references and index.
  ISBN 978-1-60907-516-3 (paperbound)
  1. The Church of Jesus Christ of Latter-day Saints—Doctrines. 2. People of God. I. Moody, Steven P., author. II. Title.
  BX8635.3.R43 2013
  289.3'32—dc23   2013003089

Printed in the United States of America
Edwards Brothers Malloy, Ann Arbor, MI

10 9 8 7 6 5 4 3 2 1

Contents

Introduction

Members of The Church of Jesus Christ of Latter-day Saints often hear they are a chosen people, a royal generation, and the elect of God. In a broader culture that is more focused on the special qualities, potential, and accomplishments of the self than ever before, it is possible that a Latter-day Saint's understanding of being God's chosen people could be conflated with the broader culture's view of being special, which might lead to a number of problematic consequences, including narcissism. Consistent with President Boyd K. Packer's assertion that a proper understanding of doctrine will do more to change behavior than will the study of behavior,[1] a scripture-based truth about human nature is needed to clarify the Lord's meaning of being chosen and to help members of the Church and others understand and live according to the true origin of their special feelings.

The truth, simply put, is that we are special, each and every one of us, because we are all children of a loving Heavenly Father with whom we shared a close personal relationship prior to coming to Earth. As a consequence of our necessary separation from Him and the veil of forgetfulness, we are each left with a vague but deeply felt sense of absence, of something missing, or, for lack of a better term, of a kind of homesickness. We also have a latent awareness that we are more than just mortal beings owing to our very special divine heritage. Knowing we would sense and feel these things and seek out ways to fill the void that results from our separation from Him, our Heavenly Father provided the means for us to learn the truth about ourselves (revelation) and to feel of His love for us on a regular basis through the Holy Ghost.

There is also a lie competing for our attention—whispered into our ears by the adversary through many means and various media— which tells us that these vague feelings we sense actually signify our uniquely special nature and our superiority to others, that our being chosen means that we are better than others. As with the truth, the adversary's lie offers us a way to fill the void created by our separation from God, but the adversary's way only ever acts as a counterfeit of that which can truly fill our lack: the love of God. In his cunning, the adversary knows that when we indulge the lie and are lifted up in selfish pride, the Spirit necessarily withdraws and our feeling of a void is enlarged. Without corrective repentance and the renewed companionship of the Holy Ghost, we are likely to return to the very artifices which enlarge the void in our lives and lead to emptiness, despair, and often addiction.

The truth and the lie present us with four options:

1) We can believe the truth and believe the lie and become lifted up in self-righteous pride.
2) We can deny the truth and believe the lie and pursue egoistic gratification.
3) We can deny the truth and deny the lie and retreat into hopelessness.
4) We can believe the truth and deny the lie and press

forward with "a love of God and all people" (2 Nephi 31:20) as humble disciples of Christ.

Each of us spends some amount of time living according to each of these four responses to the truth and the lie during the course of our lives. Our goal should be to move more regularly into the way of living marked by discipleship and to remain there for a longer period of time when we are there.

The solution to the problems of the three other ways of living and the key to remaining true to the way of living marked by discipleship is the Atonement of Jesus Christ. When we sincerely repent and genuinely forgive others, the Atonement purifies our motives and removes any trace of the lie from our lives. Like Lehi, we are filled with the pure love of God and we are freed from the lie to act from a place of gratitude and charity—to do what is right for the right reasons. With the feeling of the void genuinely filled, we turn outward to others to help them taste of the exceeding joy of which we have tasted (see Alma 36:24), and we know true and enduring happiness, which is the design of our existence and the desire of our loving Father in Heaven.

As we explore together the true nature of what it means to be special, first, we can gain *insight* into what it means to be a chosen people of God and how to fill the void in our lives. We develop greater confidence as we learn how to separate the truth from the lie and to clearly discern the many artifices the adversary props up to lead us away from the truth. Second, we can receive clear and concrete *guidance* as we learn to discern between the truth and the lie. By identifying the ways of living that tempt us the most, we will naturally desire to move into the way of discipleship and stay there longer. Anyone can increase his or her time in the way of discipleship, even if by slight— but still increasing—degrees. Finally, with a clear understanding of the truth, we may have tender spiritual experiences and receive *inspiration* for how we can personally improve through the Atonement of Jesus Christ. As we come to accept the truth and deny the lie about who we really are, we will feel the Lord's love for us and see His tender mercies in our lives, but we will also look outward as we are filled with "a steadfastness of hope" and "a love of God and all people" (2 Nephi 31:20).

CHAPTER 1

The Culture of "Special"

"Maybe we all just want to feel special, even for a little while, to be fooled for a bit into feeling something besides the truth of our own ordinariness."—DEB CALETTI[1]

In October 2009, several news reports featured the story of a family who concocted an elaborate hoax. They called 911 one morning and claimed one of their sons had somehow hid himself in a large, helium-filled weather balloon that had come loose from its tether and was floating hundreds of feet overhead. Only after the costly deployment of National Guard helicopters and hours of TV news coverage was the boy finally found—not in the balloon but in the family garage! It turned out that his parents had staged the entire event, hiding their son in the garage and telling their other children to act distressed and lie along with their parents about their sibling's true whereabouts. Why would these parents do such an outlandish thing? To bring themselves attention, of course. As the story unfolded, it was revealed that the family had been on a reality television program not long before and missed the limelight they once enjoyed. So they conceived a crazy stunt to get the cameras focused back on them in the hopes that the news coverage would act as a kind of audition tape to endear them to reality television producers, secure them a new reality show contract, and get back the special attention they so desperately wanted.

In a university psychology class, a professor was discussing our culture's fear of death. After asking students which ways of dying scared them the most, the professor posed the question, "If you had your choice, how would you most like to die?" As expected, most students desired to die quietly in their sleep, but to the professor's surprise, one student stated that she would like to be eaten alive by a school of hammerhead sharks. When the professor asked her why she would ever want to die in such a horrific way (hammerhead sharks have fairly small mouths and it would take many of them biting her many times for her to die and be consumed), she answered immediately and matter-of-factly—as if she had thought this all out already—that she wanted to die that way because it would be noticed by the press and remembered for a long time. In short, it would make her famous.

The professor was so surprised by this response that he asked the rest of the class to raise their hands if they also wanted to die a famous death, even if that meant greater suffering. A good number of them raised their hands. Several added that they would like to die in some heroic manner, such as through rescuing someone, because it would make them famous *and* remembered for their altruism. This was all hypothetical of course, but the mere fact that such a morbid thought would even occur to these students is an indication of the lengths some people might be willing to go in order to leave this life in a special way.

On June 17, 2010, a man named Reid Stowe set a new world record for the longest time spent at sea, floating on his seventy-foot schooner for an incredible 1,152 days straight (which means he made no landfall after embarking on April 25, 2007). When asked why he had attempted this incredible feat, the man answered, "I needed to do

2

something great in order to be able to live the way I wanted." When asked what he felt he had achieved, he replied, "I'm in a different state of mind than is normal, and this has allowed me to surpass my human powers and discover my superhuman powers. I'm at the top of evolution."[2] Perhaps he was at sea a little too long.

Nevertheless, his belief in his superhuman powers is not that unusual. Consider the number of athletes who pursue superhuman strength through performance-enhancing drugs or the thousands of women who have undergone scores of plastic surgeries to achieve superhuman beauty. The History Channel even features a show titled *Super Humans* that spotlights people with "special," superpower-like abilities that set them apart from others. Many people desire or even seek superhuman qualities and abilities or special achievements that would land their name in the Guinness Book of World Records among the most unique people in the world.

For the low price of just $2,499.99 (plus tax), you can purchase the "Mega Star Package" from a website named *Celeb 4 A Day*, which buys you two hours of six personal paparazzi following you around, asking you questions, shouting your name, and vying for your attention. You will also receive a bodyguard to keep the paparazzi at a distance, a publicist to answer the paparazzi's questions for you, a limousine, an 8"x10" print of *Celeb 4 A Day*'s gossip magazine cover with your picture on it, and a DVD containing videos and pictures of your experience. You name the time and the place, and the fake paparazzi will be there, cameras in hand, to make you feel what it is like to have celebrity status. The *Celeb 4 A Day* company's mission statement reads: "Our belief is that the everyday person deserves the attention as much, if not more, than the real celebrities and nothing makes us happier than to be able to provide that service to each and every one of you."[3]

What is going on here? These behaviors, though extreme, are not anomalies. Instead they represent a shared cultural concern with being unique, special, and famous that some psychologists think may be unmatched in history.[4] Surely in the past there have been emperors, kings, queens, and dictators who have thought of themselves as being somewhat closer to a god than a mere mortal, but they made up an infinitesimal percentage of the world's population at the time. Today, it is not just those of royal blood who believe they are special, but many of us "common folk" as well.

Psychologists Jean Twenge and Keith Campbell make the case in their book *The Narcissism Epidemic* that "we are a nation fixated on the idea of being the exception to the rule, standing out, and being better than others—in other words, on being special and narcissistic—and we're so surrounded by this ethos that we find it shocking that anyone would question it. Fish don't realize they're in water."[5] Their research suggests that the feelings of being special that accompany narcissism, which for centuries had been a unique luxury of the wealthy, famous, beautiful, and powerful, have now become a full-blown cultural epidemic sweeping over our society, afflicting young and old, rich and poor, male and female alike.

This social epidemic has become sufficiently widespread that it was selected as the cover story of the American Psychological Association's *Monitor on Psychology*. Twenge and Campbell and other psychologists discuss how this increase in narcissism in individuals in the United States might be an outcome of a shift in our culture toward a greater focus on self-admiration. They suggest that we have become a generation so focused on ourselves that we feel entitled to the best of everything in life. We think we are special and deserve special things.[6] Twenge points out that in the United States, narcissism rose faster in the 2000s than in previous decades, such that by

2006 one out of four college students agreed with most of the criteria on the standard measure of narcissistic behavior.

The Pew Research Center reports that 51 percent of eighteen- to twenty-five-year-old Americans said that becoming famous was their most or second-most important life goal.[7] Responding to this pervasive trend, *Time* magazine put a mirror on the December 2006 cover of their magazine, making each and every one of us the Person of the Year.[8] Such an aggrandized view of ourselves approximates and parallels the diagnostic criteria for Narcissistic Personality Disorder, which include such symptoms as requiring excessive admiration, a grandiose sense of self-importance, a sense of entitlement, and "believ[ing] that he or she is 'special' and unique and can only be understood by, or should associate with, other special or high-status people (or institutions)."[9] Perhaps Thom Yorke of the rock band Radiohead was tapping into this cultural epidemic with the song "Creep" when he sang, "I don't care if it hurts / I want to have control / I want a perfect body / I want a perfect soul / I want you to notice when I'm not around // You're so very special / I wish I was special . . ."[10]

What is it that would lead so many people of such different backgrounds, classes, and pedigrees to believe they are special? In what follows, we consider a few possible and popular sources of this cultural epidemic.

Parenting

"Parents may have always thought their children were special, but until recently they did not expect the rest of the world to treat them that way."—JEAN M. TWENGE AND W. KEITH CAMPBELL[11]

According to psychologists Twenge and Campbell, "one of the most popular current cultural messages is telling kids they are special. 'I am special' appears on T-shirts, stickers, and even car seats."[12]

Parents may unintentionally reinforce this message by the unconditional and sometimes unrealistic praise they give their children. Promises of "You can be anything you want to be" and "There's nothing you can't do if you set your mind to it" may sound like the sort of supportive comments that loving parents should give their children. But when parents give those comments in excess, without also acknowledging the real limitations such pursuits will likely entail, and when they refuse to offer constructive criticism to their children, they facilitate an unrealistic view of the child's potential and an underestimation of the challenges of the world that awaits them.

Parents may become so focused on building their children up that they also actively work to guard them against unwanted negative feedback from other sources. Consequently, it is now the norm for every child on a sports team to get a trophy, regardless of their team's season record or how well they individually played. Everyone's a winner! Where negative feedback still might occur, parents may deflect it away from their children by telling them that an apparent failure was not their fault, or that other people were to blame. As a result, children are not inclined to take responsibility for their actions or own up to their mistakes. Indeed, in their parent's eyes it would appear they don't make any mistakes. Consequently, parents' exaggerated emphasis on success and high achievement is rarely coupled with any guidance about how to deal with failure and rejection when they occur. This leaves children ill-equipped for the setbacks and difficulties of the world. It is as if some parents believe they are raising child superheroes endowed with a multitude of superior gifts and abilities who are invulnerable and destined for greatness. Any preparation for failure is simply unnecessary.

To make matters worse, in such a scenario parents' sense of their own specialness may become intertwined with that of their children.

After all, they did contribute 50 percent of their children's genetic makeup, and they did raise them, so any success their child achieves inevitably reflects positively on the parent as well. Thus, shouts of "that's *my* boy" or "there goes *my* girl" are bound to accompany a successful solo trumpet performance or the scoring of a goal. Their child's success is especially important for parents who feel as if their own childhood potential was stymied in some way. Perhaps their parents were not supportive of them when they were children. Their parents may have been critical, or may have discussed failure as a real possibility. They may have even told them they weren't good enough to succeed at something or weren't cut out for it. Maybe their team came in last and they didn't get a trophy, or maybe they didn't make the cut in tryouts.

If their children can succeed where they as parents failed, perhaps they can vicariously experience the glory they've always desired. Freud first labeled this typically unconscious defense mechanism *identification*. Identification helps people defend against painful feelings of guilt and shame associated with their own failures and feelings of inadequacy through identifying with the successes of their children. It is this defense mechanism that leads some parents to insist that their children, from a very young age, play baseball, enter beauty pageants, study hours per day for the spelling bee, take voice lessons, and so forth. It is this same mechanism that is involved when two fathers get into a fight at their four-year-old daughters' soccer game, each convinced *his* daughter will be the next Mia Hamm. The girls probably don't even know which goal is theirs, let alone who Mia Hamm is. They may not even *like* soccer, but they are going to play soccer and they are going to be the best if it's the last thing they—or their fathers—do!

Perhaps these parenting-related features of specialness are best illustrated by the tryouts for *American Idol, The X Factor, The Voice,* and other popular television shows that promise to find the next great singing sensation in America. Thousands of contestants show up to each tryout, certain they will be the next great superstar. Many would-be idols wait in line, their doting parents primping their hair and guiding them through vocal scales. Some of these parents have spent thousands of dollars on vocal lessons, dance instruction, and piano or other instrument lessons, and all of them believe their son or daughter is the real deal. One of the highlights of these shows—and part of the reason for their popularity—occurs when the contestants sing the songs they've prepared for so carefully in front of the judges. Most contestants clearly believe they are nailing the song but the judges are absolutely appalled. Finally, unable to stand it any longer, the judges stop a typical contestant and tell her frankly how bad she sounds. The contestant retorts that the judges, with all their experience and reputation, are simply wrong. Then the contestant dramatically storms out of the room and into the arms of her mother, who tells her the judges are idiots and she is still the greatest singer of this generation.

Media

> *"The celebrity media industry projects the image of a life where all participants are privileged, powerful, beautiful, and charismatic."*—Drew Pinsky and S. Mark Young[13]

"The media" is often described as a reflection of societal values, trends, and desires as well as a potential contributor, if not creator, of such things. In all its forms, the media plays a powerful role in facilitating the culture of "special." As just one example, consider the sorts of stories the media regularly tells us through movies, books, and television.

One prevalent type of story centers on a main character who has a special quality that makes him or her "the chosen one." This character has a special destiny that lies in a mission that only he or she can fulfill which will bring about the salvation of the world. We put "the chosen one" in quotation marks because these are often the very words that are used. For example, in *Star Wars: Episode III—Revenge of the Sith,* Obi-Wan Kenobi used these words when he spoke to Anakin Skywalker during their final, climactic battle.[14]

Consistent with the "special" archetype, Anakin was unlike any other Jedi knight. "The Force" was stronger with him than almost anyone else, even as a child, and it was his destiny alone to overthrow the Empire and bring peace to the Republic. Granted, it took him six movies to realize and achieve that destiny, and his path wasn't always a clear or direct one, but in the end, he fulfilled his destiny as "the chosen one."

Similarly, in the movie *The Matrix,* Neo has a name that is an anagram of the word "one," signifying that he alone was destined to destroy the machines that had taken over the world and to restore humanity to its rightful place on Earth. He too had a special quality, an ability to read and create computer code with such speed and competency that his virtual self was able to act with nearly unlimited power in the cyber world.[15]

Harry Potter, the main character in J. K. Rowling's immensely popular book series, was chosen as an infant to be the one and only wizard who would have the power to defeat the evil Voldemort.[16] Bella, the main character in the popular Twilight book series, has a special kind of blood that makes her extremely attractive to vampires, but also impervious to many of their powers. She alone can live with them, understand them, and even love one of them with a love that is truly unique in all the world.[17] Frodo, an otherwise unassuming and unremarkable hobbit, is the only character in the Lord of the Rings trilogy who is able to stave off the temptations of the One

Ring and fulfill his unique destiny of destroying it.[18] The latest craze in Hollywood filmmaking is taking superhero stories off the pages of comic books and putting them on the silver and the flat screen. Superman, Spiderman, Batman, the Avengers, the Fantastic Four, and others have special gifts and unique destinies to fulfill that entail fighting evil, saving the innocent, and protecting their towns, cities, or even the world.

Each of these stories and hundreds of others like them in ancient and contemporary texts, plays, movies, comic books, and songs alike have long shared this one clear theme—there is a chosen one with a special mission that only he or she can perform who will save the world (or some portion of it) if he or she but follows the path of destiny. What is it about this theme that makes it so prominent in our culture? Why haven't we grown tired of it? Why does the media keep repeating it over and over again, albeit with different characters in different settings and times? Perhaps what makes these stories so compelling is that they resonate with something deep within each of us that we believe might just be true of ourselves. Perhaps we are the chosen one with special attributes and destinies to fulfill. Perhaps we see something about ourselves in these characters and live out our own special missions vicariously through them.

I'll[19] be honest; the night after I watched *Star Wars* (*IV—A New Hope,* the first movie released) for the first time at seven years old, I tried to use the Force to turn off my light switch from my bed for several minutes. I thought maybe—just maybe—*I* might have the same special ability that Luke and Obi-Wan had. I also remember the exciting feeling I had when I watched Neo awaken to his gift in *The Matrix,* stopping bullets in midair in the cyber world. What if I could do something like that? What if I have some superpower-like ability that has been dormant and needs only to be awakened? What if I'm the chosen one?

Then again, what if everyone sitting in the theater with me and everyone else in all the theaters around the world watching the same movie has that same feeling? We can't *all* be the chosen one, can we? How is it possible that so many of us, if not all of us, would have this special feeling? We will speak to these questions further on. Suffice it to say for now that the media may not know where this feeling comes from, but it does know that many, many people respond to it, and that the more products it puts out that appeal to that feeling, the more successful those products will be.

Celebrity

"Don't you know who I am?"

It should not strike us as too surprising that, with the oft-repeated theme of a character who is the "chosen one" pervading the media, some people have come to associate the actors who play those characters in movies and television shows with their characters' special qualities. These actors are already attractive and talented enough to get a highly sought-after role in a cutthroat business, but when they go on to play the character so compellingly that they actually become that character in the minds of the audience, then it is difficult not to see them as worthy of a special form of praise, if not worship. In this way, the media has contributed to an aggrandized celebration of celebrity.

Of course, there has long been fame (and its attendant problems) in our world. The Greek poets praised the fabled bravery of Achilles, Odysseus, and Jason, names we still recognize and value today. Medieval bards sang tales of the conquests of Charlemagne and Barbarossa, and nickel books in the late 1800s practically made outlaws like Jesse James a household name. But *these* celebrities were thought to have actually carried out the brave and noble actions that might have warranted the praise they received (even if the stories exaggerated their deeds). Today, our society celebrates those who only play the role of someone who accomplishes incredible, even superhuman feats.

Our society has become infatuated with celebrities to the point that it could be described as a kind of sickness. We've become celebrity worshippers, putting them on pedestals and hoping to share in the glow of their fame, and even to the point of wanting to dress like them, talk like them, act like them, and even look like them. We see extreme cases of celebrity infatuation on MTV's *I Want a Famous Face,* which features young adults getting plastic surgery to resemble their favorite celebrity. Entire magazines are devoted to detailing the latest news and photos of movie stars, and television programs like *Access Hollywood* and *TMZ* (even an entire cable network, E! Entertainment Television) show us which actors ate what for lunch, where they buy their groceries, and how they look in a formal gown or tuxedo.

We can also enhance our own feelings of being special by making even the remotest of connections to celebrities. I[20] worked in the main office at my high school with another student who was absolutely in love with the pop star Michael Jackson. One day she brought in a photo album with pictures from a trip she had recently won to Jackson's Neverland Ranch in Santa Barbara. Her most prized picture was of her hugging the "King of Pop" himself. When she showed it to the office staff she was actually crying. She had proof that she had met, talked to, and touched the one and only Michael Jackson, and it was clear that this "connection" enhanced her own self-esteem considerably.

Social psychologists call this prevalent self-esteem enhancing technique "Basking in Reflected Glory" or "BIRGing."[21] BIRGing occurs when we can claim a relationship to someone who is successful, famous, or powerful, as obscure or superficial as this connection might be (e.g., "My cousin's best friend walks Tom Hanks's personal chef's dog"), and thereby enhance our own self-esteem. I[22] have a friend who is an unabashed celebrity worshipper. Without fail, she will let me know via phone call, text, or e-mail every time she sees a celebrity. She follows them on Twitter and feels compelled to tell me what they are doing and where they are eating, shopping, and jogging. Much of my friend's time is spent celebrity watching; she is completely up to date on all the breaking stories about celebrities. Without necessarily recognizing it, my friend is trying to feel special by being associated with someone who has been granted celebrity status by the media. Sadly, the association is based on nothing more than mere proximity; that is, on seeing the celebrity or knowing where the celebrity is. My friend has no actual relationship to any of them, but still seems to believe that I and others will think more highly of her if she is in their vicinity or knows their whereabouts.

Research and experience show that this BIRGing phenomenon is particularly pronounced with athletic teams. When "our" team is doing well, then "we" are having a great year and everybody feels good and wears "our" team's colors—hats, shirts, and so forth. However, when the team performs badly, then "they" are having a bad year; in order to keep our own self-esteem from plummeting along with the team, we don't wear "their" colors at all. We dissociate from "them." Social psychologists refer to this latter behavior as "Cutting Off from Reflected Failure" or "CORFing," which we do in order to protect our self-esteem. In light of BIRGing and CORFing, I[23] often wonder how my high school acquaintance whose self-esteem was so strongly tied to Michael Jackson was affected by the events that marked Jackson's later life, including allegations of pedophilia, drug abuse, and his eventual death. Did she CORF and adopt a new, less controversial celebrity to follow, or did she stick with him through it all and experience a roller-coaster ride of self-esteem highs and lows? Either way, she spent, as many others have, a good deal of time and effort hitching her capacity to feel special to the special status afforded celebrities whose glory can come and go.

Another significant consequence of linking our self-esteem to celebrities is that it skews our understanding of what we see as normal behavior. Dr. Drew Pinsky in his book *The Mirror Effect* states, "As we study the photos in magazines, absorb hours of 'entertainment' and reality programming on TV, and stare at our computer screens, we absorb the images, and our perception of what is normal begins to change."[24] When we take our cues for how to live our lives from the celebrities we admire, we adopt an unrealistic view of the good life. For example, the program *Cribs* on MTV shows in considerable detail the living conditions of various celebrities: how many expensive cars they have, how large their houses are, how many pools they have, how much granite is in their kitchens, and how many square feet their entertainment rooms are. Flaunting celebrities' over-the-top affluence shows the audience how special they are—and also creates a false connection between wealth, being special, and a good life in the minds of the viewers. The result is that many in the audience believe they can only be special and happy if they become rich and famous.

The reality show phenomenon may best represent just how absurd our celebrity worship has become. We live in a culture where many embrace vanity, feel entitled, and practice unapologetic selfishness. Reality TV shows have made a fortune by celebrating the most extreme examples of these self-indulgent forms of living. In addition to shock value, part of what makes reality television shows so popular is that they star supposedly everyday people just like you and me, giving them the opportunity to experience the special status normally reserved for "real" celebrities. That is, they get a chance to just "be themselves" in front of a camera and, if they are interesting, attractive, or offensive enough, they may gain a following and perhaps achieve a celebrity status that extends beyond the reality show. It is hard to believe that previously unknown names like Kim Kardashian, Kate Gosselin, and "The Situation" have suddenly become familiar to so many people. Some reality stars have become national celebrities, millionaires who charge hundreds of thousands of dollars just to make an appearance at a party or movie premiere.

For many in our society, watching reality TV and its newly crowned celebrities has become an obsession. If we look at what these shows really promote, we find self-entitlement, greed, selfishness, love of money, backbiting, gossip, envy, and vanity. Jean Twenge, author of *Generation Me,* sees a desire for fame at the heart of the popularity of the reality show phenomenon:

"Many reality TV shows feed on this obsession with celebrity and fame. Flip channels for a few minutes during prime time, and you'll see *Survivor* contestants barely getting enough food, *Fear Factor* participants with bugs crawling all over them, and *Rebel Billionaire* CEO wannabes falling off cliffs. Why do people do these crazy things? Ostensibly, it's for the challenge and the money, but everyone knows the real attraction: You get on TV. For many people—particularly GenMe—instant fame is worth eating bugs."[25]

Technology

"The very act of creating an artfully crafted image of oneself, in words, photos, or video, and posting it for universal consumption

can make the poster feel suddenly important, gratified, glamorous, even powerful. Ultimately, these sites act as incubators for those who harbor narcissistic traits.—DREW PINSKY AND S. MARK YOUNG[26]

Modern technology provides a new way for people to obsess over feeling special and important. Facebook, Myspace, Twitter, and YouTube all present the same message: Look at me and pay attention to what I do. Pinksy and Young observe that "All these innovations in technology and media programming have fueled today's narcissistic notion that everyone is entitled to be famous."[27] *New York Times* writer Alessandra Stanley asserts that Twitter is a "gateway drug to full-blown media narcissism."[28] Essentially people can put themselves on display and create for themselves a grandiose sense of self-importance by gaining followers who make them feel special and important. In an article entitled "Twitter Is a Narcissism Machine" on fusedlogic.com, Walter Schwabe wrote, "With each tweet are we not saying, look at me, think of me, respond to me, FOLLOW ME?"[29]

To illustrate the power of this social media technology to create instant fame, talk-show host Conan O'Brien conducted an experiment. On March 5, 2010, Conan O'Brien tweeted: "I've decided to follow someone at random. She likes peanut butter and gummy dinosaurs. Sarah Killen, your life is about to change."[30] Indeed, Sarah Killen's life did change. She became famous overnight because she was the only person Conan O'Brien decided to follow on Twitter. She started out with three followers and now has more than 16,000. Conan brought her into the spotlight of fame, and soon she started receiving all the perks that fame entails. For instance, a Florida-based online retailer contacted her and gave her a brand new iMac. She was married on September 25, 2010, and was given custom-made shoes and a dress from Kelima in New York. The designer offered her the gown in exchange for promoting their favorite charity, the Children's Hunger Fund. She and her husband were provided with a limousine for transportation for free, the jeweler Classic Creations gave them wedding bands, and a vineyard in California sent them complimentary wine.[31]

YouTube is based on the concept of broadcasting yourself to the cyber world and seeing how many views you can get from other people. The more views you get, the more famous you can become, and the more your self-esteem might increase. The title of YouTube is not coincidental; it is all about "You" and how everyone wants to see "You." Some of the people who have broadcast themselves on YouTube doing the most absurd and outrageous things have become YouTube celebrities and their fame has spread across all strata of society.

With regard to the social media giant Facebook, psychologists Lauren Buffardi and W. Keith Campbell randomly surveyed 130 Facebook users, analyzed their Facebook profiles, and asked untrained strangers to assess the users' profiles. They found a significant correlation between high numbers of Facebook friends and wall posts and narcissism.[32] Some Facebook users update their status every five minutes, letting everyone know what they are doing at almost every moment. It would appear that these individuals believe their "friends" are interested in the most mundane details of their lives, and their assumptions are confirmed whenever they get comments or likes on their status updates. With each comment comes the opportunity to increase their feelings of being special and important. Not only are they special, but so are the chips and salsa they had that day, or the place where they got their nails done, or the mud pie their child made in the yard. Anything that evokes a comment (or a like) from others reaffirms that others care, even if they care about the most jejune of details.

Psychologists have long identified the Spotlight Effect among adolescents, which is a tendency to think that everyone is watching them and is aware of what they do. Now, not only adolescents but also many adults who seem to have regressed to this same adolescent tendency can find proof that they are in fact in the spotlight. After all, if someone takes the time to comment on the picture of my hangnail, I must really be somebody! An absence of comments, on the other hand, indicates a lack of interested and invested friends. A person's life must not be that special if people don't comment on the picture of the homeless guy he gave change to that day or her kid's tooth that just fell out. For those whose self-esteem has become tied to the quantity of friends, comments, and likes from their Facebook friends, a paucity of responses could wreck their fragile egos.

Pinsky and Young warn us that when our self-esteem becomes wrapped up in technology in this way it can lead to "an *urge/compulsion/reinforcement cycle* [that is] very similar to what happens to those who crave drugs or other addictive substances."[33] Thus it is possible that "without appropriate monitoring, these social networking platforms are subject to abuse by those who are most vulnerable to the endless feedback loop they create." We are the first to admit that having a Facebook page can be a good thing. It allows people to connect with friends, both past and present, and establish and maintain relationships that might otherwise not be possible. Our concern is the obsessive yearning to feel special through the use of social media.

Society

"Society drives people crazy with lust and calls it advertising."
—John Lahr[34]

American society's focal point is the individual. Unlike collectivistic cultures which emphasize the interdependence of persons within groups such as the family, community, or country, individualistic societies like America focus on the independent, unique self.

There are many ways in which individualistic and collectivistic cultures differ, but one obvious contrast is manifest in sports. Consider the Olympics. In the 2008 Summer Olympiad, all of America was focused on the swimmer Michael Phelps, who was trying to achieve an unprecedented record of winning eight gold medals in one Olympic games and sixteen medals overall. With each race he swam, fellow Americans cheered him on, in awe of his unique abilities. But it was all about Michael Phelps, not about the US swim team, or about the coaching staff, or about his family or his home country. Can you even recall the name of another American swimmer from that Olympics? It would be Phelps's picture on the Wheaties box and his fame alone that would be celebrated when he got home.

At the same time that Michael Phelps was swimming for gold, the Chinese diving team was pulling off an almost perfect sweep, winning seven of eight available gold medals in their events. Leading this effort was female diver Guo Jingjing, who won two gold medals in Beijing and became the most decorated Olympic diver in history. Despite this great personal accomplishment, when she was interviewed after winning her second gold medal of the games, she only gave credit to her team and her country, never drawing attention to herself.

It is important to bear in mind that neither of these forms of societal living is necessarily better or worse than the other. Each has its strengths and each has its limitations. We focus on individualism in America only because it is the focus of our society.

One limitation of an individualistic society is that it tends to overemphasize what psychologist Philip Cushman calls the "bounded, masterful self,"[35] which is supposed to "function in a highly autonomous, isolated way . . . to be self-soothing, self-loving, and self-sufficient."[36] In this view, relationships, context, and inter-dependence are underemphasized and even viewed as hindrances to a healthy, fully-functioning, independent self. Thus, individualists often strive to assert their autonomy. I[37] had a student in a class once whose parents had named her "Unique." This young woman spent much time and effort trying to live up to her name, trying to be different from every other student in the class. She felt she had to prove that she was her own autonomous self. So she would come to class with her sweatshirt turned inside out and on backwards or with her hair colored neon green. She would blurt things out in class without raising her hand or she would sing out loud in the middle of a quiz. It became a distraction, to say the least, and eventually I had to pull her aside and talk to her about her "unique" behavior. As we talked, I couldn't help but feel badly for her. What a burden it must have been for her to be named Unique. She had to continually find new ways to violate societal norms and be different.

I also could not help but think how representative Unique was of the great paradox of individualistic culture, which is that individualists are all trying to be different and unique together. They all conform to the social norm of non-conformity as they try to pursue their autonomy en masse. I remember driving around BYU's campus with a family member and her friend who were visiting from California. As we drove through campus these two girls commented about the students they saw: "They are like sheep. They all dress and act exactly alike. I could never go to school here." I adjusted my rearview mirror so I could see the two of them. They both had the same pink highlights in their hair, the same black fingernail polish, the same thick eyeliner, and the same style of clothes. They used the same words and the same voice inflection. Frankly, they looked like twins. *Even non-conformists have social norms about how to be a non-conformist,* I thought to myself. What a contradiction individualism can be.

The psychologist Frank Richardson asserts that individualism has another downside. He has studied the consequences of individualism for many years and concludes from his study that "there is evidence that this inflated, would-be autonomous self almost inevitably collapses into an 'empty self,' whose characteristics of fragility, sense of emptiness, and proneness to fluctuation between feelings of worthlessness and grandiosity are often said to be the hallmarks of neurotic psychopathology in our day."[38] He argues that by striving to be autonomous, our focus turns inward and as a result, we inevitably devalue or ignore the social world and lose touch with important communal forms of living. The absence of the social and communal aspects of our lives is in part responsible for the sense of emptiness we feel. It "leaves individuals quite vulnerable to influence from cultural forms such as advertising and psychology, both professional and 'pop,' which emanate authority and certainty."[39] In other words, there is a vacuum created by our loss of communal interdependence and relational responsibility that becomes filled by the messages of advertising and psychology. What are the messages of advertising and psychology? Self-satisfaction, self-reliance, self-sufficiency, self-help, self-interest, and self-actualization. Focus on yourself and yourself alone.

This fixation on the self easily supports a form of narcissism that is shared across our culture. As individualistic society continues to promulgate messages of self-improvement, self-enhancement, and self-actualization we begin to take egocentrism for granted. The problem, as Richardson points out, is that a continual focus on oneself cannot fill the empty self. The empty self can only be filled by an outward focus on meaningful interdependent relationships and communal commitments that extend beyond self-interest, the very things that autonomy and individualism eschew. In this sense, Richardson and Cushman and other psychologists argue, psychology, advertising, and individualistic society in general perpetuate and exacerbate an emptiness in people by contributing to a narcissistic, inward focus on the false pretense of a unique, autonomous self.

What is it that drives society, technology, media, parents, and individuals toward this special status? Is it possible that there is some deeper, less recognized, but ever-present sense that a mundane existence is not our ultimate purpose for living? Might there be, as the humanistic psychologists Carl Rogers and Abraham Maslow have asserted, some potential in each of us that we are not fully aware of and have not yet achieved, but that we feel calling us and pulling us forward out of obscurity? Could each of us feel a kind of void or lack in ourselves that we can't quite comprehend or articulate that feels as if it can only be satisfied by our having a special quality, mission, or destiny? Do we resonate with the story of "the chosen one" because we have this vague sense that it is *our* story, that *we* might be chosen for something greater than just an ordinary life? Are we "empty selves," striving to soothe and heal the feeling of a void within us by striving for special achievements and attributes? At the end of the day, are we special or not?

CHAPTER 2

The Truth

I want to tell you . . . that you are well acquainted with God our Heavenly Father. . . . You are all well acquainted with him, for there is not a soul of you but what has lived in his house and dwelt with him year after year. . . . We are the sons and daughters of celestial Beings, and the germ of the Deity dwells within us."—PRESIDENT BRIGHAM YOUNG[1]

Pre-Earth Life

The truth is that we are special because we are God's children. In word and vision, the prophets were made aware of our divine origin. Abraham, for example, was shown all of God's creation, among which were the spirit children of God, the "noble and great ones" (Abraham 3:22). And God "stood in the midst of them . . . and saw that they were good; and he said unto me: Abraham, thou art one of them; thou wast chosen before thou wast born" (Abraham 3:23). Similarly, the prophet Jeremiah was told by the Lord, "Before I formed thee in the belly I knew thee" (Jeremiah 1:5), letting Jeremiah know that he had a personal relationship with the King of Kings prior to his earthly conception. And to the great prophet Moses, the Lord proclaimed his divine heritage with the words, "Behold, thou art my son" (Moses 1:4). God then showed Moses the spiritual creation of all things, including the creation of His spirit children, the spirits of men and women made in His own image and after His likeness (Moses 2:26–27) prior to their earthly creation (Moses 3:5).

Following Christ's earthly mission, the Apostles assured the early Saints that they were spirit children of the "Father of spirits" (Hebrews 12:9) and that it is "in him we live, and move, and have our being; as certain also of your own poets have said, For we are also his offspring" (Acts 17:28). Here we are taught not only that we are God's spirit children, but that He is always with us, in our every action, sustaining us, supporting us, and giving us life, as any loving father would. Finally, in his epistle to the Romans, Paul makes our divine origin and potential perfectly clear. "The Spirit itself beareth witness with our spirit," he writes, "that we are the children of God: and if children, then heirs; heirs of God, and joint-heirs with Christ; if so be that we suffer with him, that we may be also glorified together (Romans 8:16–17).

Modern prophets affirm these visions and prophecies of old. The prophet Joseph F. Smith, for example, was given a vision of the spirit world that is recorded in D&C 138. Like Abraham, he saw many of the noble and great ones, including the prophet Joseph Smith and other early church leaders. Of these great leaders he stated, "Even before they were born, they, with many others, received their first lessons in the world of spirits and were prepared to come forth in the due time of the Lord to labor in his vineyard for the salvation of the souls of men" (D&C 138:56). Adding his witness of our divine origin and our divine potential, President George Q. Cannon stated, "We descend from this Father. We are His offspring. We possess His attributes. It is true they are not developed, but we possess them; and

24

He desires to lead us forward until we shall be like Him. This is the object of the Gospel."[2]

President Boyd K. Packer described our premortal relationship with God in this way: "He knew you there. Because he loved you, he was anxious for your happiness and for your eternal growth. He wanted you to be able to choose freely and to grow through the power of correct choice, so that you may become much as he is."[3] Finally, Elder Robert L. Simpson poses the question from Psalm 8:4, "What is man, that thou art mindful of him?" His response is clear and resonant: "A loving Father in heaven, concerned for the welfare of his child, might well answer: 'Why, you are my son, . . . I love you very much. I listen carefully each day, hoping to hear from you. I want so to one day have you back where you belong.'"[4] This is but a sample of the many visions and revelations given to prophets that show both them and us that we lived with our Heavenly Father before coming to this world as His spirit children and that we do indeed have a special relationship with Him.

Separation

These verses and quotations make it clear that we lived with our Heavenly Father before we came to this earth. There, we developed a close relationship with Him and knew Him intimately as our loving Father. We formed an attachment to Him much like a child forms an attachment to his or her parents here on earth. He made us feel special, and we loved being His children. We were with Him when the plan of salvation was presented and we chose to come to earth and fulfill our mission. However, coming to earth to fulfill our mission also meant that there would come a time when each one of us would have to leave him. President Boyd K. Packer explained: "It was necessary for us to leave his presence. Something like going away to school. A plan was presented, and each agreed to leave the presence of our Heavenly Father to experience life in mortality."[5] As Matthew O. Richardson has explained, "God's requirement that we leave His presence did not diminish His love for us, nor did it diminish our love for Him. In truth, this act accentuated the deep bonds of our love. Leaving the premortal estate was necessary for our development and growth."[6]

As we passed through the veil of forgetfulness and came into this phase of life, we experienced a separation from our beloved Father and left the direct affirmation of being special that we enjoyed in our close association with Him. Because of the veil, we have no clear memory of our premortal existence, but we do maintain a vague, felt sense of awareness of our spiritual life with our Father. Although many psychologists do not share our belief in a premortal existence, their research shows that even very young children do. A recent article by Beth Azar in the American Psychological Association's *Monitor on Psychology* reports that "children as young as age 3 naturally attribute supernatural abilities and immortality to 'God,' even if they've never been taught about God, and they tell elaborate stories about their lives before they were born, what Barrett calls 'pre-life.'"[7] Not surprisingly, psychologists attribute the children's thoughts and stories to evolutionarily derived cognitive mechanisms, but such attributions are not any more scientifically supportable than the possibility that the children are actually remembering in some unclear way their Father in Heaven and their premortal experiences with Him.

As painful as our separation from God may have been for each of us, and as vague as our memory of our premortal existence may be, it is, as Elder Neal A. Maxwell teaches, a temporary separation. He states, "We define the veil as the border between mortality and eternity; it is also a film of forgetting which covers the memories of earlier experiences. This forgetfulness will be lifted one day, and on that day we will see forever—rather than 'through a glass darkly' (1 Cor. 13:12)."[8]

A close analogy to the experience of our separation from our Heavenly Father can be found in the departure of young missionaries to their different fields of labor. As these young men and women give their parents a final tear-filled embrace, they and their parents know they have an important mission to fulfill and that a necessary and wonderful opportunity for them and for the people they will serve awaits. However, it is still a painful separation. When I[9] taught at the Missionary Training Center, I would observe the last moments these brave young men and women spent with their parents and siblings. Watching them, I couldn't help but feel I was witnessing an echo of a previous departure and another touching embrace. I could almost feel that moment when I—and each of us—left the presence of our Heavenly Father. We knew we needed to leave Him in order to fulfill our mission, and we knew we could see Him again after mortality, but it still had to be difficult to leave. Perhaps at that time tears were also shed by both parent and child. The love of parents for their children is so great and the desire of parents and children to be in each other's lives is so strong that it is hard to imagine it having been at all easy for our Heavenly Father to let us go, or for us to leave. Yet because the mission was so important and because it would allow us to grow and mature, He let us go and we willingly came to earth knowing we would miss Him dearly.

I[10] have a particularly poignant appreciation for the pain of parent-child separation. As a young child, I developed a very close relationship with my mother and she made me feel very special. I would fear any separation from her while I was growing up, whether it was a sleepover at a friend's house, scout camp, grade-school outdoor education, summer camp, you name it. It all made me fear the separation. I would worry for months and months before any event that would separate me from my mother. I shed many tears and came up with many excuses to avoid becoming separated from her. It got to the point that my mother had to be creative and invent what she called "the homesick pill." As everyone else knows, there is no such thing as a homesick pill. Little did I know at the time that I was only taking my daily supplement of vitamin C. However, my mother guaranteed that this pill would remove my homesickness and eliminate my anxiety and worry about separating from her. That little made-up pill made life a lot easier for me. I carried my bottle of "homesick pills" with me whenever I had to be separated from my mother. I tell this story not only to laugh at myself and commend my mother on her brilliant idea, but to show how hard it can be for children to separate from a parent with whom they have established such a strong attachment.

The Void

At some level of awareness, each of us experiences the feeling of a void created by our separation from Heavenly Father. This void is a necessary part of God's plan. By divine design, our Heavenly Father anticipated our feeling this void and knew that this feeling, when properly understood, would incline us toward Him and help us be receptive to the gifts He provides us to fill the void. "We are separated from God in order that we may *voluntarily* return to him," asserts Arthur Henry King.[11] The void prompts at least two feelings in each of us that will aid us in our return to God. First, it leads us to feel as if something is missing in our life. We are not quite complete. There is something lacking and unfulfilled about us. Second, it creates a desire in us to fill this void. The feeling of the void makes us restless and unsettled. We are not content. We need to fill the void even if we don't understand its origin.

In her aptly titled *Ensign* article, "Filling the Void," clinical psychologist Victoria Anderson described an evening where she prayed and wondered aloud with God about why she felt "a yearning—almost a need—to fill every minute with music or television or something to satisfy the void." As she questioned her own need to satisfy the void, she wondered about her clients' needs. "Why," she wondered, "does Sherry seek to fill her void with food? Why does Susan feel a need to fill her void with drugs, and why does Bert seek to fill his void with sex? Why does there sometimes seem to be a giant hole in our lives, even when we want to do what is right?"

The answer to her question came to her as it has to so many prophets and other humble followers of Christ before. She recounts that "after these questions, thoughts, and feelings filled my heart and soul, the answer came in a peaceful awareness. I had lived with my Heavenly Father in the premortal existence. In that realm I was filled with His divine love for me as His daughter. When I came to earth, I left His presence, and a void was created. I felt the void was placed in my heart for my earthly journey so I would seek Him again. As I seek to know and love my Heavenly Father, the void can be filled."[12]

Many people describe their life before conversion as being marked by a particularly poignant feeling of uneasiness or a vague awareness that something was missing. One woman described her adult life prior to finding the gospel in this way: "My life had come so far since my early childhood, but I still felt incomplete; something was still missing."[13] Another convert who had been agnostic notes that prior to her conversion, "uneasiness and self-doubt haunted me constantly, and even at the happiest of occasions, the sad prospect of death and the pointlessness of life marred my joy."[14] A young man who left home at twenty and joined the army states that before he found the gospel, "I began to experiment with living, however, I thought that there must be something more to it than simply working, eating, socializing, sleeping, and then doing it all over again the next day." His uneasiness prompted "a desire to find purpose for my being" and eventually led to his conversion.[15] In each of these cases, we see that a feeling that something was missing prompted a desire in the person to find fulfillment.

Existential philosophers and psychologists have long recognized the *angst* (or anxiety) that accompanies the feeling of the void. This angst, though potentially debilitating, can become a powerful motivation to find genuine meaning and purpose for one's life. In the case of these converts, it motivated them to listen to missionaries or friends of faith, to read scriptures, and to be baptized. We are reminded of the prophet Enos, who wrote of his conversion experience, "And my soul hungered; and I kneeled down before my Maker, and I cried unto him in mighty prayer and supplication for mine own soul; and all the day long did I cry unto him; yea, and when the night came I did still raise my voice high that it reached the heavens" (Enos 1:4). It is hard to imagine a person more strongly motivated to find purpose and meaning than someone praying all day and all night.

Perhaps no conversion story better relates the feeling of the void than that of Joseph Smith. As a fourteen-year-old boy living in a time of religious revivalism, Joseph's "mind was called up to serious reflection and great uneasiness" (Joseph Smith–History 1:8). The young Joseph had met with the various churches in his area but did not find fulfillment in any one of them. His feelings of uneasiness and uncertainty prompted him to follow the admonition of James in the Bible. As he described it, "At length I came to the conclusion that I must either remain in darkness and confusion, or else I must do as James directs, that is, ask of God" (JS–H 1:13). Motivated by his desire to join the right church—but more deeply by the feeling of something missing in his life, namely a meaningful and correct religion—the young boy went into a grove of trees and prayed. The result of his effort was nothing less than the personal visitation of God the Father and His Son and the restoration of the true Church of Jesus Christ.

We also know that Christ Himself experienced the full depth of the void when He atoned for our sins. Having taken our sins upon Himself, He could not be in the Father's presence because God cannot tolerate the least degree of sin. Thus, it was precisely at the moment of His greatest anguish, when He experienced all the sins of all humanity, that He had to also endure the absence of His Father. When Christ needed Him most, His Father could not be there. No wonder He asked, "Father, if it be possible let this cup pass from me" (Matthew 26:39). He was not only concerned with the weight of our sins but also with the separation from the Father that bearing our sins would create. Nevertheless, He did partake and suffered an unimaginable depth and darkness of separation from His Father. In His words, this "suffering caused myself, even God, the greatest of all, to tremble because of pain, and to bleed at every pore, and to suffer both body and spirit—and would that I might not drink the bitter cup, and shrink" (D&C 19:18).

Of this darkest hour, Elder Jeffrey R. Holland has said, "Now I speak very carefully, even reverently, of what may have been the most difficult moment in all of this solitary journey to Atonement. I speak of those final moments for which Jesus must have been prepared intellectually and physically but which He may not have fully anticipated emotionally and spiritually—that concluding descent into the paralyzing despair of divine withdrawal when He cries in *ultimate* loneliness, 'My God, my God, why hast *thou* forsaken me?'" Elder

Holland continues, saying, "For His Atonement to be infinite and eternal, He had to feel what it was like to die not only physically but spiritually, to sense what it was like to have the divine Spirit withdraw, leaving one feeling totally, abjectly, hopelessly alone."[16]

Along with these powerful scriptural and personal examples of the void, we can find a helpful analogy in the many social science studies concerning the effects that the absence of a father or parental figure has on children in the home. Referring to this disturbing trend, Elder Holland stated, "I suppose no book I have read in recent months has alarmed me more than a work entitled *Fatherless America.* In this study the author speaks of 'fatherlessness' as 'the most harmful demographic trend of this generation,' the leading cause of damage to children. It is, he is convinced, the engine driving our most urgent social problems, from poverty to crime to adolescent pregnancy to child abuse to domestic violence. Among the principal social issues of our time is the flight of fathers from their children's lives."[17] In their book *Surviving the Breakup,* Judith Wallerstein and Joan Kelly found that fathers who had jobs that required them to be away from their children for long periods of time had children who experienced numerous negative reactions, including anger, rejection, depression, and low self-esteem.[18]

Similarly, the US Department of Health and Human Services found that children who grow up without a father are at an increased risk of mental illness, drug and alcohol abuse, criminality, suicide, poor educational performance, and teen pregnancy.[19] In the journal *Adolescence,* Stern, Northman, and Vanslyck write that "the absence of the father in the home affects significantly the behavior of adolescents and results in the greater use of alcohol and marijuana."[20] Seventy-two percent of adolescent murderers grew up without fathers,[21] and Knight and Prentyky studied 108 violent rapists and found that sixty percent of them came from single parent homes.[22] Adams, Milner, and Schrepf found that adolescent males who grow up in fatherless homes are more likely than those in father-present homes to have trouble establishing appropriate sex roles and gender identity.[23] Harper and McLanahan add, "Youth incarceration risks were elevated for adolescents in father-absent households."[24]

As a therapist, I[25] have observed these negative consequences first-hand. Early in my career, I had the opportunity to work with incarcerated youth at a juvenile detention center. Many of these young men had been abandoned by their fathers at a young age. Each individual experienced a negative reaction to this and filled this fatherless void through deviance. During my counseling sessions with them you could actually see the void when you looked them in the eye, after you got past the rough and tough exterior. There was a sadness, a longing for something that was missing in their lives. Many joined gangs because the gang made them feel special, it made them feel significant, and it covered up the negative feelings of being abandoned. It is typical for people to mask feelings of a void in their life with feelings of self-importance; it is a classic narcissistic defense.

Filling the Void

The analogy of fatherless children, though helpful in illustrating the powerful feelings associated with the void, falls critically short of describing our relationship with our Father in Heaven, because He is in no way an absentee or neglectful father. On the contrary, He has provided all the resources needed to fill the void with His love. We list seven of these wonderful resources for genuine void fulfillment below.

Holy Ghost: In preparing the Apostles for His eventual departure, the Savior promised them that He would not leave them comfortless, "but the Comforter, which is the Holy Ghost, whom the Father will send in my name, he shall teach you all things, and bring all things to your remembrance, whatsoever I have said unto you" (John 14:26). In the same way, when we left our Heavenly Father's presence, He promised us that we would have the light of Christ to help us know good from evil, and the power of the Holy Ghost to help us recognize His voice and come unto Him. Following the cleansing immersion in water that is our baptism, we receive the greatest of gifts, the personal companionship of divinity, a member of the Godhead, even the Holy Ghost who accompanies us through our trials and tribulations and reminds us with His comfort that we are indeed children of a divine King. If we continue to practice faith and repentance, and renew our covenants each week by humbly and sincerely partaking of the sacrament, the Holy Ghost will continually fill the void in our lives and we will not feel empty and alone.

Patriarchal Blessing: Each of us has an opportunity to receive a patriarchal blessing and hear and feel the veil parted as a loving Father speaks to each of us, His own children, directly through one of His mouthpieces on earth. Like those precious letters missionaries receive from their loving parents, affirming their love for their child and offering support and guidance while they are away, a patriarchal blessing is our Father's missionary letter to each of us to lift us up, remind us of our divine heritage, and offer us guidance and hope for our lives while we are away from Him. President Thomas S. Monson said, "The same Lord who provided a Liahona for Lehi provides for you and for me today a rare and valuable gift to give direction to our lives, to mark the hazards to our safety, and to chart the way, even safe passage—not to a promised land, but to our heavenly home. The gift to which I refer is known as your patriarchal blessing. Every worthy member of the Church is entitled to receive such a precious and priceless personal treasure."[26]

Parents: Heavenly Father also gives us earthly parents to care for us and love us in a manner similar to what we experienced with Him in our premortal existence. While serving as Presiding Bishop, Elder Robert D. Hales said, "In many ways earthly parents represent their Heavenly Father in the process of nurturing, loving, caring for, and teaching children. Children naturally look to their parents to learn of the characteristics of their Heavenly Father. After they come to love, respect, and have confidence in their earthly parents, they often unknowingly develop the same feelings toward their Heavenly Father."[27] Not just during our early years, but throughout our lives, our parents can be a vital source of advice, guidance, and revelation. They can comfort us when we feel alone or discouraged. They are particularly helpful when we struggle to feel our Heavenly Father's presence and to hear His answers to our prayers. At these times, when our Heavenly Father seems distant, our earthly parents can be close, a vital support and a reservoir of strength. They can bear us up when we feel let down. Like Moses, whose weary arms were held up by the elders of Israel (see Exodus 17:8–16), we can lean on our elders when we tire and falter. They can help us endure the dark nights of despair until we again feel the brightness of hope that comes from feeling the close proximity of our Heavenly Father.

Friends: Heavenly Father has also given us a community of fellow servants in and out of the Church. Elder Charles Didier teaches that, "Whenever the Lord's Church has existed on the earth, it has been the organization to help believers bond together spiritually and socially and, by the authority of the priesthood, participate in the ordinances of salvation. . . . At church we develop caring relationships with others—relationships that can help sustain us during times of crisis."[28] Paul wrote to the Ephesians, "Now therefore ye are no more strangers and foreigners, but fellowcitizens with the saints, and of the household of God" (Ephesians 2:19).

When we[29] moved to Georgia, we were far away from our parents and family and did not know anyone. Yet we trusted that when we joined the then-little branch of members in Carrollton, Georgia, we would be welcomed as brothers and sisters in the gospel. Sure enough, when our family walked into church for the first time, we knew we were not alone. So many members greeted us, smiled, and told us how excited they were to have us there. Within days my wife and I had callings, my children were making friends in Primary, and we were invited to dinner at members' homes. Similarly, we were literally welcomed with warm embraces at my new workplace (I worked in a department that loved to hug!). In this community, membership in the Church was not the binding influence, but we were united by a shared passion for a psychology that valued the potential in all persons to actualize goodness in themselves and others. Among the good people we met in Georgia, both members of the Church and those of other faiths, we found some of the closest friends we have ever known. Our feeling of the void was filled by the love of God manifested by their love, their kindness, and their goodness.

Prophets, Seers, and Revelators: God has also provided us with modern-day prophets who guide us with divine revelation from our Father and watch over and protect us. These good brethren are a trustworthy spiritual anchor to help us weather the stormy seas of our earthly sojourn. President Joseph Fielding Smith explained: "I think there is one thing which we should have exceedingly clear in our minds. Neither the President of the Church, nor the First Presidency, nor the united voice of the First Presidency and the Twelve will ever lead the Saints astray or send forth counsel to the world that is contrary to the mind and will of the Lord."[30] Quite the opposite, a prophet is like a lighthouse shining forth the light of truth to pierce the clouds of confusion and guide us through the stormy seas of temptation.

Scriptures: Through His prophets, the Lord has revealed clear and comforting doctrines of the gospel which have been written for us to remind us of our divine potential and God's love for us. As Elder Neal A. Maxwell described it, "Deep within us, [the Savior's] doctrines do strike the promised chord of familiarity and underscore our true identity. Our sense of belonging grows in spite of our sense of separateness, for his teachings stir our souls, awakening feelings within us which have somehow survived underneath the encrusting experiences of mortality."[31]

Atonement: The most important resource that God has provided to remind us of our special nature and connection to Him is His Only Begotten Son and His atoning sacrifice for us. The Atonement literally fills our hearts, souls, and minds with the pure love of our Father in Heaven and Jesus Christ, and the feeling of the void disappears altogether. It is impossible to simultaneously feel this love in its fulness and feel the void. Like light and darkness, they are mutually exclusive. Think of a time when you have been filled with God's love and you will recall that at that time you did not feel empty or incomplete. You were made whole by the Atonement, meaning you were again in a close intimate relationship with your Father through His love. It may have lasted for only a brief time, but it is sufficient evidence that we can be filled with that peace that "passeth all understanding" (Philippians 4:7) during our time of separation from our Father.

Our experiences with the Atonement also reassure us that we can return to our Heavenly Father and again be in His presence and feel of His love on a constant basis. Without that assurance, our lives would be like flying on a one-way ticket to an unknown destination with no return ticket. We would feel anxious, uncertain, and fearful about not being able to have a return flight back home. The Atonement of Christ is like God providing us that returning flight back home. The knowledge that we can go back to Him when our earthly journey is complete helps calm those feelings of uncertainty.

With these and many other divine resources provided for us, there can be no doubt that we are indeed special to our loving Heavenly Father. He wants nothing more than to help fill the void created by our separation from Him.

CHAPTER 3

The Lie

"Behold, here am I, send me, I will be thy son, and I will redeem all mankind, that one soul shall not be lost, and surely I will do it; wherefore give me thine honor."—MOSES 4:1

Along with the truth there is a lie competing for our attention, whispered into our ears by the adversary through many means and various media. The lie tells us that the void we feel signifies some unfulfilled personal destiny for greatness, and that we have a special quality, purpose, or power that makes us unique in the world and more important, special, and better than everyone else. We have only to realize our special potential and then we will achieve the fame, admiration, success, wealth, and prestige that accompany those who are the elite in this world. The lie comes in many forms but each form has the same goal, which is to lead us to think we have to stand out from among others and stand above others to prove to ourselves and to others that we are special. The lie turns us inward, focuses our attention on our unique and autonomous self, and directs our attention away from the divine relationship we have with our Father in Heaven.[1]

Satan, the father of all lies, knows that we each experience the void, and he has designed his lie to lead us away from the truth of our Father and toward pride and selfishness. The ultimate purpose of the lie is to create within us an ever-expanding sense of the void that approximates his own misery, which resulted from his prideful downfall and his eternal separation from his Father. C. S. Lewis had a particularly clear understanding of Satan's lie, which he shares with us in *Mere Christianity:*

"The moment you have a self at all, there is a possibility of putting yourself first—wanting to be the centre—wanting to be God, in fact. That was the sin of Satan: and that was the sin he taught the human race. Some people think the fall of man had something to do with sex, but that is a mistake. . . . What Satan put into the heads of our remote ancestors was the idea that they could 'be like gods'— could set up on their own as if they had created themselves—be their own masters—invent some sort of happiness for themselves outside God, apart from God. And out of that hopeless attempt has come . . . the long terrible story of man trying to find something other than God which will make him happy."[2]

At the center of the lie is the proclamation, "Glory be to me!" The lie turns us away from our special relationship with our Father in Heaven toward the presumed special nature of our self, which is, at its heart, pride. President Dieter F. Uchtdorf stated that pride is a "gateway sin" that leads to an abundance of other weaknesses. He continues, "It leads some to revel in their own perceived self-worth, accomplishments, talents, wealth, or position. They count these blessings as evidence of being 'chosen,' 'superior,' or 'more righteous' than others. This is the sin of 'Thank God I am more special than you.' At its core is the desire to be admired or envied. It is the sin of self-glorification."[3]

Many of the examples and potential sources of the culture of "special" we talked about in the first chapter are rooted in the lie. We can also find many scriptural illustrations of those who believed the lie. Here are a few notable examples:

Judas Iscariot was hand-selected by the Lord Himself. As an Apostle, he had ample opportunity to feel his Heavenly Father's love, yet he betrayed the Savior for thirty pieces of silver. We can't be sure of Judas's intentions. Perhaps he was jealous of Christ, or he may have been consumed by greed, or he may have just hated himself and anyone's happiness was his despair. Whatever his intentions, he allowed himself to believe the lie that led him to betray his Lord and allowed Satan to "[enter] into him" (John 13:27). Because he hearkened to the lie and not to the truth, "it had been good for that man if he had not been born" (Matthew 26:24).

Cain came to believe the lie when he put more emphasis on earthly concerns than on heavenly virtue. So powerful was his jealousy that he sought the guidance of the adversary to gain power over his brother and even to rule over Satan (see Moses 5:23). On this latter point, Hugh Nibley writes:

"Cain rule over Satan? Yes, that is the arrangement—the devil serves his client, gratifies his slightest whim, pampers his appetites, and is at his beck and call throughout his earthly life, putting unlimited power and influence at his disposal through his command of the treasures of the earth, gold and silver. But in exchange the victim must keep his part of the agreement, following Satan's instructions on earth and remaining in his power hereafter. That is the classic bargain, the pact with the Devil, by which a Faust, Don Juan, Macbeth, or Jabez Stone achieve the pinnacle of earthly success and the depths of eternal damnation."[4]

The Zoramites were made up of two groups. 1) The poor, who were humbled by their poverty and ostracism, and 2) the wealthy, who became a prideful people, boasted about their worldly treasures, and began to worship idols. The wealthy Zoramites prayed atop their Rameumptom to be seen and admired by their peers, to mistakenly thank God for being special and chosen above all other people, and to brag about their righteousness. They excluded and persecuted the poor among them and did not allow them in their churches. They truly believed they were blessed with wealth because of their "righteousness" and chosen status. In Alma 31:16–18, we read the words of their vain prayers: "Holy God, we believe that thou hast separated us from our brethren; . . . we believe that thou hast elected us to be thy holy children; . . . and thou hast elected us that we shall be saved, whilst all around us are elected to be cast by thy wrath down to hell. . . . And again we thank thee, O God, that we are a chosen and a holy people. Amen." Clearly, they believed the lie.

The Nephites as a whole were a people who often believed the lie and were eventually destroyed because of it. In Helaman 4:12–13, we read of the consequences of their believing the lie:

"And it was because of the pride of their hearts, because of their exceeding riches, yea, it was because of their oppression to the poor, withholding their food from the hungry, withholding their clothing from the naked, and smiting their humble brethren upon the cheek, making a mock of that which was sacred, denying the spirit of prophecy and of revelation, murdering, plundering, lying, stealing, committing adultery, rising up in great contentions, and deserting away into the land of Nephi, among the Lamanites—and because of this their great wickedness, and their boastings in their own strength, they were left in their own strength; therefore they did not prosper, but were afflicted and smitten, and driven before the Lamanites, until they had lost possession of almost all their lands."

Enlarging the Lie

As with the truth, the adversary's lie offers us a way to fill the void created by our separation from God, but the adversary's way only ever acts as a counterfeit to that alone which can truly fill our lack, which is the pure love of God. In his cunning, the adversary knows that when we indulge the lie and are lifted up in selfish pride, the Spirit necessarily withdraws and our feeling of the void is enlarged. Satan tries to convince us that indulging desires to be better than others is the way to be happy; that happiness is found in realizing our uniquely special potential. However, what the lie conceals from us is the real consequence of our selfish pursuits. As we pursue worldly ambitions and look for happiness in prideful comparison and self-satisfaction, we inevitably end up feeling more empty and incomplete than we did before.

It is at this point that the adversary increases his efforts to ensnare us by whispering the lie again in our ears and trying to persuade us that we have to work even harder now to achieve our goal of being more special than others, or that we need to change our goals to other selfish pursuits that will bring happiness. Either way, the lie convinces us that we need to do more to realize our unique potential. As we focus on the next set of prideful achievements and increase our efforts to feel special and unique, the Spirit continues to withdraw and the feeling that something is missing, the feeling of the void, grows even larger. Our appetites become insatiable. Those caught in this lie-fulfilling cycle who do not humble themselves and change become locked into a never-ending, void-enlarging tragedy, continually seeking artifices or idols that are empty substitutes for the pure love of God, which can only be received and felt through the Holy Spirit.

Each of us can identify in ourselves our own tendency toward falling into this void-enlarging tragedy when we allow ourselves to think the words, "Once I _____, *then* I'll be happy." Some of us can remember thinking as a freshman in high school how awful it was not to have the freedom of the juniors and seniors who could drive to and from campus and leave for lunch. We can recall the words coming to our minds, "Once I get my license and can drive, then I'll be happy." Then we turned sixteen and received our license and that was great—for a while. But then we realized a license isn't really enough. We still had to ask our parents if we could borrow the car, and that was a pain. So we began to think, "Once I get my own car, then I'll be happy." And for some, the cycle continues on and on. "Once I graduate high school," "once I marry," "once I get my master's degree," "once I get a job," "once I have kids," "once I get my dream house," "once I make my first million," "once I retire."

Despite all our efforts to obtain these things that are supposed to make us happy, the happiness we desire continues to elude us. Our desire for happiness grows larger than it was before because our feeling of being incomplete, our sense of something lacking, enlarges. What is so surprising about this void-enlarging tragedy is that we often don't see how caught up we have become in the lie and how futile our efforts to fill the void with the next material good or worldly accomplishment prove to be. This is the cruel self-deception of the void-enlarging tragedy. We actually believe things *will* be different once we achieve our next goal.

While there are many counterfeits that Satan uses to substitute for the truth, none have been more effectively used than wealth, power, fame, and sex. Religions have long recognized the temptation of these four idols and their potential for self-destruction. The Hindus teach a parable called "The Wish-Fulfilling Tree" that illustrates the void-enlarging tragedy created by the pursuit of these four artifices. The wish fulfilling tree is described as a magical tree that a person can stand under and wish for whatever they want. And they get what they want—"and with it its opposite, guaranteed." Children, first introduced to the tree, wish for candy, which they receive in abundance, and then they get stomachaches. They give up on candy and wish for toys. They get toys, and with the toys they get boredom. Then they wish for "bigger and better toys," and with the bigger and better toys they get even more boredom.

Eventually, the children become young adults and their wishes change to the four fruits that hang from the branches of the tree, which are wealth, power, fame, and sexual pleasure. As with the candy and the toys, with the granting of each wish the young adults also receive its opposite, guaranteed. So they ask for "wealth, power, fame, sexual pleasure—and they get these, but also cupidity, insomnia, anxiety, and frustration/disease."[5] And the young adults become miserable, and now there is nowhere else to go. The tree is everywhere—they can't get out from under it. They are caught in the void-enlarging tragedy, what one storyteller refers to as "the cosmic swindle of life."[6] This is where we all are, the storyteller suggests. There is no way to escape it. Or is there? "Yes there is," the storyteller assures us. "Parables don't end like that."[7]

We will return to this parable of the wish-fulfilling tree in the concluding chapter of this book and will discuss the answer it gives for a way out of this cycle of attachment there. For now, suffice it to say that the void-enlarging tragedy that results when we pursue counterfeits for the love of God is well-known among religious faiths as it is among a growing number of psychologists. It is so well-known and so difficult to avoid because, as the Savior taught, when we place the desires of our hearts on these things and lose sight of the truth, we become entangled in the lie and our heart belongs to Satan: "And thus he whispereth in their ears, until he grasps them with his awful chains, from whence there is no deliverance" (2 Nephi 28:22).

Perhaps no one understands the captivity of the void-enlarging cycle better than those who suffer from addiction. The addict lives by a false belief that if he could just get his fix he'd be fine. However, the fix is never enough; more is always needed. The addict begins with the same void we all experience. As one drug addict put it, "I had always had this feeling of sort of insecurity and, I don't know, like there was this hole inside of me."[8] At some point the addict is presented with an apparent opportunity to feel better, a way to escape the feeling of a hole inside of her. It could be a friend offering a drug, an image or video encountered on the Internet, or it could be the comfort found in overeating after a difficult day. Of the myriad temptations toward addiction, clinical and forensic psychologist Dr. Stephen Diamond explains that "we all have our personal addictions: workaholism, rationalism, shopaholism, perfectionism, etc. This is our futile attempt to fill a spiritual and emotional emptiness within, to gratify some long-buried need, to heal or at least numb some festering psychological wound."[9]

By indulging these temptations, the addict feels such things as temporary relief, distraction, or excitement that give him or her a false and fleeting feeling of fulfillment. Elder M. Russell Ballard notes the expertise of the adversary in using these things: "Satan knows how to exploit and ensnare us with artificial substances and behaviors of temporary pleasure."[10] A post on a food addiction blog shares the experience of a woman struggling with overeating. The post states that "one of her main triggers is loneliness" and that she ate to fill a void in her life. She continues, "Many times we eat to replace something that is missing in our lives. It only feels good for a short period of time and, depending on what we eat, we can end up feeling much worse and depressed. We think of food as some treat that will make everything better—but it never does—we are just left feeling sick and fat."[11]

As this post reveals, the false fulfillment that an artifice for God's love provides is short-lived. As its effects wear off, the feeling of the void quickly returns, only now the feeling is exacerbated by the guilt and shame we feel for indulging the lie. The feeling of the void has grown larger, making our feelings of something lacking more poignant and our desire to fill the void stronger. Our mind recalls our previous indulgence and, against all reason, we convince ourselves that the very food, pornography, or drug that ultimately increased our unhappiness before will now magically make us feel better, and we go after the artifice with increased vigor. We pursue the artifice without realizing that the void has enlarged and we will need more of the artifice to achieve the same level of false fulfillment as before.

Beyond the biological tolerance that may develop, the increase in the void that follows each addictive act can itself necessitate our "upping the dosage" of whatever artifice we mistakenly pursue. Eventually, we will hit the upper limit of the artifice's ability to provide sufficient pleasure to temporarily offset the now very large feeling of the void in our heart, and we will be left fully exposed to the feeling that results from our separation from our Father. People suffering from addiction refer to this experience as "hitting rock bottom." At this point, the addict can no longer live the false pretense that the artifice can fill the void. Consequently, he or she must either give up on the possibility of pleasure or happiness altogether, as some do, which can lead to giving up on living, or the addict will turn his or her attention to another artifice and perpetuate the void-enlarging cycle, fully believing things will be different this time. Or addicts will turn toward the truth and begin to accept the genuine resources of God's love and true void fulfillment in their lives.

The Quadrants

Four Ways of Living in Response to the Truth and the Lie

As illustrated by our addict example, our response to the truth and the lie will have significant consequences for our agency. On the one hand, when we yield to the enticing of the truth, the feeling of the void is attenuated and we are freed from our concern with ourselves to serve God and others (see figure 1). In other words, our agency is maximized. On the other hand, when we listen to the adversary's lie, the feeling of the void enlarges, filling the void becomes an obsession, and we grow ever more dependent on Satan's artifices (see figure 2). Our agency is severely compromised.

Knowing what is at stake in our response to the truth and the lie, the prophets have always taught the importance of using our agency wisely. Lehi taught his son Jacob that, "men are free according to the flesh; and all things are given them which are expedient unto man. And they are free to choose liberty and eternal life, through the great Mediator of all men, or to choose captivity and death, according to the captivity and power of the devil; for he seeketh that all men might be miserable like unto himself (2 Nephi 2:27). In this verse, Lehi first assures his son that his Heavenly Father has provided all the resources needed to feel His love and make the right choice. Then, Lehi lets his son know what the consequences of the choices available are: liberty and eternal life, or captivity and death. Finally, Lehi teaches Jacob the motivation behind Satan's lie: The adversary is miserable and wants us to be miserable like unto himself.

For Satan, the feeling of the void is all-consuming. He was cast out of the presence of his Father because he rebelled against Him and chose darkness over the light. Believing his own lie, he pursued the artifices of power, glory, and superiority. He tried to be special, above all others, even God. By so doing, he lost all hope of ever reuniting with his Father and other loved ones. The feeling of the void created by his separation from the Father is eternal and cannot be reduced. Thus, he is left to his own devices, to his artifices, but they are of little comfort. He can feel pleasure, as he surely does when we become "miserable like unto himself," but he cannot feel joy. He can feel power, as he does when he holds us captive with his chains, but he knows nothing of the liberating power of Christ's mercy and forgiveness. And he can receive a modicum of worldly glory from those who follow him and serve him, but he can never know the glory of being reunited with the most glorified One of all, our Father in Heaven, and feeling again His warm embrace. He is perpetually at "rock bottom"; his only consolation is found in getting others to join him there.

The enticements of the truth and the lie provide us with four choices—or ways of exercising our agency—that we have organized into quadrants (see table 1).

1) We can accept the truth *and* accept the lie. When we accept the truth and accept the lie, we believe that we are chosen of God and we believe that we are better than others because of it. The exemplar we will use to illustrate this way of living is the Pharisee.
2) We can deny the truth and accept the lie. When we deny the truth and accept the lie, then we seek only to pursue our own special destiny or satisfy our selfish desires. By

doing so, we deny the existence of God in our life. The exemplar of the Egoist illustrates this way of living.

3) We can deny the lie *and* deny the truth. When we deny the lie and deny the truth, we dismiss the very notion of being special in any way, either from God or our own special achievements. The Nihilist will be our exemplar of this way of living.

	Accept the Truth	Deny the Truth
Accept the Lie	Pharisees	Egoists
Deny the Lie	Disciples	Nihilists

4) We can accept the truth and deny the lie. When we accept the truth and deny the lie, we acknowledge that we are special because we are children of God, but we deny that this makes us better than others. Our exemplar for this way of living is the Disciple.

We will address each exemplar in the chapters that follow, but before doing so we issue the following caveat: These quadrants and their respective exemplars do *not* represent distinct personality types. The four ways of living in response to the truth and the lie are not character traits or inherent attributes of a person. Rather, they represent choices, or more exactly, ways of exercising our agency that are usually fluid and changing. Indeed, as our circumstances change, so do the possibilities for living out our response to the truth and the lie. Thus, we are always choosing our response to the truth and the lie and are therefore regularly moving through and among all four of these ways of living.

This is not to say that a person cannot feel stuck or locked into a particular quadrant for an extended period of time. Indeed, this is likely the case when we accept the lie and pursue artifices for God's love, as in the case of the addict. Still, we caution readers against placing themselves or others in solely one of the quadrants. All of us spend some amount of time responding to the truth and the lie in each of these four ways, often on a daily, if not hourly, basis.

We also warn readers against equating the exemplar with the quadrant it represents. The exemplars are illustrations of different ways of living in relation to the truth and the lie. There are many other representative groups we could have used to exemplify the

Agency and the Void

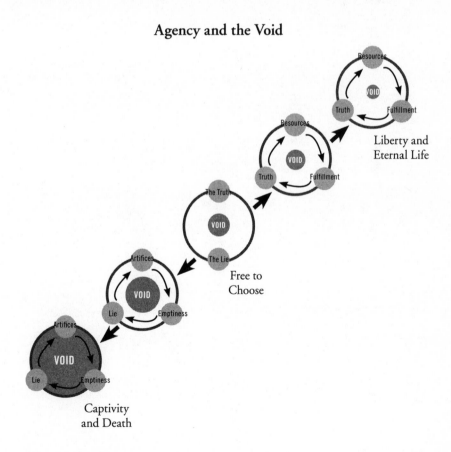

quadrants. We chose these exemplars because they obviously illustrate each way of living and are most likely to resonate with the readers' own choices in response to the truth and the lie. We expect there are numerous other ways to live the truth and the lie that we will not cover and we encourage the reader to identify those ways that apply to him- or herself.

CHAPTER 4

The Pharisee

But woe unto you, scribes and Pharisees, hypocrites! for ye shut up the kingdom of heaven against men: for ye neither go in yourselves, neither suffer ye them that are entering to go in.
—MATTHEW 23:13

The Pharisees of Christ's time accepted the truth that the Jews were chosen by God to be His covenant people. Their holy scriptures confirmed their special status: "For thou art an holy people unto the Lord thy God: the Lord thy God hath chosen thee to be a *special* people unto himself, above all people that are upon the face of the earth" (Deuteronomy 7:6; emphasis added). The Pharisees also accepted the lie that their special status made them superior to other people, even other Jews. The Bible dictionary teaches that the Pharisees were "a religious party among the Jews. The name denotes separatists. They prided themselves on their strict observance of the law, and on the care with which they avoided contact with things gentile."[1] The Pharisees did not believe they had been separated from other equals; they believed they stood above the sinner and the heathen, the unchosen and the uncircumcised, and ultimately even above

Christ. Consequently, the Pharisees "were a major obstacle to the re-
ception of Christ and the gospel by the Jewish people."[2]

Although the Pharisees were lifted up above all others by the lie,
they shut up the kingdom of heaven against themselves. As we will
see throughout this chapter, one of the great paradoxes of Pharisaism
is that Pharisees demand strict adherence to a law that they themselves are not capable of living. This is why Christ said, regarding the
Pharisees and the kingdom of heaven, "ye neither go in yourselves."
This paradox lies at the heart of their famed hypocrisy and shows the
Pharisees to be prototypical perfectionists. They can be the chosen
people of God and live closer to perfect obedience to the law than
anyone else, but they still fall short of the absolute standard of flawlessness that the law demands.[3]

Because they inevitably fall short of the unattainable standard of
perfect obedience to the law, the Pharisees' only consolation is found
in the lie that they are closer to perfection than others. They can
look down their noses at the sinner and the Gentile and know that
even though no person is justified by the law, they are closer to being
justified than these depraved souls. Their only solace, then, meager
though it might be, is the pride they take in being more righteous
than others, even if that righteousness does not ultimately count.
In this way, the Pharisees take their reward in this life because they
have no hope for a reward in the next.[4] And how do they take their
reward? By lording their moral rectitude over others. In doing so,
Pharisees are reminiscent of Satan himself, against whom the kingdom of heaven is truly shut and who can only find the slightest consolation in holding the souls of other men captive by claiming his
lordship over them.

This brings us to a second way in which the Pharisees shut
up heaven—they will not "suffer them that are entering to go in"

(Matthew 23:13). This phrase has three important meanings. One is that the Pharisees deny others the possibility of getting into heaven. Their attitude is one of, "If I am not able to get into heaven with all of my obedience and righteousness, then you, a lowly sinner, certainly have no chance." This keeps the sinners down and the Pharisees up, maintaining their separatist status quo.

A second, more subtle meaning in the phrase is that the very sinners the Pharisees will not suffer to go in "are entering" the kingdom of Heaven. This turns the whole perspective of the Pharisees on its head and shows the self-defeating hypocrisy of their belief system in bold relief. Christ, through the Atonement, allowed the very people the Pharisees tried to shut heaven against to enter the kingdom where the Pharisees themselves were not worthy to go. Even with all their imperfections and inadequacy before the law, the sinners, because they trusted wholly in the grace of their Savior, repented of all their sins and gained entry into heaven. This means that the law that justifies the Pharisees' separatism in this life is of no real effect in the kingdom of heaven. All who come unto Christ are acceptable to Him. Only the Pharisees, because they have been deceived by the lie of the adversary, exclude themselves from entry into their Heavenly Father's presence.

Finally, this phrase shows that the Pharisees made the critical mistake of acting as if they had control over the gates of the kingdom of heaven. Their hubris led them to put themselves in the place of God and behave as if people's entry into heaven was somehow up to them, as if it was their place to stand in final judgment on others—and themselves. It also fueled their strong resistance to Christ's claims of divinity and inflamed their anger toward Him, resulting ultimately in their call for His crucifixion. They fancied themselves the judges of men's souls and would not surrender themselves and their judgment seat to the true judge, especially when He seemed so willing to forgive and let those into heaven who, from the Pharisees' perspective, had absolutely no right to go there. How dare Christ forgive the unforgivable sinner? More importantly, how dare He judge the Pharisees, the chosen vessels of God, so harshly when it was their right to judge? Who was He to do such things? Time and again we read how Christ's strait way collides with the Pharisees' crooked paths.

Christ makes clear the difference between the strait way of His gospel and this crooked path of the Pharisee in the Parable of the Pharisee and the Publican found in Luke 18. Christ shared the parable with those who thought they were more righteous than others to teach them the consequences of their actions. Christ related, "Two men went up into the temple to pray; the one a Pharisee, and the other a publican" (Luke 18:10). It is important to note that publicans (tax collectors) were not well-liked by the people and were especially disliked by the Pharisees because they were suspected of being dishonest in their collections and charging too much for their services.

When the Pharisee arrived at the temple and prayed to God, he did not repent. There was no need. Instead, he thanked God that he was not a sinner like the publican, and then went on to boast in his prayer about how much he fasted and how he paid an honest tithe. He pretended perfection.

The publican also offered up a prayer to God at the temple, but his was much different from that of the Pharisee. The publican humbly bowed his head, genuinely accepted his sin, was sincerely sorry for it, and asked God for forgiveness. The publican knew he had sinned and wanted to repent for it but the Pharisee acted as if he had no sins and did not need help from God. God granted the publican forgiveness and he "went down to his house justified." The Pharisee, on the other hand, was "abased" for his pretense of perfection and for his one-upmanship toward the publican.

Modern-Day Pharisees

Members of the Church are susceptible to the way of living represented by the Pharisee because, like the Pharisees, we have been taught that we are a special and chosen people. We have been adopted into the House of Israel and, along with the Jews, are members of the covenant people of God. As Peter taught, we are "a chosen generation, a royal priesthood, an holy nation, a peculiar people" (1 Peter 2:9). What does this mean? To the Pharisee who accepts both the truth and the lie, this means that God loves us more than He does others. We are like the favorite child of a parent who has been let in on the secret that he prefers us to his other children. This leads us to feel better than those around us. Whether in secret or flaunted openly, modern-day Pharisees believe they are indeed superior to the "unchosen."

But is this what being chosen means to God? A closer look at the scriptures indicates something very different. The scriptures reveal that God's chosen people have a special responsibility to be servants to others and to be humble followers of Christ. To be chosen is to have a special duty to mourn with others, to comfort others, to serve others, to invite all to come unto Christ, and to show charity and compassion to "the least of these" (Matthew 25:40), wearing ourselves out in the service of others, losing ourselves in that service for His sake, not our own, if only to bring save it be one soul unto Him.

Given these divergent meanings, members of the Church are faced with the same challenge as the Pharisees of old. We may know the truth that we are counted among God's chosen people, but we can be deceived about what that truth means. We can believe the adversary's lie and try to fill our void with the false belief that we are better than others rather than lowly and humble servants of all. This challenge is particularly pronounced when we consider revelations like D&C 1:30, which states that our church is "the only true and living church on the face of the earth." Do we take these words to mean that our church is better than other churches because we have more truth, more power, ongoing revelation, and so forth? Or do we see this phrase as an invitation and responsibility to share our faith, our love, our joy in the gospel with others by word and deed? In other words, does this verse mean that our church is to be a servant to all other churches just as members of it are to be servants of all other people?

We urge the reader to be very circumspect in answering these questions. We issue the caveat that Pharisees also believe they should share the gospel with others, but always do so from above, from the position of the haves deigning to give aid to the have-nots. This results in a condescending form of "sharing" from a place of presumed superiority, where one claims a monopoly on truth and greater righteousness.

In subtle ways, we can confuse our being a member of the Church with being a member of an elite group, and so lift ourselves above others. Almost without awareness we may send the message to others that they are inferior to us. Like the Pharisees of old, we can shut up heaven against others and by so doing shut it up against ourselves. Given the subtle manner in which we can easily fall into this way of living, we must be vigilant against the forms of Pharisaism that can easily beset us. In what follows we provide a top-ten list of examples of modern-day Pharisaism to illustrate its pervasive and subtle influence, several of which we, the authors, have both personally experienced and practiced.

1. A Pharisee thinks membership in the Church makes him or her better than "nonmembers."

Compared to Pharisees, nonmembers are necessarily deficient because they do not have the ordinances, priesthood, gift of the Holy Ghost, and covenants afforded to God's chosen people. Thus, no matter what nonmembers do to live good lives, to worship God, and to help others, in a Pharisee's eyes, nonmembers can never be as good as a member. They will always come up short. Granted, members may come up short too, but their shortcomings are still superior to those of the nonmembers. To a Pharisee, those outside the Church can never know full joy and happiness, never experience the same depth of the Atonement, and never achieve the level of exaltation afforded to God's chosen people. Members who do not keep the commandments and live in sin may fall, but as long as they keep their Church membership and repent, to the Pharisee they are still a step above the nonmember. The obedient and diligent member who avoids all sin is the best of all.

We find it interesting that the Pharisee draws this line of separation according to membership in the Church. On the one hand, this appears to be the only logical line to draw. After all, it is by virtue of baptism that we are adopted into the Abrahamic covenant and receive the gift of the Holy Ghost. Without baptism and the other ordinances of the gospel, it is impossible to return to Heavenly Father. In that way, members really are different from nonmembers. Or so it would appear. The mistaken logic of the Pharisee is to think that these ordinances secure the blessings of exaltation for each individual member. In fact, the ordinances secure nothing of themselves without the accompaniment of a contrite heart and a broken spirit and the grace of God. Thus, whenever members are lifted up in pride and fail to repent, forgive, and depend completely on the Savior for their life and their hope of eternal life, then the ordinances are of no effect—and the pretense of a separation of the chosen from the unchosen is nothing more than a Pharisaical facade.

Given that any sin keeps us from God, the only line worth drawing, if there should be a line at all, is the one between the repentant and the unrepentant of any faith. Like the Pharisee and publican in the parable described earlier, if a member is proud and unrepentant and a nonmember is humble and repentant, then it is the nonmember whose sins will be forgiven through the Atonement. The member will be abased. Rather than draw lines of separation that are meaningless unless we are yoked to Christ in faith, repentance, and love, the disciple, as we will describe in a later chapter, acknowledges our shared dependence on God and the lack of any justified place for prideful separation. At the most, being a member means being a servant to all, in humility, as a fellow sinner who depends fully on Christ for everything. With the Apostle Peter, the disciple-servant humbly and sincerely proclaims, "Of a truth I perceive that God is no respecter of persons: But in every nation he that feareth him, and worketh righteousness, is accepted with him" (Acts 10:34–35).

2. A Pharisee thinks of church callings hierarchically and associates "higher" church callings with greater righteousness.

We are told that it is the mantle, not the man or woman, that we honor, and that we should not think of callings and worth as positively correlated. But the Pharisee who first believes he is part of a chosen people standing above others can't help but think that there are those who are *more* chosen than others. One way to measure that added chosenness is to look at Church callings hierarchically. The "higher" the Church calling which a Pharisee holds, the more confident he is that he was one of God's most special and valiant spirit children in the premortal existence, or that he was foreordained to do something great and significant in this life. Callings provide Pharisees the signs of assurance they need to feel special and chosen.

As a new missionary I[5] wanted very much not to care about whether I had a leadership role in the mission, but the thoughts were always there. My oldest brother had been a zone leader and the second oldest an assistant to the president. My father had been a bishop and was at the time a stake president. How could I not wonder, at least a little, if I would measure up? Was I less special than they? Maybe I wasn't foreordained to be one of the truly chosen, a leader in the church? I tried to keep these questions out of my mind and to focus on doing the work. I did a pretty good job of it, even as my MTC cohort of elders were called as trainers, senior companions, and district leaders while I was still a junior companion. I remember thinking, "I know these guys and they are no better than I am. Some of them don't even take their mission seriously and goof off a lot. How could they be in leadership positions before me?"

The first year of my mission passed and I was still a junior companion. These questions came back to my mind with the full force of a spiritual crisis. Why was I still a junior companion? Was I inadequate? Were there sins of which I had not fully repented? Did the mission president not see how committed I was to working hard? Maybe he just didn't like me? What had I done wrong? I had worked as hard as anybody. I hadn't goofed off. Why was the Lord punishing me? More deeply, the questions centered on the possibility that maybe I was not special. Perhaps I wasn't one of the truly chosen; maybe I wasn't one of the Lord's leaders. Perhaps, dare I think it, I was just an average person with no special foreordination to speak of. It was this haunting thought, more than any other, that kept me up on the night of the one-year mark of my mission.

I got out of bed that night and got on my knees, pleading with the Lord to let me know if I had done something wrong and if there was some reason why I did not deserve to be at least a senior companion. I told Him I did not need or want to be a district leader or zone leader or AP, but I felt like I had been ready to be a senior companion for some time. Was it too much to ask for Him to give me a little trust and a little more leadership over the work I gave up two years of my life to do? I decided that I was not going to stop praying until I got an answer, and it was and still is the longest time I have ever spent on my knees. Several hours went by and I began to fall asleep as I prayed. I finally gave up and decided I wasn't even special enough to get an answer to a prayer and I went to bed.

The next morning, the mission president called and announced a change in our companionship. My companion was being transferred and I would be getting a junior companion. The president then called me to be the district leader. A Pharisee would be tempted to see this phone call as an answer to my prayer, but I knew it wasn't—at least it wasn't the one that really mattered. The true answer came the night before in the absence of an answer. It was wrong, as I knew it was, to complain to the Lord about my status. How could I forget the words of the Lord to Joseph Smith: "The Son of Man hath descended below them all. Art thou greater than he?" (D&C 122:8). It was wrong for me to connect the Lord's love of me or confidence in me or estimation of me to a calling. Even though I consciously resisted that temptation, I had done exactly that. I believed that a position, a calling, a role mattered to the very God who forsook all those things to condescend for all of us and come into this world "with no beauty that we should desire him" (Isaiah 53:2). It was vanity, nothing more, nothing less.

Twelve years later when I was called to be a bishop, those old proud feelings started to come back, but only for a very brief moment.

The fleeting thought returned to my mind that maybe this calling showed that the Lord was pleased with me. Perhaps I am one of His truly chosen. Whatever false and Pharisaical sense of pride I allowed myself to entertain in that brief moment was quickly dashed to pieces by the hardship of that calling on me and my family. Five years later, when I was released and looked into the eyes of the next bishop and knew that he hadn't sought the calling either, but the same questions were in his head, I gave him a hug and knew that he too would quickly lose whatever vanity was in him. I now understood why so many bishops say that anyone who wants to be bishop should be given the opportunity—"for fools . . . shall mourn" (Ether 12:26).

I had also learned by the end of my tenure as bishop who the truly valiant and humble followers of Christ really were. They sought no calling, no attention for themselves. They simply went about quietly doing good. Before being a bishop I hardly knew them or appreciated them, but by the end I realized that they were the Lord's anointed. They were the Saviors on Mount Zion. They were His humble disciples, seeking only to do His will in whatever way they could. I love these good people and aspire to be like them. They were my heroes as a bishop and still are.

3. A Pharisee thinks scriptural warnings to Pharisees don't apply to him or her.

In Matthew 23, the Lord chastised the Pharisees for worshipping past prophets and claiming they would never have killed them as their forefathers did, for at that very time they were casting prophets of the Lord out of the city of Jerusalem or crucifying them, including eventually Christ Himself among those killed. The Pharisees' belief in the truth and the lie blinded them to seeing their Messiah right in front of them. Modern Pharisees do likewise. Their belief that they are chosen disallows their acknowledgment that the Lord's warnings apply to them here and now just as they did to the "chosen" in the past. They cannot acknowledge their commonality with other "chosen" people who have fallen in the past (such as the children of Israel in the Old Testament, the Jews at the time of Christ, or the Nephites when they became lifted up in pride). The modern Pharisee is heard to say, "How could those people be so stupid after all the signs the Lord showed them and the warnings of His prophets? We would never do that today. We are different. We know better. We were saved to come forth in these latter days because we are a royal generation, more righteous than those who lived before. We won't make their mistakes."

In social psychology we understand this false belief to be made up of two related biases—hindsight bias and overconfidence bias. Hindsight bias is a tendency to assume from a perspective taken after an event that one would have behaved at the time of the event in a manner that is consistent with what they now know after the fact. Of course, this is mistaken reasoning because one could not have predicted the outcome at the time of the event and therefore one necessarily lacks the knowledge required to make the choices that lead to the desired outcomes that are recognized later down the road. It is easy to forget that the Nephites, the early Saints, our own parents, and others were acting without perfect awareness of the outcomes of their actions at the time. Pharisees second-guess others from their lifted-up, hindsight perspective without realizing that their decisions about what to do in the present are just as prone to error as the decisions were of those they criticize.

The other bias is an overconfidence in one's judgment that social psychologists have found almost always outstrips accuracy. Pharisees are sure they won't make the same mistakes as their ancestors because they believe they are better judges than they were. They think they can see the warning signs of their times and will make smarter decisions than their less-skilled forebears. We won't review all the literature on overconfidence bias here, but there have been numerous studies on human judgment in various categories—including impression formation, attitudes, eyewitness testimony, and introspection—which show that our accuracy is not very good and is especially prone to error when our confidence in our judgments is high. Anytime we think we are above error or are too smart to fail we are in jeopardy. Heeding the scriptural warnings and recognizing their absolute applicability to ourselves, here and now, is the only antidote to this Pharisaical faux pas.

4. A Pharisee thinks the Lord blesses him or her with money.

It is difficult to imagine that, with all of the scriptural warnings about riches and all of the scriptural examples of those whose hearts became set upon their wealth and turned away from their God, the Lord would choose money as a means to bless His chosen people. It seems more likely that riches are used to test the faith of God's people; that is, to see whether they will choose Him over wealth. More often, it is the poor who are described as blessed. It is true that at times the scriptures speak of having one's heart set upon riches as a sign of sin, but there are also verses which plainly state, "Woe unto the rich" (see Luke 6:24; 2 Nephi 9:30), with no reference to the state of one's heart. The Pharisees see the "blessing" of wealth as evidence of their righteousness and as a sign that they are God's chosen people. They forget the words of Isaiah 55:8, where the Lord revealed, "My thoughts are not your thoughts, neither are your ways my ways." Thus it is likely that the Pharisee's idea of a blessing is something very different from the Lord's, and Pharisees may deceive themselves when they define blessings in terms of worldly riches.

There are many dangers in affluence, one of the greatest of which is that economic class becomes the dividing line that allows one to be lifted up in pride. This was the case among the Zoramites in the Book of Mormon, a people who saw riches as evidence of God's love and their specialness. The poor among them were not just seen as unlucky, they were viewed quite literally as unloved by God. After all, if they were loved, they too would have been blessed with wealth. The poor Zoramites were kicked out of the synagogues and were not allowed to worship with the righteous rich. This confounding of wealth with righteousness is among the most abhorrent forms of Pharisaism, as the poor Zoramites were now shut out from the places of worship where closeness to God could be achieved. They literally had to buy the right to worship God, like buying tickets to a grand gala or other event, and if they didn't have the money they couldn't afford God, His grace, or His kingdom.[6]

King Benjamin taught another danger in believing that the Lord blesses His chosen ones with riches. It can lead Pharisees to draw a line between what they consider the deserving or the undeserving poor. If the Pharisee is willing to give of his or her substance at all, he or she will only give to those who through no fault of their own have fallen on hard times. A widow who is left without an income by her husband's death, orphaned children, or a family whose home was destroyed by a tornado are clearly not responsible for the poverty that has befallen them. In such cases, Pharisees may be willing to lend a hand, especially if their gift giving is seen by others. However, if the poor are poor because they have made bad decisions and misused their finances, then they are in no way deserving of the Pharisees' contributions. "How will the undeserving poor ever learn their lesson if they keep getting handouts?" goes the Pharisee's reasoning, so they keep their substance to themselves.

As a bishop with responsibility for distributing fast offering contributions to the poor in the ward, I[7] often found myself thinking in terms of the deserving and undeserving poor. Many of the ward leaders who aided me with ward welfare inevitably struggled with these distinctions as well. At some point, after helping me minister to the needs of struggling families by reviewing budgets, meal plans, and food orders, these good leaders would usually come to me and express concern that many of these families had gotten themselves into their situation through bad habits and bad choices and by depending on others for help, including the ward. The leaders doubted whether our efforts were going to pay off because these people had made their own suffering. They wanted to help people who really deserved it and would appreciate it. They wanted to help the deserving poor.

When this concern arose, I would tell each one of them that I understood their concerns and that I felt much the same way myself at times, but that if I were to only help the "deserving" poor—the innocent whose poverty was not in any way self-inflicted—we would be helping very few people. The fact was that many people who were poor had made some bad decisions in their lives in addition to having some difficult circumstances befall them. Many of them had developed bad habits and several were not making good choices to change their circumstances. I would then ask each leader a couple of questions I asked myself many times as well. "Who did the Lord have in mind when He commanded us to give to the poor and the needy? Did the Lord have only the innocent and deserving poor in mind?"

To help us answer this question, I would turn to Mosiah 4 and read the words of King Benjamin on the subject. I would tell each of them that I had to read these verses regularly to remind me of the Lord's position on the distinction people draw between the deserving and undeserving poor. Speaking of how we might respond to a beggar asking for assistance, King Benjamin stated (as if reading my and my leaders' minds), "Perhaps thou shalt say: The man has brought upon himself his misery; therefore I will stay my hand, and will not give unto him of my food, nor impart unto him of my substance that he may not suffer, for his punishments are just—but I say unto you, O man, whosoever doeth this the same hath great cause to repent; and except he repenteth of that which he hath done he perisheth forever, and hath no interest in the kingdom of God. For behold, are we not all beggars?" (Mosiah 4:17–19).

These verses and the ones following them are some of the most powerful in scripture; as I read them with each ward leader, it became very clear to them as it was made clear to me that our decisions to help the poor cannot be made on the basis of our assumptions about who brought upon themselves their own circumstances and who did not. Thank the heavens that our Father doesn't treat us likewise, but instead forgives us willingly whenever we sincerely repent, even when we have brought upon ourselves our own grief and suffering through sin. He forgives us even when He knows we will sin again, sometimes even committing the exact same sin that got us into trouble in the first place. His arms are outstretched still. He pours out His mercy in abundance and we receive an excess of joy, though we have done nothing to deserve it.

There are not deserving and undeserving poor, just as there are not deserving and undeserving rich, or deserving and undeserving sinners. We all are undeserving of God's mercy and His blessings, yet He grants them to us in exceeding abundance. The poor may seem to be undeserving of our substance, but following the example of our Father, we must not refuse them on that basis. Granted, as a common judge in Israel, the bishop must decide whom to give sacred funds, how much to give, and what to require of those to whom funds are given, but as the ward leaders and I learned from King Benjamin, the bishop can't wait until just the deserving poor arrive at his door to provide assistance. The bishop must seek out all the poor and assist them all in the Lord's way.

5. A Pharisee thinks he or she is a Disciple (or doesn't know he or she is a Pharisee).

Before going any further we must issue a caveat. If you have been reading these forms of modern-day Pharisaism and you think they don't apply to you because you haven't sinned, broken a commandment, or given into temptation, then you are most likely living as a Pharisee. The criterion for recognizing yourself as a disciple is not one of negation. That is, you do not know you are a disciple by identifying the sins you do not commit. You recognize you are a disciple by what you do—by seeking others' well-being, loving God and those around you, repenting willingly in order to be closer to God, and becoming as a child. Unlike the Pharisees, who see discipleship as a zero-sum game only attainable by a chosen few, the disciple wishes nothing more than to help all the people he or she can to taste the love of God.

The disciple doesn't concern him- or herself with attaining salvation and exaltation, but wears him- or herself out trying to help others attain it. As we will illustrate in the disciple chapter, if you are a disciple you wouldn't think of yourself as a disciple—you wouldn't think of yourself at all. You would live for others' sake, to help them become disciples and to "taste of the exceeding joy of which [you have tasted]" (Alma 36:24). Thus, if you think you are a disciple, you are most likely in the Pharisee quadrant, where identifying yourself as a disciple and making other people aware that you are a disciple is of utmost importance.

6. A Pharisee thinks he or she doesn't sin, not really.

A Pharisee's sins are small sins, the kind that don't weigh as much as the bad ones that others commit, and besides, those little sins are offset by all the acts of righteousness a Pharisee performs. A Pharisee keeps the commandments more than he sins, so the scales tip in his favor. But sinners, those who commit the real sins and violate the commandments, cannot tip the scales their way because their sins are too grievous and their obedience too inconsistent. The Pharisee fails to see that we could never tip the scales in our favor, because "all we like sheep have gone astray" (Isaiah 53:6); none is deserving of God's mercy and grace. As King Benjamin taught, we are unprofitable servants no matter how hard we try to earn heaven by our good deeds. None is good but God and so it is always His goodness that merits our salvation and exaltation, not our own.

One day in one of my[8] psychology classes, while my students were taking a quiz at the end of class, I noticed one of my students let his eyes wander to his neighbor's paper. I watched as he looked at her paper several times and wrote down her answers on his paper. I decided I would pull him aside after class and confront him about his misbehavior. When class ended, he approached me first and told me that he needed to talk to me about an important issue that he hoped I could help him with. I decided to wait to address the cheating until after I heard him out.

We went up to my office and he proceeded to tell me about an experience he had had a few days before. He had needed to borrow his roommate's computer and discovered pornographic material on it. He told me he was shocked and appalled that his friend was viewing such things. He did not immediately confront his friend or let him know that he knew what he was doing. Instead, he first contacted the friend's bishop to let him know what he found. But he didn't feel like that was enough. He felt that he also needed to talk with the friend about his sinful behavior. I asked him what his motives were for confronting the friend. He responded that he wanted to let the friend know that he was aware of what he was doing and that it was wrong and he should stop. He wanted him to know that his behavior would ruin his life and maybe endanger his eternal soul.

I asked him if he thought of himself as being as sinful as his friend. He replied quickly that he was not at all the same as his friend. He didn't look at pornography at all. I asked him if he thought of sins as being hierarchical, as if some sins were worse than others. He said that he did think viewing pornography was worse than other sins, so yes, there were degrees of severity. I then asked him how he thought his roommate would respond to him if he came to him from that position—that is, of not being guilty of such a heinous sin as his friend was. He agreed that his friend might not take it too well if he approached him from a place of greater righteousness, but he couldn't help it if he was living more righteously than his friend. He told me that his friend didn't attend church very much and had some other bad habits, whereas he (my student) was totally active and kept the commandments.

I then asked him if he believed that any sin, regardless of its apparent severity, keeps us from God's presence unless we sincerely repent of it. He agreed that it did, and then asserted that he did repent of his sins so he was in fact living more righteously than his unrepentant friend. I asked him if cheating was a sin. He said that it was. I then told him that I had just watched him cheat a few minutes earlier on the quiz and that I had planned to approach him about it before he approached me. I asked him if he had any plans to repent of his cheating; and if he would have sought me out to tell me he had cheated if he hadn't been caught. Extremely embarrassed and obviously ashamed, he began to realize, all too painfully, that he was no better than his friend, no more righteous or deserving of God's forgiveness—that he too was a sinner as much in need of God's grace as his friend or anyone else. He was humbled; I can promise you that he took a very different approach to talking with his friend as a result.

I think of how things would have gone if he hadn't realized his own sinfulness and his equal dependence upon the Lord's mercy as his friend. I can imagine his friend, already struggling to overcome a powerful temptation, being fully aware of his sinfulness and probably feeling undeserving of the Atonement. Then his "righteous" friend catches him in his sin and adds to his despair by condemning him and chastising him for not doing better. As we will see in the Nihilist quadrant, my student's friend, like many who struggle with pornography, probably already believes he can't be forgiven and is defective compared to his more worthy roommate. Rather than being supported in finding the resolve to take Christ's hand and repent and be forgiven, he would likely drift further into the darkness, in part because his friend, in the manner of a Pharisee, mistakenly orders sins into different categories of severity and too easily forgets that the *least* degree of sin, including his own, keeps us from God's presence—unless we repent.

7. A Pharisee counts and measures his or her good deeds *and* the bad deeds of others.

If it hasn't become obvious by now, it is important to a Pharisee to keep track of the score of his or her righteousness compared to the righteousness of others, adding up every church meeting attended or missed, every sin committed, and every commandment kept. It may not be a coincidence that there is a book in the Old Testament titled Numbers. The law of Moses was in many ways a quantitative law; sins and good deeds were added up and reckoned and even footsteps were counted. The law of Christ, on the other hand, is a qualitative law; the sincerity of our actions and the contrition of our heart matters most. With quality, it is less a question of whether one has attended church or not. It is a question of whether one has experienced a transformative spiritual experience in the church attended. Were we kind to others and meek and gentle? Were we long-suffering with those we served and merciful to those who wronged us? Did the sacrament ordinance work a mighty change in our heart; did our countenances shine forth the Spirit of the Lord? Did we recognize that we can't add up enough good deeds or obedient acts to warrant salvation, that we depend wholly on Christ for all that we have and can have? Did our hearts turn toward repentance and forgiveness, seeking it for ourselves and working through it with others? Do we recognize along with King Benjamin that "if ye should serve him who has created you from the beginning, and is preserving you from day to day, by lending you breath, that ye may live and move and do according to your own will, and even supporting you from one moment to another—I say, if ye should serve him with all your whole souls yet ye would be unprofitable servants" (Mosiah 2:21).

In his wisdom, King Benjamin understood that even our capacity to enact service (that is, our breath and our living and moving) comes from God and manifests our infinite indebtedness to God, such that our thoughts, words, and deeds could never generate enough profit to "earn" His mercy. Thus, for those in the Pharisee quadrant who are keeping track of their good deeds and comparing them to the deeds of others, there are only two false options. On the one hand, they think their good deeds have earned them a greater portion of God's blessings than others and they are entitled to His kingdom. They actually think their works add up to win God's favor.

I[9] met with a man once who was contemplating suicide. His wife had just left him and his life was in shambles. He could not understand how this misfortune had befallen him. He recounted with me all the good deeds he had done, all the commandments he had kept, and the acts of service he rendered to others on God's behalf. He even exclaimed that he had never even had a sip of Coke! He had done so much for God. How could God let this suffering happen? It became clear that he had tried to use the quantity of his "good" deeds and his obedience to the commandments to hold God hostage to his will. He believed God was bound by his righteous deeds to protect him from suffering and to bless his life in the manner he desired. When God didn't do that, he believed He broke his word and there was no reason to keep living. What a shame that he believed his good deeds could ever add up to compel God to never let him suffer. What a mistaken understanding of blessings and suffering as well. He did not understand that no matter what he might do, he is still an unprofitable servant.

The other false option is the path of guilt. We will have more to say about this in the Nihilist chapter, but at this point suffice it to say that when Pharisees count their good deeds and keep track of their obedience, they leave themselves vulnerable to the guilt of always coming up short. They will inevitably not do everything they are supposed to do and will always feel inadequate as a result. Of course, we are all inadequate, but the issue for Pharisees is that they misattribute this inadequacy (in others primarily, though also in themselves) to not doing enough rather than to their complete dependency on Christ's grace for all that they are.

8. A Pharisee worships the gift and not the altar (see Matthew 23:16–22).

Pharisees miss the mark with their worship. They talk more about the miracles and blessings they have received than the Lord who provides the miracles. It would seem as if the blessings, miracles, and signs of God have become more important than God Himself.

Comments like "I don't want to lose the blessings of the Lord so I had better continue to pay tithing" are evidence of worshipping the blessings and not the Lord who supplies them. How often have "testimonies" been borne which are completely focused on the signs of God's mercy, the blessings of His love, and the miracles of His goodness rather than the merciful, loving, and good Savior Himself? Sometimes a miracle or blessing is so fantastic and "special" that the God who granted it is overshadowed by the miracle's awesomeness. When miracles and blessings become our focus, they fuel our actions rather than faith and can become a great stumbling block to ourselves and others.

A Pharisee would be wise to remember the story of Job, who had great wealth and prosperity but lost it all and suffered immensely in both body and spirit. Unlike the Pharisee, Job's heart was not set upon the blessings of the Lord but was centered on the Lord Himself. Thus, when the blessings ran out for Job and suffering came, he did not give up hope but continued to worship his God as he did before, even exclaiming "though he slay me, yet will I trust in him" (Job 13:15). The Pharisee fails to do that. The Pharisee's heart is attached to his or her prestige, prosperity, and pretended piety, and anything that threatens those "blessings," including even the Lord who provides them, is to be cast aside.

A meeting I[10] attended featured a member of the Church sharing an absolutely incredible story in which she and her family were in real financial trouble and had no idea how they were going to keep their house, pay for food and utilities, and manage to survive. The woman told how she and her family were led by the Lord through dreams and other unbelievable events to purchase a lottery ticket which ultimately won them a million dollars. Many who heard the story were amazed at this incredible miracle and seemed reassured that the Lord blesses His children who follow Him. I found myself having a very different reaction. I wondered if there weren't people in the audience who had been in similarly troubling circumstances in the past, or even currently, and had also prayed for help and were also good, worthy people and who were not similarly blessed. I thought of the many people who prayed over their sick child or dying spouse and pleaded with the Lord not to take their loved ones, and they died. How would they be affected by other people's miracle stories of healing? These miracle stories could cause them to question their faithfulness, their worthiness, their deservedness of God's mercy.

Blessings or miracles do not truly uplift us or encourage us. They might just as well discourage us. It is always only the Savior, our God, whom Job loved no matter what blessings or curses came his way, whom we must worship, and from whom our encouragement comes. Like Job, our focus must be on the root, not the fruit of the branches. It must be on the altar and not the gift we receive. The Pharisee fails to learn that no matter what our circumstances, no matter whether we are clearly blessed or seem abandoned to our own devices, it is Christ, always Christ, who is our Lord and to whom we must be yoked.

9. A Pharisee thinks "power or influence can or ought to be maintained by virtue of the priesthood" (D&C 121).

Modern-day Pharisees mistakenly equate authority and power. They believe their priesthood office can be used to motivate, change, and control others. They often practice an authoritarian style as a spouse, parent, or church leader, commanding obedience and respect by virtue of their office and punishing those who do not appropriately yield to their will. As the Pharisees of old, they see strength in their priesthood pedigree and lord it over others of lesser priesthood or those who hold no priesthood office. They fail to recognize that the person after whom the priesthood is truly named, Jesus Christ, never wielded power through His most high of high offices. His power and His influence were manifest in His attributes—His mercy for the sinner, His gentleness toward the sick and lame, His willingness to eat and live with outcasts, His loving rebuke, His long-suffering and His patience—all things the Pharisee views as weakness, not power.

Satan revealed his own misunderstanding of Godly power when he tried to tempt the Lord. He kept asking Christ to manifest His power in the ways Satan conceives of it: power over nature (changing stones to bread), power over heaven (calling angels down from heaven to protect Him), and power over humankind (ruling over the kingdoms of man). This is the power Satan desires; it is the power he tempts us with. Each of his temptations represents a fundamental misunderstanding of priesthood power that is also prevalent among the Pharisees, ancient and contemporary. These false conceptions of power constitute the "unrighteous dominion" spoken of by the Lord to Joseph Smith in Liberty Jail in D&C 121:37–39, when Joseph's own temptation to call upon angels to protect the Saints being attacked and forced out of Missouri must have been at an all-time high.

The Prophet Joseph Smith, like each of us, had to learn that Christ's power is in His attributes and character. From the time of Satan's temptations up to the point of His crucifixion, He never exercised any power or influence in the ways the Pharisees expected from a true Messiah. Not a lion but a lamb, His power was in His meekness and humility. He is our great example and if we are to be like Him we too must learn that "no power or influence can or ought to be maintained by virtue of the priesthood." Instead, it is "only by persuasion, by long-suffering, by gentleness and meekness, and by love unfeigned; by kindness and pure knowledge which shall greatly enlarge the soul without hypocrisy, and without guile" (D&C

121:41–42) that we can have any real power. The Pharisee fails to comprehend that true and enduring power is made manifest by turning the other cheek, washing others' feet, and sacrificing our desires for the benefit of others.

10. A Pharisee has to do everything and do it him- or herself if it's going to be done right.

A Pharisee overemphasizes works and underemphasizes grace. We have already noted their quantitative focus and their perfectionism. The Pharisees believe that every jot and tittle of the law must be obeyed in order to earn God's greatest reward—exaltation. Thus, they are always busy with the many duties they must fulfill. For the modern Pharisee, this means being an amazing spouse and parent, teaching their children the gospel, and all but ensuring that they have testimonies and go to church and go on missions and go to the temple. It means holding important church callings and fulfilling those callings perfectly. For the Pharisee there really is no difference between doing our best (or "all we can do") and perfection. In other words, giving one's "total effort"[11] or doing one's best always amounts to living perfectly in the Pharisee's mind.

The Pharisee's belief that total effort equals perfection compels them to try to do everything—and do it without error. When we think of all the things the modern Pharisee feels compelled to do, we can't help but think of the Chinese acrobat who begins to spin a plate high atop a flexible bamboo stick. Once the acrobat gets one plate spinning, he then moves on to another plate and then another one and so on until ten or more plates are all spinning. By the time he gets the last plate spinning, the first plate slows down, wobbles, and threatens to fall. The acrobat quickly runs over to it and gets the plate spinning again, but then the second one starts slowing and the third one and so on. The scene that unfolds is exhausting to watch. The audience knows the acrobat cannot keep up the frenetic pace required to keep all the plates from falling. Eventually one plate topples into two or three others and, like dominoes, the plates all come crashing down on the exhausted acrobat and the ground. In defiance of this inevitable reality, Pharisees believe they can and should keep all their plates—the duties of their lives—spinning, and take pride in their ability to do so (or at least in the pretense that they do so).

While teaching at the University of West Georgia, I[12] faced a major employment review. During the review one of my colleagues in the department questioned how I could ever manage to keep up all the responsibilities of my life. He was aware that I had a large family, I was serving as the bishop of a large ward covering a wide area, and I was managing a heavy teaching, research, and service load in the department. To his thinking, I must be spread too thin and would certainly burn out. I must admit that when he asked this question, I initially felt some pride. It was true that I was managing all of those things and accomplishing what I needed to. It was also true, as I told him and the other faculty reviewing my employment, that my circumstances were nothing new to me. In fact, when I was completing my dissertation I was also working three part-time jobs, serving as a counselor in a bishopric, and raising very young children with my wife, who also worked. I told them this was really quite typical of my life and they didn't need to worry about burnout at all.

I felt admittedly proud to have impressed my peers, as I believed I had, with how well I balanced all the responsibilities of my life. In some sense, it was as if I was superhuman and truly special. I didn't realize until I came to know this colleague who asked about burnout better that he wasn't impressed at all, but genuinely worried that my quality of life would suffer along with the quality of my work if I tried to do it all. To his thinking, balance didn't mean doing everything. It meant learning to let some things go, to let some things fall through, and to sometimes say no. At the time, such a notion of balance never occurred to me. I thought balance meant figuring out how to get everything done with the time you had. If that meant staying up later or waking up earlier then so be it. The important thing was to meet all my obligations, to keep the plates spinning, and to do it all myself.

After all, if you want something done right, you almost always have to do it yourself. No one else can be trusted to get it right—which is another form of "special." Of course, it is a deception to think that no plates are falling just as it is a deception to think we are doing any of these things by ourselves. As Christ pointed out numerous times in His comments about the Pharisees, they clearly let a number of plates fall, especially the most important plate of all, their relation to God.

At the time of my employment review, I too was letting plates fall as I pretended to myself and others that I was getting it all done. My attention to my wife and children, for example, was less than ideal. I wasn't taking care of my body. I wasn't keeping up relationships with family and friends. Aspects of my life were not in balance and I wasn't getting it all done. If a Pharisee is being honest, he or she isn't doing it all either. Rather than pretending that one is getting it all done and doing it alone, grace teaches us that it is impossible to get it all done and what we *do* get done we can only do with Christ's divine assistance. Perhaps it is time to let grace in and do the difficult but necessary task of choosing which plates to keep spinning and which plates to let fall. After all, they are His plates, not ours.

CHAPTER 5

The Egoist

"There are two kinds of egoists: those who admit it, and the rest of us."—LAURENCE J. PETER[1]

When a person chooses the egoistic way of living, he or she behaves as a conceited, self-centered person with little regard for others. The Egoist accepts the lie that he or she is better and more special than others and disregards the truth of his or her relationship to God. The Egoist's mantra is "Eat, drink, and be merry, for tomorrow we die" (2 Nephi 28:7–8). The satisfaction of the self becomes the total focus, God is essentially squeezed out of the picture, and the truth is rendered practically irrelevant. The Lord taught, "No man can serve two masters; for either he will hate the one and love the other, or else he will hold to the one and despise the other" (3 Nephi 13:24). Thus, when Egoists embrace the lie and pursue self-satisfaction, they can't help but simultaneously deny the truth and by so doing end up despising God, even if they do not explicitly intend to. As a result, they experience the Spirit less and less and will try to compensate for that lack by filling their growing void with self-indulgence in the pleasures of this life.

Elder Dallin H. Oaks said, "A selfish person is more interested in pleasing man—especially himself—than in pleasing God. He looks only to his own needs and desires. He walks 'in his own way, and after the image of his own god, whose image is in the likeness of the world' (D&C 1:16)."[2] The Egoist is continually caught up in the selfish cycle of trying to please the self. Professor Elton O'Keeffe said, "The more egoistic individuals are, the more convinced they become that Egoism is the answer and the more blind they become to the dangers and shortcomings of Egoism."[3] Unfortunately, this type of thinking damages our relationships with others, including our spouse, family members, friends, and ultimately our God.

Christ anticipated the trade-off of egoism when He said, "For what shall it profit a man, if he shall gain the whole world, and lose his own soul?" (Mark 8:36). Christ wanted us to understand that the price of egoism is the loss of our special connection to our Heavenly Father and the eternal life that we can enjoy with Him. Egoists' hearts are placed upon their treasures and not placed upon their Lord. When people pursue their own selfish interests, they inevitably experience a greater emptiness. Consider how people who always want more material wealth and prestige are never satisfied. Instead, they are always looking for the next item or accomplishment that they believe will bring them happiness, but never does. Research shows that even lottery winners are not any happier after collecting their winnings than they were before. The more Egoists pursue and receive pleasure, the farther they distance themselves from the Lord and the greater the void grows within them. Because they believe the lie, they falsely assume that this greater void they experience is best filled with even more pleasure, resulting in a vicious cycle.

The Subtlety of Egoism

By saying that the Egoist denies the truth, we do not mean to imply that all Egoists intentionally or knowingly deny their special relationship to God. It is more likely the case that when we choose to live egoistically we find ourselves unknowingly caught up in a way of life that is ultimately incompatible with discipleship. By our actions, we implicitly make ourselves the master of our life and as a result, displace God from His rightful position of importance in our lives. This displacement can be so subtle that it is not easy to recognize when it has occurred. We offer a few guidelines here to help us identify when we are behaving egoistically and displacing God from His rightful place in our lives, and then we provide more specific examples of egoism's manifestations in the sections of the chapter that follow.

A first guideline we can follow to help us recognize the subtle forms of egoism in our lives is to examine our ultimate goals. C. Daniel Batson, a research psychologist who studies egoism and altruism, distinguishes between proximate goals and ultimate goals. Proximate goals are goals we pursue in the short-term. Ultimate goals are for the long-term, the final and most important outcomes we hope to achieve.[4] A student studying psychology may have the proximate goal of getting a high grade point average. This pursuit may entail even more immediate goals of outperforming other students in a class on a test where grades are awarded competitively or not spending time with friends and family in order to focus on studying for exams. These proximate goals might look fairly self-centered, even egoistic. However, the proximate goals don't tell the whole story.

What if the student has the proximate goal of achieving a high GPA because she is pursuing the ultimate goal of helping others? What if she hopes to fulfill her ultimate goal by becoming a clinical social worker and helping incarcerated youth become more functional, contributing members of society? Maybe she knows how hard it is to get into a social work program that specializes in this kind of therapy, and so she has to get good grades if she is going to get into the program and thereby realize her ultimate goal of helping troubled kids. Seeing her proximate goals of a high GPA and getting into a good social work program in the context of her ultimate goal of helping people makes all the difference in how we interpret the meaning of this woman's life.

When examining our potential for giving in to egoistic motivation, we as members of the Church can examine our ultimate and proximate goals in relation to each other from an eternal perspective. A member might acknowledge that he or she spends a lot of time serving others, doing good deeds, and lifting others' spirits. But without also acknowledging the ultimate goal of the member it will be difficult to interpret the meaning of the service. If this proximate goal of serving others is pursued in the service of the ultimate goal of achieving individual exaltation, it signifies a different meaning than if the proximate goal of service is carried out in order to fulfill the ultimate goal of helping those served receive exaltation. The former relationship of proximate to ultimate goals is more egoistic. The latter is more altruistic. When we apply this idea of proximate and ultimate goals to Christ's Atonement, the importance of motives and their meaning becomes particularly clear. If Christ had had the proximate goal of suffering for our sins in the garden of Gethsemane because He ultimately wanted to receive His Father's glory, it has a very different meaning than if He pursued this proximate goal because He loved us—that difference will make all the difference in how we worship Him and how we emulate Him in setting our own goals.

To recognize when we are ultimately choosing egoism, we must each ask ourselves some difficult but essential questions: "At the end of the day, am I ultimately focused on myself or others?" "Is it my exaltation that matters most or is it the exaltation of others that is my final purpose in this life?" "Do I focus on myself in the short-term so I can be a better servant of others in the long run, or am I ultimately just trying to fill my own void, and pretending to be an altruist to save face?"

A second, related examination we can undertake to guide us in identifying the subtlety of egoism is to ask ourselves whether we instrumentalize our Father in Heaven. In this case, *instrumentalize* means making something into a means to our ends. In the case of egoism, it is to try and use God in order to reach our selfish goals. If our ultimate goal is individual happiness and not glorifying God, then we will inevitably find ourselves trying to use God to achieve that egoistic end in some way. In our prayers we might ask God to bless us, meaning to make us happy as we conceive of happiness instead of asking that His will be done. From the instrumental perspective, God can become a kind of blessing distributor. We have heard members regularly say, and may have thought to ourselves, "I had better do _____ (insert any commandment here) to receive blessings," or "I don't want my blessings to end so I better keep doing ____." When the blessings become primary, God becomes secondary. He is what gets us to our destination rather than *being* the destination.

A friend of mine told me[5] that he is going to be more obedient and serve others more often because his family needs the blessings. Think about what his comment means for a moment. He might not intend it this way, but his words could mean that he will serve others and be obedient if the Lord blesses him and his family. Social psychologists have identified this "I scratch your back, you scratch mine" mentality as the norm of *reciprocity,* which is a powerful form of instrumentalization in Western culture. When we engage in this type of reciprocity thinking it is egoistic, not only because we do our good deeds in order to get something in return, but because we also try to obligate our God to reciprocate, and to do good deeds for us in a way that pleases us. He becomes like a genie in a bottle granting us wishes. We have rubbed the lamp and now He has to fulfill His part of the contract. No one who rubs the lamp ever cares about the genie in these stories, but only about what the genie can do for them— indeed *must* do for them.

Few of us intend to exploit and demean God when we behave this way, but in a subtle manner, our focus on blessings and individual happiness betrays an instrumental egoism in our actions. Surely, the Lord does promise us blessings and wants us to be happy; however, when blessings or happiness are pursued instrumentally there is a very different meaning to them and we risk serving the wrong master. To help us avoid this, we revisit Daniel Batson's work, where we find a third guideline to help us identify subtle egoism. Batson distinguishes between the terms "pursue" and "ensue."[6] For Batson, if a person is *pursuing* another's well-being by helping them, and, after the fact, as a completely unintended by-product of their service, they receive some reward, benefit, or even a good feeling, then that positive outcome that unexpectedly *ensued* from their service does not undo their pursued goal of helping someone. That is, the person does not magically become an egoist just because a good outcome happened to follow his or her good deed. If the person genuinely pursued an altruistic goal, then the person acted altruistically.

Similarly, if God is our master and we sincerely pursue His will, and blessings happen to ensue from that service, as they often do, they do not magically become our true goal after the fact. It is true that the scriptures teach that we will be blessed for our good works, but this means that blessings will ensue from our Christ-centered service, not that the blessings ought to be our goal, which inevitably makes God the means to their attainment. Psychiatrist and concentration camp survivor Viktor Frankl understood all too well and by means of great tribulation the distinction between pursue and ensue, and he will rightfully be our last word on the subtlety of egoism, as we believe there is little left to say after his very clear and cogent statement. He writes:

"Don't aim at success—the more you aim at it and make it a target, the more you are going to miss it. For success, like happiness, cannot be pursued; it must ensue, and it only does so as the unintended side effect of one's dedication to a cause greater than oneself or as the by-product of one's surrender to a person other than oneself. Happiness must happen, and the same holds for success: you have to let it happen by not caring about it. I want you to listen to what your conscience commands you to do and go on to carry it out to the best of your knowledge. Then you will live to see that in the long-run—in the long-run, I say!—success will follow you precisely because you had *forgotten* to think of it."[7]

Manifestations of Egoism

Hedonism

"I sometimes wonder whether all pleasures are not substitutes for Joy."—C. S. LEWIS[8]

At its core, egoism is driven by hedonism, the pursuit of pleasure and the avoidance of pain. British philosopher Thomas More's famous city described in his 1516 book *Utopia* is peopled with those who are "more inclinable to that opinion that places, if not the whole, yet the chief part, of a man's happiness in pleasure."[9] We believe he could not have been more mistaken in his link of happiness and pleasure. If this were the case, addicts should be happier than everyone else; however, all they are left with is pain, despair, and misery. Indeed, addiction is a perfect example of those who constantly pursue pleasure and always fall short. Craig Nakken wrote in his book *The Addictive Personality* that pleasure is something that is always temporary and that those who seek pleasure while excluding spiritual values are always ultimately seeking misery. He goes on to assert that the major by-product of a life dedicated to finding pleasure is indeed grief.[10] Elder Jeffrey R. Holland addressed the consequences of this hedonistic pursuit when he stated, "In an absolutely terrifying way, we see . . . others, roaring full speed down the dead-end road of hedonism, shout that they will indeed live by bread alone, and the more of it the better. We have it on good word, indeed we have it from the Word Himself, that bread alone—even a lot of it—is not enough (see Matthew 4:4; John 1:1)."[11]

Despite these significant issues, psychologists, economists, biologists, and other social and natural scientists by and large agree that the pursuit of pleasure and the avoidance of pain is the fundamental, natural, and even desirable motivation of human beings. Nowhere is this agreement more pronounced and more problematic than in the social science literature on marriage. A popular longstanding social science model of marriage is the equity theory of attraction.[12] According to this model, marriage is much like an economic contract, in which each participant makes contributions to the marriage and receives benefits. The model assumes a satisfying marriage occurs when each person in the marriage perceives an equity between his or her contributions and benefits and those of his or her partner. If one partner puts considerable effort into the marriage but also receives considerable benefits from the marriage, even as the other partner may put little effort into the marriage and receives fewer benefits, the marriage is perceived to be equitable. That is, pleasure and pain are relatively balanced. Contributions and benefits are not equal but they are equitable. However, if one partner perceives him- or herself as putting a great deal of effort into the marriage and receiving few benefits, while he or she views the partner as contributing little to the marriage but reaping a lot of benefits, that partner will be dissatisfied with the marriage because the pains of inequity offset any benefits, and the marriage contract is likely to be dissolved. From this perspective of economic exchange, marriage only endures when a hedonistic homeostasis is maintained.

To better identify when hedonism pervades our own marriages, consider the relevance of the following example: A husband who has been at work all day, working hard to provide for his family, comes home to a wife who has also been working hard all day by taking care of the kids and meeting her household duties. Thinking of their own circumstances, both the husband and the wife would appreciate it if their spouse would give them a break from the evening labors of making sure the kids do their homework, are fed and bathed, brush their teeth, and say their prayers, as well as such household chores as doing the dishes and taking out the garbage. Each one thinks, "It would sure be great if just this once my spouse would take care of all that and let me rest." Each is thinking of their difficult, exhausting day and is not really considering the day their partner may have endured. When neither partner says to the other, "I can tell you have had a hard day. You rest and let me take care of everything tonight," feelings of being unappreciated may arise and resentment may even emerge because one or both partners will not get the desired benefit of a break. They may even get into an argument about who is more deserving of the break, which will only add to the pain and resentment they already feel and decrease their hedonistic satisfaction even more.

The problem, as this example illustrates, is that in any marriage there are times like this when both partners are exhausted, there is an overwhelming number of responsibilities to be met and jobs to be done, and there are few if any hedonistic benefits to either partner in the marital relationship. Often, both spouses suffer together under the burden of childcare challenges, financial problems, housework needs, and so forth.

When I[13] was working on my doctoral dissertation, my wife and I were both swamped with work, childcare, education, financial worries, church callings, extended family concerns, and more. (Come to think of it, we are still swamped!) We were in survival mode much of the time. We were exhausted, with little time for or thought about our benefits and contributions. We were just trying to endure to the end of graduate school, let alone this life. Sometimes marriages are like that. Sometimes being parents feels like all contribution and no benefit. A hedonistic exchange model of marriage makes no allowance for such occurrences and can only understand them as running counter to marital well-being. From that perspective, if your partner and your children are not providing benefits to you that are comparable to all the contributions you are making, then you should leave the relationship. For the hedonist, staying in a pleasureless relationship is not only unhealthy, it is irrational.[14]

The hedonistic model also allows little room for empathy or altruism. From its perspective, the husband only sees his hard day at work and the wife only sees her hard day at work, and it is only their personal accounts of their own pleasure and pain, as they themselves see them, that ultimately matter. When we see our marriage in this hedonistic, economic way, we foreclose on the possibility and potential value of shared suffering, empathy, and self-sacrifice.

From the hedonistic perspective, most spouses can tolerate

inequity occasionally, but when they see it as being typical of their relationship, they will not be satisfied with their marriage because their pain outweighs their pleasure on a consistent basis. Because hedonism is thought to be their fundamental motivation, the unsatisfied partner is likely to end the marriage or look outside the marriage for alternative sources of pleasure which may include infidelity, pornography, drug use, spending more time with friends than with a spouse, obsessive video game play, gambling, working too much, shopping, and so forth.

Eventually, one or both partners often become utterly dissatisfied with the lack of perceived equity in the marriage and enter marital therapy as a last resort. Once in therapy, they readily list all the evidence of unfair treatment, their partner's lack of attention to their needs, and all the unreciprocated effort they have put into making the marriage work. They often summarize their view of the marriage with phrases like, "I'm just not happy and I don't see things getting any better," or "Don't I deserve better than this?" and "Why would I stay in a marriage that makes me so sad all the time?" and finally, "If he or she doesn't change his or her behavior soon, I'm outta here!" Implicit in each phrase is the hedonistic message that the pain far outweighs the pleasure. Unless the partner who is viewed as responsible for the inequity invests significantly in the relationship to balance the accounts of pleasure and pain, the dissatisfied spouse is going to leave.[15]

We have focused on marriage because it so profoundly illustrates the problematic effects of hedonism, but we want to acknowledge in concluding this section that there are many other subtle and perhaps more everyday ways in which Church members may also be tempted to behave hedonistically. For example, we may be hedonistically motivated when we attend church for our own personal pleasure of seeing friends, finding ourselves in the hallway during Sunday School talking with friends because we think the teacher is boring or not smart enough to make class enjoyable and interesting. We may pay tithing to receive the financial blessings that we believe tithing will bring. We may skip a service project or welfare assignment because we don't believe we will gain a benefit from it.

We are not saying church shouldn't be enjoyable or that we can't enjoy the company of friends there. We are simply asking: If there were no friends at church, if the talks and lessons were consistently dull, and the blessings from tithing or service difficult to discern, would we continue to go to church and keep the commandments? That is the fundamental question of hedonism. And if it is true that pleasure is our ultimate goal and we displace God, making him into the means to our pleasure, it is hard to imagine why we would answer the question affirmatively, unless, of course, we can find some other form of pleasure in doing these things. This is the problem of the hedonistic approach—we must always find some form of pleasure because pleasure has become our God. When that occurs, the Spirit necessarily withdraws, we feel the pain of the void increase, and because we are acting hedonistically already, we are likely to try to minimize the increasing pain of the void by seeking more pleasurable blessings and gifts from God, all the while distancing ourselves from Him.

Vanity

"God is forgotten out of vanity."—President Henry B. Eyring[16]

When the pursuit of pleasure becomes an obsession we open ourselves up to vanity. As an article in the *New Era* tells us, "The Hebrew word that the word *vanity* is translated from literally means 'vapor' or 'breath,' implying something that has no substance or permanence, such as the worship of idols or worldly things."[17] Vanity is self-worship. It is to make the self an idol and to become its servant and even its slave. Consider pagan idol worship as an analogy. Great care and effort went into building the idol and adorning it with the finest raiment and jewelry. Gifts were to be brought to the idol, sacrifices were to be made for the idol, and edifices needed to be built to protect the idol and provide the idol with a surrounding adequate to its beauty.

When we make ourselves into an idol, we too become obsessed with perfect beauty, adorning ourselves with the best clothing, makeup, and jewelry we can buy. Some may go as far as to undergo plastic surgery, suffering long and painful recovery periods and expending considerable funds and even going into debt to create the illusion of perfect beauty. Many suffer from an increasingly prevalent psychological disorder known as body dysmorphic disorder and spend all their time obsessing over the slightest blemish on their faces and bodies. All our labors and earnings are put into providing gifts to the idol of ourselves. The idol becomes everything and our vain obsessions with serving it begin to destroy us. We sacrifice our relationships, our concern for others' well-being, and neglect our responsibility to others and to God.

By being a slave to ourselves we really have no time to be servants of our Lord. Recall Christ's warning that no man can serve two masters; eventually one will be displaced. When we think we can have both God and ourselves as masters, "we try to live the impossible—having one foot in the kingdom of God and the other in the world, hoping to be accepted by both. Truly we are caught up in vanity—futile, worthless behavior in which we find excessive self-satisfaction in thinking that both God and the world are pleased with us."[18] Eventually God loses, we serve ourselves, and the void from our separation grows larger, leading us to worship the idol of ourselves even more, bringing it more gifts, more sacrifices, and more adornment and making us even more captive to ourselves. As President Henry B. Eyring put it, "Pride creates a noise within us which makes the quiet voice of the Spirit hard to hear. And soon, in our vanity, we no longer even listen for it. We can come quickly to think we don't need it."[19]

We can learn from those who came before us how vanity can completely consume and destroy people. At several places in the Book of Mormon we read of the wealthy Nephites adorning themselves with "costly apparel" and fine jewelry to be seen of others and to lift themselves above those who were not as beautiful and were less privileged (see Alma 32:2; see also Moroni 8:36–37). As they became their own idols, their self-worship supplanted the proper worship of their God, making them "gods unto themselves." Each time they became consumed by vanity, they ignited the jealous anger of the one true God and experienced hardships, captivity, and ultimately destruction as a result. As the scriptures had warned, they lost "even that which they [had]" (2 Nephi 28:30). They lost their beauty, their wealth, and their costly apparel, but more importantly they lost their souls, their salvation, and their love of God and their neighbor. They were emptied, hollowed out. There was no substance to them beyond the superficial veneer of what they once were.

Looking over all of his fallen people, the prophet Mormon recalled the true beauty of the Nephites that had been completely marred by their vain pride when he repeated, "Oh ye fair ones, how could ye have departed from the ways of the Lord! O ye fair ones, how could ye have rejected that Jesus, who stood with open arms to receive you!" (Mormon 6:17). Mormon calls out to his own people in futility, but in great hope for us who would read this book many years later. He counsels us not to place our trust in the vain things of the world but to recognize that we are already "fair ones" because of our special relationship to our God and our Savior, Jesus Christ. Perhaps Mormon would have us know that as God's spirit children we are already beautiful. We are heirs to the beauty of His love and His goodness. When we remember that, we no longer feel a desire to pursue worldly attraction and make ourselves into vain idols.

In these latter days we have received similar warnings from our leaders regarding vanity, as Douglas Bassett reminds us:

"For us, the disease which encompassed the Zoramites takes on more than clothing; it can include cars, houses, boats, diplomas, and anything else that has a foundation in which the need for the approval of others carries more weight than the need to be accepted by God. President Benson referred to this problem in general conference . . . : 'Are not many of us status-seekers—measuring the worth of a man by the size of his bank account, his house, his automobile? . . . This is a sad commentary on a civilization that has given to mankind the greatest achievement and progress ever known. But it is an even sadder commentary on those of us who call ourselves Christians, who thus betray the ideals given to us by the Son of God himself.'"[20]

The prophets today, like the prophets of old, pose the same question found in Alma to all of us, "Will ye persist in . . . setting your hearts upon the vain things of the world?" (Alma 5:53).

Greed

"Earth provides enough to satisfy every man's needs but not every man's greed."—MAHATMA GANDHI[21]

When we live as the Egoist, it can also lead to unbridled greed, which is an overwhelming desire to have more of something than is actually needed. Greed is perhaps the quintessential example of the lie because by definition, greed means to never be satisfied with that which we have. Oftentimes we think the more we have of something the better off we will be. On the contrary, Elder William R. Bradford asserts, "That which a man serves himself upon the platter of selfishness and greed may appease his mortal appetite, but it will leave him spiritually starved and malnourished."[22] We are seeing greed today destroy families, ruin lives, and lead people down immoral and unethical paths. Brother Quinn McKay said:

"The allure of the 'good life' and associating with those who are preoccupied with expensive cars, big houses, luxurious travel, vacation homes, and big investments causes people to think and feel differently. As Nephi, the son of Helaman, proclaimed, 'How could you have forgotten your God? . . . Behold, it is to get gain, to be praised of men, yea, and that ye might get gold and silver.' . . . (See Hel. 7:20–21.)"[23]

From television to newspapers to the Internet, we have read countless stories of so many individuals falling victim to greed; however, we cannot say we have not been warned. The warning was given to Timothy from Paul in 1 Timothy 6:7–10:

"For we brought nothing into this world, and it is certain we can carry nothing out. And having food and raiment let us be therewith content. But they that will be rich fall into temptation and a snare, and into many foolish and hurtful lusts, which drown men in destruction and perdition. For the love of money is the root of all evil: which while some coveted after, they have erred from the faith, and pierced themselves through with many sorrows."

Paul is not concerned with people having money. He is concerned with people setting their hearts upon money. As we mentioned earlier with regard to blessings, it is certainly not wrong if financial benefits ensue from our living a life that is focused on glorifying God. It is when we pursue money for its own sake that our ability to keep our eye single to the glory of God is called into question. In the Lord's words, we "cannot serve God and mammon," an Aramaic word meaning "riches" (Matthew 6:24; see also Luke 16:13; 3 Nephi 13:24). Succumbing to greed is the choice to serve mammon.

The challenge of greed for members of the Church comes primarily in the form of prosperity. Many of us are aware of the promise in Alma that states, "If ye will keep my commandments ye shall prosper in the land" (Alma 37:13), but it is only the greedy Egoist who equates prosperity with wealth. In fact, prosperity may come in many forms. There is no reason to assume that our understanding of "prosperity" is the same as the Lord's. Prosperity could mean receiving an abundance of the Spirit, having healthy children, living in close proximity to temples, having sufficient resources available to meet our basic needs, having healthy and close relationships, and so forth. Thus, when we become wealthy we ought not assume that it is necessarily evidence of the Lord prospering us. We see many examples in the scriptures of people who mistook wealth for the Lord prospering them (the Zoramites, for example). These people became greedy and prideful as they equated their desire for wealth with God's desire to prosper His righteous disciples.

Imagine if the greedy Egoist's equating of wealth and prosperity were true. This would mean that people who are poor are not being prospered by the Lord, which would mean that they must not be keeping the commandments of the Lord, because if they were they would be prospering in the land. In a 1989 *Ensign* article, Richard Tice responds to this problematic misunderstanding:

"There is no doubt that the Lord does bless us—but in *his* way. Many who diligently try to keep the Lord's commandments do not flourish financially. Many, in fact, may find themselves at times unable to make ends meet. Yet they can point to spiritual riches the

Lord has given them that they would never trade for a new car or a more luxurious home."[24]

Tice also says:

"The Lord has promised that if we serve him, we will prosper and have sufficient for our needs. But wealth is another matter. With so many millions in the world who don't have enough for their daily needs, why should we expect the Lord to make us wealthy?

"And yet, many of us continue to expect that our material conditions will automatically improve if we remain faithful."[25]

In addition to mistakenly equating wealth and prosperity, the greedy Egoist regularly engages in what social psychologists describe as *social comparison,* which is the tendency to evaluate ourselves by how we compare to others. Downward social comparison occurs when we compare ourselves to people who have less than we do and appear to be worse off. It results in an increase in our self-esteem. Upward social comparison occurs when we compare ourselves to people who appear to be better off and have more than we do, which results in a decrease in our self-esteem.

Not long ago, an acquaintance of ours decided to build her home high up on the hill overlooking the valley so she could literally look down on all the people who were worse off than she was. In a 2010 general conference talk, President Dieter F. Uchtdorf discusses how this type of social comparison is a sin of pride, noting that pride usually begins with "'Look how wonderful I am and what great things I have done,'" and "always seems to end with 'Therefore, I am better than you.'"[26]

For a time our acquaintance's "higher" living did enhance her feelings of self-worth. However, her pleasure was short-lived. A family began to build a home next door, and she noticed that they were installing tubing under the driveway that would run hot water beneath its surface and melt the snow in the wintertime. She did not have such a luxury. She had to shovel her snow. She also noticed (she actually measured it) that the neighbor's roof was exactly one foot higher than her own. With each amenity added to her neighbor's house—and she noticed them all—her "happiness" decreased until she began to despise her home. She focused on everything that was wrong with it to the point that she decided to put it up for sale. While this example may appear somewhat extreme, each of us can recognize similar feelings in ourselves when our neighbor comes home with a new car or boat or installs new granite countertops. When we allow ourselves to act as the greedy Egoist, our self-esteem takes a tumultuous roller coaster ride of ups and downs. President Gordon B. Hinckley could not have been more right when he said, "It is when greed takes over, when we covet that which others have, that our affliction begins."[27]

The greedy Egoist's only method of regulating his or her self-esteem is to "keep up with the Joneses," or even better, to surpass the Joneses. Thus, to offset the upward social comparison brought about by her new neighbor's better and taller house, the only thing our acquaintance could think to do was to move to a higher plateau on the hill and install the newest technologies into her home. This would allow her to social compare downward once again and again raise her self-esteem, at least until another new neighbor started building their taller, bigger, or better house, and then the cycle would repeat itself again.

In their incisive book *Affluenza: The All-Consuming Epidemic*, John De Graaf, David Wann, and Thomas H. Naylor define this self-esteem–affecting comparison cycle and its effects on behavior as "a painful, contagious, socially-transmitted condition of overload, debt, anxiety, and waste resulting from the dogged pursuit of more."[28] To their thinking, greed afflicts people as any disease and is rapidly transmitted from person to person until it becomes a societal, and even global, crisis.

Manufacturers, salespeople, and advertisers are fully aware of this greed-based epidemic, its causes and its symptoms, and know how to exploit it regularly to their gain. Consider technology as one compelling example. Many people have become completely enamored by, if not obsessed with having the latest technological invention or innovation, and manufacturers and advertisers know this all too well. As soon as they present a new product they are already preparing the next updated version to be sold soon thereafter. Those who own the original version will experience lowered self-esteem due to upward social comparison when the newer version comes out with its new bells and whistles.

Oftentimes the consumer is caught up in this cycle without even considering how noticeable the benefits of the new model are over the old one. We are sure our examples will be grossly outdated by the time the book is published, but one of our favorite symptoms of affluenza is the "more is better" symptom. In my[29] classes, when we discuss technology and ethics, I will ask my students whether it is more desirable to have a car with a single overhead camshaft (SOHC) or a double overhead camshaft (DOHC). They unanimously agree that the DOHC is preferable to the SOHC. I then ask them what an overhead camshaft is and what effect it has on a car's performance. With few exceptions, none of them have any idea whatsoever.

Like my students, most people just assume that having two of something is better than one. So, they favor a dual core processor in their computers over a single core processor (a triple or quadruple processor would even be better), a dual-bandwidth Internet router over single bandwidth, and double-strength Tylenol over regular strength. The higher the number, the better the product—regardless of whether any noticeable improvements can be identified or if we actually understand what the numbers mean. And we *have* to have these products even if we don't fully use their "improved" features. Thus, we want the four terabyte hard drive instead of the one terabyte hard drive, even if we will never use more than an eighth of its storage capacity. We have to have a TV with 1080p resolution instead of 720p resolution, even if we can't actually see the difference. We must have the 4G network instead of the 3G network on our smartphones if we are ever going to communicate effectively with the world.

At its worst, greed may even infect our marriages and families. Infidelity, for example, tends to germinate through thinking that things could be better in our marital relationship. When we see our friends and family with more attractive spouses, enjoying better financial stability, living in bigger homes that they own, or traveling the world, we can easily engage in upward social comparison and our marital esteem decreases. We become dissatisfied with our current spouse and we may begin looking elsewhere for someone more physically attractive, more funny, more emotionally sensitive, more financially stable, or more sexual. The key word in these statements is "more." When we are caught up in this cycle of wanting more we convince ourselves that the grass will be greener with someone else and we begin looking for something better.

We see this cycle time and time again when we counsel with couples. We hear husbands and wives say things like, "I am just not attracted to my spouse anymore," "He doesn't make enough money," "She has put on a lot of weight since we got married," or "It's just different from when we first got married." These comments betray the self-deception of marital greed, which is the belief that our marriage isn't enough. The spouse having an affair, for example, gets caught up in the excitement of a fresh new relationship. This new person seems so interested in them and so fun to be around; it is exciting to find someone who listens to you and wants to spend time with you. The self-deception is that they forget that they felt the exact same way about their spouse when they started dating many years ago. Moreover, they fail to recognize that this new relationship will also one day become less exciting—perhaps even boring—years down the road. If they do not learn this lesson, when that day comes they will start looking again for someone "better," fully believing that this time things will be different. With each "new model," the cheating spouse deceives him- or herself into thinking this time he or she will finally be truly fulfilled.

The sad consequence is that the self-deception of greed manifest in infidelity trivializes the sacred bonds of the marriage covenant, turning our spouse into just another commodity that becomes obsolete whenever a newer, better model comes out. Only too late do we realize that our pursuit of "more" breaks up our family and breaks the hearts of our spouse and our innocent children.

The philosopher George Santayana once said, "Those who cannot remember the past are condemned to repeat it."[30] When it comes to greed, we give no thought to the past or the present, but only to the future where the next thing or accomplishment is to be found. By focusing only on what is coming next, we ignore the God who was with us in the past, reaches out to us in the present, and will judge us in the future. We also fail to learn the lessons of the past that are taught in the Book of Mormon. Elder F. Burton Howard said, "[This book] speaks directly to members of the Church who have been blessed with more than they need."[31] May we be slow to forget the warning from President Brigham Young to the Saints about the dangers of greed in prosperity, "The worst fear I have about this people is that they will get rich in this country, forget God and his people, wax fat, and kick themselves out of the church and go to hell."[32]

CHAPTER 6

The Nihilist

"Nihilism is not only despair and negation, but above all, the desire to despair and to negate."—ALBERT CAMUS[1]

The nihilistic way of living is marked by feelings of hopelessness and despair. The Nihilist sees life as pointless and devoid of meaning. If a Nihilist has hope for an afterlife, it's not one that is any better than this life. These feelings of despair, however deeply they are felt and however long they last, ultimately stem from the same underlying—and likely implicit—response to the truth and the lie: *denial.* The Nihilist denies the truth that he or she is a chosen and beloved child of God, an heir to a King. The Nihilist sees no divine birthright, no divine plan, and no divine concern for him- or herself.

Whenever we experience any of these feelings, even for a moment, in that moment we inevitably, and perhaps even unintentionally, deny the truly special relationship we have with our Heavenly Father and dismiss the great plan for us that He has provided. We forget, however briefly, that He is dedicated to both our current and ultimate well-being and that He has provided us an abundance of resources, including the Comforter, a member of the Godhead, to help us fight off despair and to remind us of His love for us and of our divine potential. We lose track of the fact that God, like any loving father but to a celestial degree, is constantly seeking to buoy us up and to fill us with "a perfect brightness of hope" (2 Nephi 31:20), having His arms always outstretched to embrace us with His love. It is this truth, this most essential of all truths, sung by Primary children all around the world every Sunday, "I Am a Child of God,"[2] that is lost on the Nihilist. It is that loss that lies at the center of the Nihilist's despair.

Unlike Pharisees and Egoists, Nihilists find no consolation for their suffering in the lie. They deny themselves the pretense of any superiority over others and do not believe they deserve anything more than anybody else. On the contrary, they see themselves as the lowest of the low, the dregs of society. Nihilists see only their inferiority, inadequacy, and worthlessness in comparison to other people. Unlike the Egoists and the Pharisees who use downward social comparison to lift themselves above others, Nihilists are experts in upward social comparison; that is, comparison with people they perceive as being better than they are. The result of upward social comparison is self-deprecation and self-loathing. Nihilists are not jealous of those who are more successful, beautiful, or famous than they are because they don't feel like they have any right to expect that they should be like them. They genuinely believe there is nothing special about them in either the godly or the worldly sense of the word. Believing neither the truth nor the lie, the Nihilist is without hope of any kind, including genuine hope in God and His love.

A Word of Caution

Before going further with our description of the Nihilist exemplar, we issue a caveat to the reader. There is already a great deal of denial at play in this quadrant; in fact, more than with any other quadrant. It will be difficult for some readers to admit to any association with this way of responding to the truth and the lie because it is a painful and dark quadrant that is difficult to look at and can engender sorrow and despair. Many of us have been taught to look on the bright side of life and to accentuate the positive. Why would we ever want to focus on the dark side of life and highlight the negative? To do so runs counter to our culture and for some may even feel like a violation of a basic tenet of our faith, analogous to a sin.

We caution the reader against taking this perspective on the content of this chapter and suggest instead that feelings of sorrow and despair are an inevitable aspect of life, and more importantly, these feelings mark the path of discipleship. It is important to remember that Isaiah characterized the Savior, whom we emulate in every respect, as "a man of sorrows, . . . acquainted with grief" (Isaiah 53:3). We know that He, the greatest of all, condescended below all, and that in that condescension He fully drank the dregs of human suffering, cruelty, and despair. We also know that His Father allowed Him to feel the withdrawal of His presence and to be utterly alone. Our greatest example, the Savior of the world, did not turn away from the darkness. He allowed Himself to experience its full force and as a result can now truly succor each one of us. He can now reach out to us however far we may have fallen and however dark our view of the world may appear. If we are to follow Him, should not we be willing to do likewise?

Consider how helpful the experiences of prophets who were acquainted with grief and sorrow and who experienced moments of despair have been to so many people in times of hopelessness and suffering. Many of us have commiserated with Job, who was subjected to terrible tribulation and suffering and genuinely considered the possibility that he was cursed by God, saying: "He hath fenced up my way that I cannot pass, and he hath set darkness in my paths. He hath stripped me of my glory, and taketh the crown from my head. He hath destroyed me on every side, and I am gone: and mine hope hath he removed like a tree" (Job 19:8–10).

There have been times when many of us have felt abandoned and alone, much like the Prophet Joseph Smith, who suffered greatly during his life, culminating in his martyrdom, and whose despair was expressed most poignantly in Liberty Jail, where he cried out in anguish over the suffering of the Saints, "O God, where art thou? And where is the pavilion that covereth thy hiding place?" (D&C 121:1). Whether we like it or not, it appears that sorrow, grief, and despair are an important aspect of discipleship, an aspect we are exposed to time and again in the scriptures, and not an aspect from which we are supposed to turn away. Why would it be any different with our own nihilistic feelings? Shouldn't we also expect to experience them as part of our efforts to follow the Savior?

It is true that these exemplars did not stay in the nihilistic quadrant indefinitely. Job, after speaking of his suffering and loss of hope, is quick to declare, "I know that my redeemer liveth, and that he shall stand at the latter day upon the earth: and though after my skin worms destroy this body, yet in my flesh shall I see God" (Job 19:25–26). The Prophet Joseph also did not dwell on his despair for too long, but was comforted by the Lord's response to his cry for help, in which he declared, "My son, peace be unto thy soul; thine adversity and thine afflictions shall be but a small moment" (D&C 121:7).

While it is true that periods of suffering and moments of despair will befall even the prophets, the Lord's anointed who know Him best, it is not the case that these feelings will have no end. Indeed, as we will describe in a later chapter, the key to moving out of the Nihilist quadrant into discipleship is to lift our gaze toward the heavens, lay hold upon the words of the Lord, and through His mercy and grace, regain our hope in the Savior and in God's love for us. However, before we can talk about how to move out of the Nihilist quadrant, it is important that we understand the ways in which we move *into* it. If we can learn to recognize the signs of nihilism and our tendencies toward denying the truth and the lie, we can be more vigilant against nihilism gaining a habitual hold on us.

We have already learned from the examples of the Savior, Job, and Joseph Smith that trials and tribulation can precipitate feelings of despair—as can feelings of sorrow over the wickedness of the world. Finally, and perhaps most importantly, as Christ experienced to a degree we will never know, we tend to enter the Nihilist quadrant whenever we feel abandoned by our Heavenly Father. But there are more easily accessed entry points into nihilism as well, and most of them are not as dramatic as watching the persecution of your people because of wickedness. For example, when someone we care about rejects us and hurts our feelings, we can feel a nihilistic sinking sadness. When we don't perform up to our expectations at work, school, or church we can begin to question our worth. When we are excluded, put down, mocked, and judged we may begin to feel despair. When we continue to sin, even after we have tried to repent and forsake the sin several times before, we can start to feel hopeless about our capacity for forgiveness and righteousness.

Nihilistic feelings can and will befall all of us, and probably do so more often than most of us realize or are willing to admit. For example, many people go through periods of low-grade nihilistic spiritual stagnation. They do all that is required of them. They read their scriptures, pray every night, attend their church meetings, and go to the temple, but their actions are not accompanied by a spirit-filled vitality that uplifts and edifies them. They are just doing what they are supposed to do without much feeling or thought. They do these things primarily out of a feeling of duty or to avoid guilt. If we keep the commandments out of duty or to avoid feeling bad we may not be moving further from God necessarily, but we are not growing closer to Him either. We can check off all the boxes that show that we are a member in good standing, but we are quite stagnant in our relationship with God.

For a number of reasons that we will discuss in this chapter, people in spiritual stagnation often have difficulty feeling God's love. They can usually recall having felt it before, like when they were converted or served a mission or had a particularly good experience fulfilling a calling. But now some time has gone by without their feeling much of anything. Questions about God's love for them may arise. They still keep the commandments, hold callings, and have family night because they know it is right to do so. They may even have felt the love of God when they did such things in the past. But now they are doing these things out of habit and because it is expected, with very little spirit-filled vitality.

Our personal prayers often fall into this stagnant rut. Many of us pray much of the time out of habit, using many of the same words and phrases in a daily ritual that we do because we are supposed to and we would feel guilty if we did not do it. In such cases, it is hardly a heartfelt communication with our Father in Heaven. BYU professor Chauncey Riddle said, "One fundamental distinction between the saint and what the scriptures call the 'natural man' is in their use of prayer. The natural man may say prayers, but it is not a spiritual experience for him. He is only reacting to his physical environment as he has been instructed or as he thinks prudent."[3] Similarly, with scripture reading we may develop a tendency to focus on quantity over quality, just trying to get through the chapter so we can say to ourselves that we did our reading for that day. However, if we don't feel God's love and inspiration when we do this, what have we really learned? The psychodynamic theorist Erik Erikson asserts that stagnation of any type can lead to feelings of being stuck in a rut and uselessness.[4] When we feel these things in relation to the gospel and our relationship to God, it can create feelings of emptiness and lead us to doubt our divine nature and our special relationship to Him. It becomes easier to deny the truth and to lose our hope.

In order for us to see our own nihilistic tendencies, it is important to break the popular stereotype of the Nihilist who only wears black, isolates him- or herself, engages in self-destructive behaviors such as cutting on him- or herself, and entertains thoughts of suicide. Such persons only represent the more extreme and obvious form of nihilism. Each and every one of us has felt the darkness of despair and self-loathing creep into our thoughts, raising the question, "Am I of any worth?" It may take the form of a slow-burning spiritual stagnation or a full-blown crisis of faith, but whenever we find ourselves in that nihilistic frame of mind, however briefly, we tend to experience, as we describe in the next two sections, doubts about our worth and feelings of alienation.

Doubts about Our Worth

When we deny our divine nature, even momentarily, we sever our ties to God and detach our anchor from the proper and true source of our worth. Once decoupled from the love of God, we are susceptible to being tossed about by the storms of life. Dizzied by the swirl of challenges that toss and turn us, and feeling lost and alone, we seek out moorings that we hope will provide some semblance of the stability and security of the love of God we have lost. Though these alternative moorings may hold us steady for a time, they always ultimately fail when the tempests of life gain strength and tear us loose from whatever artificial mooring we have attached ourselves to.

We may attach our anchor to people, prestige, fame—any number of things. It is even possible to attach our anchor to loved ones, even our own spouse, which seems like a perfectly reasonable thing to do, until we consider what happens when our spouse gets angry with us, disappoints us, or rejects us. In our experience as therapists, we have seen spouses who depend on one another for their self-esteem, which seems great when things are going well, but often turns disastrous when conflict arises. When you put your trust in other people, no matter how close you are to them, your self-worth will always depend on how they treat you, and that treatment will change because even the best of us can err, hurt, and let us others down. A wise spouse, parent, and friend knows this and does not play into the other person's effort to anchor his or her self-worth in their relationship. In psychotherapy we call this "maintaining appropriate boundaries in the relationship." Proper boundaries are essential to a healthy, flourishing relationship, and no boundary is more important than those that point us, our spouse, our children, and our friends back to the true source of worth, our Heavenly Father, whose love never fails.

Perhaps this is why Nephi cried out, "O Lord, I have trusted in thee, and I will trust in thee forever. I will not put my trust in the arm of flesh; for I know that cursed is he that putteth his trust in the arm of flesh. Yea, cursed is he that putteth his trust in man or maketh flesh his arm" (2 Nephi 4:34). Because Nihilists continually anchor themselves to something other than God and are consistently let down and ultimately disappointed by their trust in the "arm of flesh," they often experience a feeling of being cursed, as Nephi put it. That is, as they continue to be disappointed by others, even loved ones, they start to wonder if something is fundamentally wrong with them—perhaps they are unlovable or undesirable to others, even God. In our work, we see people all the time who are seeking approval from others and, because they trust in the arm of flesh, they constantly need to see evidence from others that they are acceptable.

Who among us has not sought the approval of a teacher, boss, friend, bishop, or even a therapist? It feels almost normal to desire such things. Yet as helpful and supportive as these individuals may be, they can disappoint us, let us down, and even hurt us. Only a divine Father whose love for us is eternal and without end, whose arms are always outstretched to embrace us, can provide the sure foundation needed for us to know our true worth. Perhaps we need to be reminded of the lesson we teach our children with the Primary song "The Wise Man and the Foolish Man."[5] Recall that when "the rains came down and the floods came up," it was the man whose home was built upon the sandy foundation whose home was washed away. Only the man who built his home upon a solid rock foundation weathered the storms. Similarly, only the rock-solid foundation of our relationship to God and our total trust in Him will keep the edifice of our worth intact. Anything short of that, whether it be a person, accomplishment, wealth, or fame will ultimately erode beneath us and the feelings of worth we have erected upon that basis will wash away with the flood.

The habits of attaching our worth to other sources than God can be hard to break, even when we know better. As a beginning therapist, I[6] sometimes found myself slipping into the nihilist way of responding to the truth and the lie, especially when I felt unsuccessful in effecting change with clients in counseling. I remember one couple specifically that was unwilling to do the work to change their marital situation. I internalized their lack of effort as somehow being my fault. Even though I knew full well that I was not going to be able to help everyone I saw in counseling, in my mind, it was because of my deficiencies that the couple was not improving. I questioned my efficacy as a therapist and even contemplated changing my practice from work with couples and perhaps even counseling in general. I remember questioning the time and effort I'd spent in graduate school and wondering if I had chosen the right path as a therapist. I was at a low point in my nihilism that made me feel inadequate and doubt my worth as a therapist, a person, and also a provider.

Whenever my anchor of worth becomes grounded in success as a therapist and not in God, when that success does not come I start to question both my ability as a therapist and my decision to become a therapist. In Nephi's words, I begin to see myself as cursed. I wonder if I am deficient in some fundamental way that will always keep me from my goal of success. This cursed feeling is at the heart of nihilism. It is marked by the belief that there must be something basically wrong with us and by the feeling that we are just not cut out for our role as a spouse, or a parent, or at work. Once we feel cursed and doubt our self-worth, we begin to experience ourselves as unacceptable and we distance ourselves from God, the Spirit, and the Atonement, as well as our families, congregations, and communities. In short, we feel alienated.

Alienation

In *Merriam-Webster's Collegiate Dictionary,* the term *alienation* is defined as "a withdrawing or separation of a person or a person's affections from an object or position of former attachment."[7] When we feel cursed or deficient, we tend to withdraw from God and others. Much like the lepers of Christ's time, whose horrible disease led to self-imposed isolation and a loss of hope for any cure, when we feel cursed we can alienate ourselves from Christ and tell ourselves that

His Atonement can't reach us, that we are beyond redemption, that we will not be exalted, and that we will not be with Him in the next life. We can isolate ourselves from the Spirit and believe that the Holy Ghost will not be our companion because of our unworthiness. We may come to believe that God will not answer our prayers because we are undeserving of His assistance and may also feel undeserving of His blessings.

Once we feel cursed or inadequate in this way we also no longer feel like we belong with family, good friends, our local congregation, or our community. We see them as good people, whom God loves and who are deserving of that love. They all appear to be anchored to God and seem happy. The Nihilist feels like he or she is the only outlier, the only one who doesn't fit in. When we feel cursed in this nihilistic way, we sit in church thinking we are the only person who struggles with sin, or yells at our kids, or has bad thoughts at times. These beliefs in our uniquely ungodly nature inevitably create distance between us and those whom we believe are righteous, even when many of those we presume are righteous may struggle with exactly the same feelings we do.

The Nihilist too easily forgets the verse in Luke 5:31, which reads, "They that are whole need not a physician; but they that are sick." As a bishop, I[8] used to tell ward members who expressed feelings of alienation that a ward is like a hospital where everyone—even the nurses and orderlies—are sick, and only Christ, the great and merciful physician, can heal us. I also told them I wished everyone's sins had an odor. Members can always detect when a smoker walks into church because the smell of his or her sin is so strong. Heads turn to look toward the origin of the smell and people often avoid sitting near the sinner who smokes. What if all our sins smelled so strongly? We wouldn't be able to hide our sins, but we would also realize that we are not alone in our sins, because everyone would smell, at least until we repent and partake of the sacrament together. Nothing would be more desirable than a chapel that stinks to high heaven every Sunday because it would signify that we all, as fellow sinners before our God, are there for the same reason, forgiveness from the Savior.

We have a soft spot in our hearts for one group of church members because they often suffer from feelings of alienation—mothers who struggle all week with their difficult children and sometimes their difficult spouse and feel as if they've failed. Exhausted by their challenging week, they then go to church on Sunday, where their kids continue to misbehave, and they receive glares and negative comments about their family's irreverence. These mothers may come to believe that they alone are the ward's example of parental failure and that the other mothers in the ward have parenting all (or mostly) figured out. On top of struggling with real challenges with their kids they also have to deal with feeling as if they are the least effective mothers in their wards.

What these poor, discouraged mothers may not realize—and we wish we could show them—is that many of the mothers sitting in that sacrament meeting on Sunday have similar feelings of inadequacy and worry about failing as a mother, as do many of the fathers. Perhaps their issues with their children or spouse don't show at church on Sunday as some mothers' do, but these mothers certainly are not alone in their feelings of alienation regarding parenting. After all, parenting is difficult, often thankless work. God knows that better than anyone. He lost a third of His children to willful rebellion and sin. He had to bring a cleansing flood to wipe out a good number more. Should any of us, with all our imperfections, expect it to be easier with our own children? When we do, we sit squarely in the Pharisee quadrant, pretending that we are better than others or blaming others for their children's challenges. As we will discuss in the next chapter, the path of discipleship follows God's path, so we should not expect to escape from some degree of the parenting highs and lows that God has been through with His own children.

The mother who feels like a failure doesn't need to be told what she can do to be a better parent. You can bet she has already read every parenting book she can get her hands on and has tried to implement all sorts of practices to help her children do better. She obsesses over such things to the nth degree. She already knows all her weaknesses and what she needs to do to improve. What she *doesn't* know is that she is not alone, that she is not a failure, that God is not disappointed with her. She doesn't know she is loved.

For you parents reading this who feel alone in your struggles, we assure you, you are not alone. When our[9] first child was born, we were so excited to have her and she was so good—for the first few days. Then came inconsolable bouts of crying that would last for hours. Nothing we tried worked, and we tried everything in and out of the book, all our parents' ideas, the experts' recommendations, everything—but she wouldn't stop crying. Of course, my wife blamed herself. "I must not be a good mother," she told me. After all, other women in the ward with new babies didn't appear to have this problem. I can still remember several of these mothers saying how surprised they were that their baby almost never cried. They expected at least a little fussiness. They meant no harm and were just grateful for their blessing, but the comparison we inevitably drew with our daughter tore my wife apart. She thought even worse of herself and was more alienated from the women in the ward than before.

Eventually, the crying got so bad and we were both so exhausted that I thought at one point, just for a moment, that I no longer wanted the baby anymore; I wanted to get rid of her. It was a fleeting thought and I never would have acted on it, but I thought it, for the briefest of moments, and then I felt really bad for it. Eventually the crying bouts resolved themselves and our daughter became a very calm and even-keeled child. She still is for the most part. We will never know what caused her inconsolable crying during those first months, but we do know that those were especially hard times for us and we only made it through those first few months by the skin of our teeth. I wish my wife hadn't felt so badly about herself as a mother when she hadn't done the slightest thing wrong.

Sometimes all it takes is one other person admitting to his or her own struggles to help us realize we are not on the outside looking in. As crazy as it may sound, when mothers admit to yelling at their children or locking them in a room or wanting to duct-tape their kids' mouths shut or drive to a far-off land to escape, it rarely pushes mothers apart but often brings them together and lessens the alienation they feel. Perhaps we are biased because we are therapists, but we feel immediately closer to people when they share their struggles with us. Of course, there is a time and place for sharing and we all have to be careful not to share too much information too often or too soon, but that shouldn't deter us completely from trying. It is risky and there will be trial and error, but if we are going to overcome alienation and have our "hearts knit together in unity" (Mosiah 18:21) like the people of Alma, we must draw closer to one another in our strengths and in our weaknesses.

Of course, alienation is exactly what Satan wants for us. He wants to divide us from God and divide us from each other. When we have sinned, for example, Satan is the first to make us feel like we don't belong with the righteous at church and that we should be alone in that dark corner of marginalization because of our badness. He knows that sin alienates us from God and that the more we sin, the greater the alienation and the more difficult it becomes to effectively tap the power of God, which alone is sufficient to save us from our sins.[10] Sin is a powerful source of doubts about our worth and feelings of alienation, but it is not the only source. There are many potential sources of nihilism that warrant our attention and awareness. In the sections that follow we consider a few that are particularly pervasive and damaging.

Sources of Nihilism

Sin and Perfection

One of the primary ways in which we can move into the Nihilist quadrant is by anchoring ourselves to a misconception of perfection as the idea that if we could live without sin we would experience true happiness. This is a misconception because sin is an inevitable aspect of life. Consequently, a hope for happiness that is anchored to the impossibility of being sinless will always elude us. The true source of happiness in relation to sin is the Atonement, and so it is by repentance and being forgiven by God and not by not sinning that we have real, lasting joy.

Yet we are commanded in Matthew 5:48, "Be ye therefore perfect, even as your Father which is in heaven is perfect." Doesn't perfection mean to be without sin? Elder Russell M. Nelson provides helpful clarification. He states, "In Matt. 5:48, the term *perfect* was translated from the Greek *teleios,* which means 'complete.' *Teleios* is an adjective derived from the noun *telos,* which means 'end.' The infinitive form of the verb is *teleiono,* which means 'to reach a distant end, to be fully developed, to consummate, or to finish.' Please note that the word does not imply 'freedom from error'; it implies 'achieving a distant objective.' In fact, when writers of the Greek New Testament wished to describe perfection of behavior—precision or excellence of human effort—they did *not* employ a form of *teleios;* instead, they chose different words."[11]

Being complete or whole can also be understood relationally. Christ is perfect because He is one with the Father. He is perfected, or completed, in Him. We become perfect when we are perfected or completed in Christ. This is why Christ pleaded with His Father in the great intercessory prayer that His Apostles might also be perfect or complete by being one in Him as He is one in the Father. As Elder Nelson makes clear, this completion in Christ is our *telos,* or final goal. We seek to have our will swallowed up in Christ's will, to have our thoughts become His thoughts, and to be ultimately united with Him and our Father in the celestial kingdom. Thus, it is by them and in them that we are perfected and made whole. Perfection, understood relationally, is not a property of the individual; it is a quality of relationship with the divine. As we will discuss in more detail in the next chapter, perfection is to be yoked to Christ, our great perfector, "the author and finisher of our faith" (Hebrews 12:2) who alone completes us through His Atonement.

Without this proper understanding, perfection remains an unachievable individual property, which will, like any other anchor that is not grounded in God, ultimately let us down and lower our self-esteem and increase our alienation from God and others. The primary way in which perfectionism damages self-worth and alienates us from God and others is through sin. Isaiah said, "All we like sheep have gone astray" (Isaiah 53:6). Sin is an inevitable feature of human life. If we are focused on being sinless but can't avoid sin, then we will continually experience ourselves falling short of our goal. We will constantly feel guilty and incapable of living up to God's standard.

Our recurring lack of success in overcoming sin will inevitably lead us to question our ability to be a righteous follower of Christ.

After all, we are commanded to be perfect, so it should be achievable. However, not only do we commit sin regularly, we even repeat the same sins we have repented of and promised to forsake. What kind of a disciple are we if we can't put our sins behind us and stop repeating them? As this question comes to mind, we may question our capacity to be good. The possibility arises that we are cursed, that somehow we are fundamentally deficient and cannot keep the commandments as we should. We begin to despair about our chances of being redeemed and saved. Once we have adopted this belief about ourselves we can't help but wonder what is wrong with us, especially when we see members of our congregation who are worthy to take the sacrament and seem to be happy and living the gospel.

This comparison to others reinforces our belief that there is something wrong with us because if they can do it, we should be able to do it. It becomes difficult to go to church and be around others when we feel inadequate by comparison. So we alienate ourselves from the very community that is there to lift us up, support us, and comfort us. At the same time, we feel we cannot be forgiven by God because we continue to sin. Consequently, we believe that we cannot have the Spirit with us as a comforter and guide, and we don't expect God to answer our prayers and assist us or bless us. In the end we don't feel we belong with God or our peers.

One thing that stood out to me[12] when I would meet with members as a church leader is that when I would ask if they considered themselves worthy (to hold a calling, to go to the temple, or to advance in the priesthood), many would get nervous and look anguished. They would answer that they weren't perfect, but they were working on it. Some even said they didn't think they could ever say yes to that question because they still had weaknesses and sins to work on. They shied away from the word *worthy*. Rarely did I hear someone say that he or she had partaken of the Atonement through repentance and forgiveness, so yes he or she did consider him- or herself worthy. Those who considered themselves unworthy had all repented, of course, multiple times, but that wasn't enough. They believed they had to stop sinning. Only when they did that could they answer that question affirmatively. Otherwise, they were not a worthy member. How sad it was to see wonderful, hard-working brothers and sisters think so badly of themselves. If only they could see themselves as Christ sees them, or even as I saw them. They are among the noble and great ones, beloved children of God.

Psychologists have expressed concerns with a fixation on flawlessness, stating that it creates "a steady source of negative emotions; rather than reaching toward something positive, those in its grip are focused on the very thing they most want to avoid—negative evaluation. Perfectionism, then, is an endless report card; it keeps people completely self-absorbed, engaged in perpetual self-evaluation— reaping relentless frustration and doomed to anxiety and depression."[13]

President Dieter F. Uchtdorf warns us of the perils of perfectionism: "I want to tell you something that I hope you will take in the right way: God is fully aware that you and I are not perfect.

"Let me add: God is also fully aware that the people you think are perfect are not.

"And yet we spend so much time and energy comparing ourselves to others—usually comparing our weaknesses to their strengths. This drives us to create expectations for ourselves that are impossible to meet. As a result, we never celebrate our good efforts because they seem to be less than what someone else does.

"Everyone has strengths and weaknesses.

"It's wonderful that you have strengths.

"And it is part of your mortal experience that you do have weaknesses.

"God wants to help us to eventually turn our weaknesses into strengths (see Ether 12:27), but He knows that this is a long term goal. He wants us to become perfect (see 3 Nephi 12:48), and if we stay on the path of discipleship, one day we will. It's OK that you're not quite there yet. Keep working on it, but stop punishing yourself."[14]

Perhaps Elder Neal A. Maxwell said it best when he said, "The Church is 'for the perfecting of the saints' (Eph. 4:12); it is not a well-provisioned rest home for the already perfected."[15] If we attach our worth to "perfection," misunderstood in these ways, it is a sure path to nihilism. Sin will happen. Mistakes and errors will emerge and doubts about our ability to be good and noble will creep into our hearts. The adversary whispers in our ears that we are deficient and cursed and that we are inferior to others and not deserving of God's love. His chains subtly tighten around us and we sink into misery and despair. Instead of becoming like Christ, we become like the adversary—hopeless. Do not forget that is what Satan's lie is all about; he wants us to become like him, separated from God and without hope of redemption. His perversion of perfection is one way he can get us there.

Addiction and Pleasure

Another one of the adversary's most successful paths to misery and hopelessness is addiction. The path of addiction is marked by an initial exposure to activities, substances, or images that provide pleasure. While several of these attractions are specifically forbidden by the Lord's commandments, many of these pleasurable experiences are not sinful, initially. Who doesn't love a good bowl of ice cream, shopping, or getting in a good workout? There is nothing inherently wrong about these activities. They provide enjoyment, and in moderation, may be perfectly appropriate. However, when we just have to eat another one or two bowls of ice cream to feel satisfied, or we don't have the money but feel we just have to get that new pair of jeans so we put it on a credit card, or when we become excessive in our exercise and obsess over our appearance, these initially harmless attractions start to test our anchoring to God. Pleasure begins to compete with God for our loyalty.

If we are not vigilant, our occasional indulgences in pleasure can turn into regular habits that we feel we must fulfill, and we pull up our anchor from God and ground it in the pleasurable activity instead. Embarrassed because we have committed ourselves to pleasure instead of our God, and stubborn because we don't want anyone to stop us, we conceal what is now a developing addiction from those around us. Because the pleasure-seeking activity is now our master, we commit an overabundance of time to it and we think about it more regularly. We rationalize that it's not that bad and we tell ourselves it is still only an occasional indulgence, not an uncontrollable habit. All the while, we develop elaborate rituals around it and give it a status and power that only enhances its attraction. Soon it has become a full-fledged addiction and, as we described in chapter 3, we become caught up in a void-enlarging tragedy that feels inescapable and we begin to despair and lose hope.

It is at this moment that nihilism takes hold of us in two ways. First, we have a cavernous void in us that we continually fail to fill which reduces self-worth and leads us to feel cursed. We question whether we can achieve goals, overcome challenges, or be helped by God in our adversity. Second, we cut ourselves off from others and feel isolated and alienated from the world. The addiction therapist Craig Nakken notes that as we become fully addicted, "There is little in the person's life that is permanent and doesn't pertain to the addiction. The person has become totally afraid of intimacy and stays away from any sign of it. Addicts frequently believe others are the cause of their problems. They think people can't understand them. Thus people are to be avoided."[16] Nakken continues, saying that the problem with the addicted person is that "the aloneness and isolation create a center that is craving an emotional connection with others. . . . the Addict wants to be alone, but the Self is terribly afraid of being alone."[17] This is the core of alienation, the paradox of feeling estranged and wanting connection but failing in the efforts to achieve it.

In our experience in working with those who suffer from addictions, many tend to eventually end up in the Nihilist way of responding to the truth and the lie. The guilt and shame they feel about themselves destroys any feeling of their being special from a worldly view and can be much more destructive from a spiritual perspective. As they hit rock bottom they feel undeserving of anything from anyone and are alone in their misery. This is a scary place to be for the addict because as they try to fill this void they fall deeper and deeper into that dark corner where, to their mind, forgiveness is no longer an option and no one can help them. The self-loathing of the Nihilist addict is almost unfathomable.

Abuse and Shame or Guilt

People who have been abused, especially as children, often suffer from a unique form of nihilism. In their case, they have done nothing to sever their relationship to God. It is the abuser who has robbed them of their innocence, ripped their anchor out of its grounding in God in the most horrific of ways, and left the person's soul feeling completely lost at sea. The innocent victim's relationship to God is broken involuntarily through no fault of his or her own. It is a sad fact of this life that one person's horrible misuse of agency can enlarge the void of another. Many who have been abused are left feeling anchorless once they feel severed from the love of God, and as a result often fall prey to the currents and winds that push them where they will. Given the size of the void created by this terrible trauma and the horrific manner in which their relationship with God was cut, these poor souls have been deeply wounded and confused. In that confusion, some may seek comfort and solace in exactly the opposite of what they need. Their world has been turned upside down, their view of themselves has been turned upside down, and they now seek comfort and solace in things that appear irrational, are unhealthy, and only worsen the problem.

Some get caught up in drugs, promiscuity, abusive relationships, and so forth, and instead of filling their void with God's love and comfort, they add their own sins on top of the sins committed against them. They feel dirty, bad, and incapable of genuine love, and they tend to think that they can never have a normal, healthy life. Some become angry with God for allowing the abuse and the devastating consequences it has created. Others feel that God has failed to protect them and live in fear of their next trauma. However manifested, this estrangement from God makes it very difficult for them to feel the Spirit's comforting power. They believe their repentance is ineffectual, forgiveness just isn't possible for them, and their prayers won't get answered.

Suffering abuse also may cause alienation from peers, family, and members of the congregation because they don't understand what it's like to have innocence taken from them. Some well-intended but misguided people try to minimize the effects of the abuse, asserting that it happened a long time ago; it's time to move on; stop letting your past control your present. Those who hold these views don't understand the depth of the wound and its resistance to healing. They don't understand that the abused person's agency is constrained by the trauma they have suffered—choices to feel good and to do good don't come easily. They can't just "snap out of it," forget it happened, and move on any more than a person who has suffered severe head trauma in an automobile accident can just behave as they did before the accident. Those who have been abused still have agency, of course, but it is constrained by what has happened. When well-meaning family, friends, and members fail to appreciate this constraint, it can be hard to be around them. Church itself can become a place to be reminded of the injustice they have suffered. As people talk about God's love, protection, and blessings, the person who has been abused is left to question why such things seem to have been withheld from him- or herself.

More than any quadrant, these wounded and tormented souls experience most acutely the feeling of the void created by their departure from Heavenly Father. The abuse doubles the distance they feel from their God. The void has become a large and infected wound that spreads to their whole being. It is for this reason that Christ spoke most decisively and angrily against those who would do harm to little children and the innocent. The damage abusers inflict is very difficult to surmount in this life. The abuser has taken that which is most precious to the Lord, the innocence of youth, and for that the Lord has this pointed response: "But whoso shall offend one of these little ones which believe in me, it were better for him that a millstone were hanged about his neck, and that he were drowned in the depth of the sea" (Matthew 18:6).

I[18] met once with a young woman in my office who wanted to end her life. She stated that no one would care if she was dead and no one would miss her. In further discussion, she revealed that she was a victim of sexual and physical abuse, abuse that she had never dealt with and always blamed herself for. Following the abuse she had developed self-hatred, taken drugs to escape pain, and had been promiscuous. Because of such sin, she explained that she did not feel worthy of the Atonement and that it did not apply to her because of her "extreme wickedness." She became hopeless and doubted that anything in her life was good. Not only did she feel undeserving of God's love, but her self-esteem was so very low that she felt undeserving of compliments or gifts from others.

With the Christlike compassion that is uniquely expressed by the Lord's special witnesses to those who suffer, Elder Richard G. Scott clarifies the true origin of the nihilism suffered by this woman and many others who have been abused:

"Satan is the author of all of the destructive outcomes of abuse. He has extraordinary capacity to lead an individual into blind alleys where the solution to extremely challenging problems cannot be found. His strategy is to separate the suffering soul from the healing attainable from a compassionate Heavenly Father and a loving Redeemer.

"If you have been abused, Satan will strive to convince you that there is no solution. Yet he knows perfectly well that there is. Satan recognizes that healing comes through the unwavering love of Heavenly Father for each of His children. He also understands that the power of healing is inherent in the Atonement of Jesus Christ. Therefore, his strategy is to do all possible to separate you from your Father and His Son. Do not let Satan convince you that you are beyond help.

"Satan uses your abuse to undermine your self-confidence, destroy trust in authority, create fear, and generate feelings of despair. . . .

"Satan will strive to alienate you from your Father in Heaven with the thought that if He loved you He would have prevented the tragedy. Do not be kept from the very source of true healing by the craftiness of the prince of evil and his wicked lies. Recognize that if you have feelings that you are not loved by your Father in Heaven, you are being manipulated by Satan."[19]

Adversity and Abandonment

Similar to the abused person, but to a less severe degree, trials and tribulations that feel too great to bear can test our anchoring to God, and when they do not relent, it can feel as if the relationship is severed. This is especially likely when we hold to an implicit belief that bad things should not happen to those who worship and serve God. After repeatedly suffering from adversity, we begin to question our worth in God's eyes and wonder if He even cares about us. We think He may not love us as much as others, we must have done something to offend Him, or that He's conducting a cruel test of our loyalty as He did with Job. Regardless of our assumptions about why we suffer adversity, when it does not relent we can feel cursed and believe that we have been given an overabundance of misfortune.

When I[20] was young I began to develop the belief that I was cursed in this way. I developed a kind of superstition about myself, in which it seemed to me that bad things happened to me more often than they did other people. When my school hosted a special trip to Disneyland or some other desirable destination, I always seemed to get sick. Of course, I was always well on test days, days I had to give a speech, and most every other day of the year, but whenever the special events came along I would fall ill. When everyone in the class was goofing off, it seemed as if the teacher always picked me to reprimand and punish with detention. When the school bully needed someone to pick on, I just happened to be nearby. When my friends and I toilet-papered a girl's house, I was the one who was caught by her parents and forced to clean it up while my friends watched from the bushes and laughed.

When my brother yelled "nice hair" out of the car window at some punk rockers on the way home from school one day, and they followed us to a stoplight, got out of their car, and came up to our open windows to confront us, it was me they accused of yelling at them. Four punches in the face later, my cheek bruised and my ear bleeding from cuts made by the rings the one who hit me wore, I couldn't help but wonder, *Why me?* In my freshman year in high school, on the first school day after Christmas break, I wore my brand-new jacket and watch to school, excited to show my friends my gifts. During PE, someone broke into my locker and stole my new jacket and watch. Why did they choose *my* locker? I had four bicycles stolen during my junior high and high school years. My fifth bike must not have been worth stealing, but someone did steal the seat and slit the tires with a knife. That made for a long and difficult walk home. My parents even called me "the boy with the little black cloud over his head" because so many bad things seemed to befall me. And these are only a few things on the list.

When it feels like there is no escape from adversity and we are cursed with a life of suffering, as I did then (and sometimes still do), we may learn helplessness. To understand learned helplessness, we look to the research of Martin Seligman, a research psychologist, who conducted a study on dogs in a cage. Initially, he would electrify the flooring beneath the dog on one side of the cage and the dog would jump to the other side to escape the pain of electrocution. He would then electrify the side of the cage the dog had escaped to and the dog would quickly move to the other side of the cage. The dog learned very well how to cope with its suffering and seemed to maintain its personality.

But then, Seligman electrified both sides at once. Then, when the dog expected the other side to be safe, it learned that it was equally painful. There was no escape. Without the possibility of escape, the dog simply gave up, laid down in a corner, and accepted the shocks, as painful as they were, without any movement. In a very short time, the dog had learned helplessness. The unfortunate consequence of Seligman's research was that he had a difficult time getting the dogs out of their helpless state. Even when he no longer shocked them and opened the cage door so they were free to walk out of the cage and leave, they continued to lay there, helpless. It was as if they didn't believe they could really escape, ever. They didn't have any hope.[21]

Similarly, when we feel we cannot escape the pain and suffering of adversity, we may give up hope that God will provide a way to escape from or cope with our trials, and we just stop trying. We feel abandoned or unloved and we surrender to our sorry lot in life. When this occurs we sense no comfort from the Spirit, we hear no answers to our prayers, and we feel lost and despised. We gain little consolation from our peers who don't seem to suffer as badly as we do. They are not cursed. On the contrary, many seem to live a charmed life. They stand up in testimony meeting and share the many blessings God has provided them, including how He has relieved their suffering, and they are now glad they went through the adversity because it strengthened them and taught them so much. This is a hard thing to hear when you are in the midst of trials and tribulations that show no signs of ending. It is hard to feel comforted by those who seem more loved and more blessed than you. Instead, it is easier just to stay away. It may be lonely, but at least your cursed status isn't being rubbed in your face.

In addition to a kind of learned helplessness that convinces us there is no relief that will come, our feelings of adversity and abandonment can lead us into a self-fulfilling prophecy, in which we primarily—or only—attend to our trials and tribulations, and we disregard evidence of Gods' blessings and our good fortune. In such cases, it can be difficult to find our way back to God because we disregard His efforts to reach out to us and ignore the love He continually shows us. My youth wasn't all bad, of course. There were times of fortune and blessings. Satan's trick is to get us to ignore those evidences that would debunk our belief that we are cursed and to focus our attention only on those events that confirm our belief that we are cursed. If we are blind to our blessings, then, like Seligman's dogs, we will see only suffering, give up, and even when good things happen and relief is available, we won't budge an inch to access that relief.

The message of the Nihilist chapter is clear. When we deny the love of God and our special relationship to Him in any way and for any amount of time, we become immediately susceptible to Satan's efforts to widen the gap between us and our God. It is hard enough to be away from Him as part of the plan. It is even harder when we put space between Him and us by doubting our worth, believing we are cursed or deficient in some irredeemable way, and alienating ourselves from the sources of His comfort and from those who love us. With our anchor uprooted, Satan, who desires to have us so he can sift us as wheat (see 3 Nephi 18:18), does exactly that. We are tossed to and fro and our self-worth rises and falls with the waves of attention we might receive from any source that is not our God. As our failures to feel worthy mount, we give up hope and become miserable. We become like that clever Lucifer who wants nothing more than for us to be as he is, utterly without hope in this world and the next.

CHAPTER 7

The Disciple

"A disciple of Christ is one who is learning to be like Christ—
learning to think, to feel, and to act as he does."
—CHAUNCEY C. RIDDLE[1]

Disciples are followers of Jesus Christ. Like the Savior, whose example they emulate, Disciples accept the truth that they are God's children, His noble and great ones, but they deny the lie that this makes them better than others. On the contrary, they are humble servants of others. The word *disciple* comes from the Latin *discipulus,* meaning "learner." What is it the Disciple is learning? Ultimately the Disciple is learning to become like Christ. Put more concretely, a Disciple is learning to fill the void which resulted from our separation from our eternal Father with God's love, even the pure love of Christ, which is charity. The Disciple is learning to practice that charity in relation to others.

Lehi learned about discipleship in his dream of the tree of life. Lehi says that in his dream:

"I beheld a tree, whose fruit was desirable to make one happy. And it came to pass that I did go forth and partake of the fruit thereof; and I beheld that it was most sweet, above all that I ever before tasted. Yea, and I beheld that the fruit thereof was white, to exceed all the whiteness that I had ever seen. And as I partook of the fruit thereof it filled my soul with exceedingly great joy; wherefore, I began to be desirous that my family should partake of it also; for I knew that it was desirable above all other fruit. . . . And it came to pass that I beckoned unto them; and I also did say unto them with a loud voice that they should come unto me, and partake of the fruit, which was desirable above all other fruit" (1 Nephi 8:10–12, 15).

In describing his dream of discipleship, Lehi first expresses the desirability of the fruit of the tree. The Spirit taught Nephi, Lehi's son, that the desirable fruit of the tree from his father's dream was a symbol for the love of God, which we all inherently desire as a consequence of our separation from Him. Our desire for God's love is the truest description of the feeling of the void. Lehi also states that the fruit filled his soul with "exceedingly great joy," which symbolizes the true fulfillment we can have when we seek to fill the void with God's love.

When Lehi partakes of the fruit, he experiences it as sweeter than anything he has ever tasted and whiter than anything he has ever seen. This symbolizes the unmatchable and indescribable fulfillment we experience when we fill the void with the resources God has provided us. When we experience His love, we realize that the artifices we have pursued in the other ways of responding to the truth and the lie are just that—hollow and inadequate substitutes, false idols. Only by eating the fruit does Lehi's soul became filled with exceedingly great joy, and only by partaking of God's love through the resources He has provided do we no longer feel the void.

Immediately following Lehi's joyous void-filling experience, symbolized by his eating the fruit, he desires to share the love of God he has experienced with his loved ones. This immediate reaching outward to others is a critical difference between the Disciple and the other ways of living in response to the truth and the lie. Because Disciples are filled with the love of God, they no longer experience emptiness or incompleteness. They are freed from the enticement of the void-enlarging artifices that Satan uses to ensnare us and lead us astray. Thus, in those moments when we are living as a Disciple, we are liberated by God's love from looking inward at our own emptiness and released from our continual efforts to fill the void.

Being truly filled, we naturally turn outward to others and are filled with a desire to share the love of God we have received with all those around us. We emanate the charity from God that fills us, and our countenance is changed as we seek to share His love with others. We become a light shining brightly before others, but it is not our light that shines (to believe it is *our* light is to believe the lie); it is His light that fills us. And once filled we are commanded to share that light with all those around us. "Ye are the light of the world," exclaimed the Lord, speaking of those who follow Him. "A city that is set on an hill cannot be hid. Neither do men light a candle, and put it under a bushel, but on a candlestick; and it giveth light unto all that are in the house. Let your light so shine before men, that they may see your good works, and glorify your Father which is in heaven" (Matthew 5:14–16).

We see the learning experience of discipleship and witness the light of charity that fills the Disciple's soul time and again in the scriptures. For example, the prophet Enos hungered and thirsted so much for God's love that he prayed both day and night to receive it. After praying for and receiving his own forgiveness, he became filled with God's love and then immediately felt a desire for the welfare of his brethren, the Nephites. He then poured out his soul on their behalf and even went on to pray for the well-being of the Lamanites, the

Nephites' longtime enemy. Enos was filled with charity and became a Disciple, whose love of God and all people shined forth as a bright example for all to see.

Alma the Younger was harrowed up with the memory of all his sins and was in utter despair until he remembered the words of his father about the Redeemer and cried out with the strongest desire for mercy. After Alma the Younger received forgiveness for his grievous sins, he was filled with joy and immediately went out and shared the joy of the Lord with others, including eventually his sons, telling his son Helaman, "Yea, and from that time even until now, I have labored without ceasing, that I might bring souls unto repentance; that I might bring them to taste of the exceeding joy of which I did taste; that they might also be born of God, and be filled with the Holy Ghost" (Alma 36:24). The light of God's love dispelled the darkness surrounding Alma and filled his soul, making him a loyal Disciple whose story of redemption has touched the hearts of millions.

Prior to becoming the great Apostle Paul, Saul was a Pharisee who participated in the persecution of Christ's followers. After being visited by Christ and being fully saturated with the love of God, Saul's transformation from persecutor to Disciple was so complete that he changed his name, his occupation, and his purpose for living. Like Enos, Alma, and all others whose feeling of the void is truly filled, Paul was inclined toward serving others. Immediately following his incredible conversion experience on the road to Damascus, Paul traveled far and wide to share the love of God he had received with all those who would listen, and even those who would not. He too emanated the light of the Savior's love for all people to see and follow, so they too could feel the sweet joy that a close relationship to the Lord brings.

This two-step learning process of discipleship—being filled with

God's love and then desiring to share that love with others—informs and edifies our understanding of the two great commandments. The first great commandment is to love the Lord thy God with all thy heart, might, mind, and strength (see D&C 59:5). We keep this commandment by partaking of our Heavenly Father's unmatchable love for us through the many wonderful resources He has provided us. His love is so abundant and effulgent that we cannot contain it. It overflows us and is returned back to Him. Paul teaches that "we love him, because he first loved us" (1 John 4:19). So it is that we can only truly love our God with all our might, mind, and strength if we have been filled with His love, which enables us to truly love Him back. Like so many other gifts we give the Lord, such as tithing, the love we return to Him is but a small portion of the great and wonderful love He has already given us.

The second great commandment, which is like unto the first, is to love thy neighbor as thyself (see Matthew 22:39). This verse can easily be misunderstood, particularly when we are in the Pharisee, Egoist, or Nihilist quadrants. We misunderstand this scripture if we believe it means that we have to focus on loving ourselves and it is only after we have done so that we can truly love others. After all, if we despise ourselves, as the Nihilist does, how can we love others? We could only despise them as we despise ourselves. So we must learn to love ourselves in order to love others, the argument goes. And how do we do that? The answer is the message of so much self-help psychology books, so many self-esteem guides, and so many "power of positive thinking" self-affirmations. We have to find satisfaction in ourselves, not be so hard on ourselves, and learn to accept ourselves as we are. We are reminded of the *Saturday Night Live* sketch where a man who struggles with loving himself looks into a mirror and tells himself, "I'm good enough, I'm smart enough, and doggone it, people like me."[2]

While we may all benefit from the occasional self-supportive pep talk, trying to talk, feel, and behave ourselves into loving ourselves is a poor substitute for God's love. As we discussed in chapter 6, when we anchor our worth in anything besides God, especially in ourselves, we will be let down and feel worse about ourselves. Moreover, trying to love ourselves is a self-centered activity, as the man looking at himself in the mirror while he tells himself he is good enough playfully illustrates. The question also arises: When will we know we have achieved self-love and are then truly able to love others as ourselves? Some people spend their whole lives trying to learn to love themselves while the people around them—their spouse, their children, their parents—wait and wait and wait for their turn. Surely, this can't be what the Savior had in mind when He gave this second great commandment.

For the Disciple, this commandment has nothing to do with focusing on the self. The Disciple doesn't have to find a way to love him- or herself so he or she can then love others. It is not about making love of self a goal. It is about partaking of the readily available love of God that fills the Disciple's soul with love for God, self, and others in the most natural of ways. When the void is filled, we see ourselves as God sees us, as His beloved children, and we see others as God sees them, as His beloved children—all at the same time. We truly love ourselves *and* our neighbors as He loves us; indeed, because He loves us. So it is that the first and second commandment are fulfilled by God's love simultaneously.

President Gordon B. Hinckley declared: "Love of God is the root of all virtue, of all goodness, of all strength of character, of all fidelity to do right. . . . Love the Lord your God, and love His Son, and be ever grateful for Their love for us. Whenever other love fades, there will be that shining, transcendent, everlasting love of God for each of us and the love of His Son, who gave His life for each of us."[3]

Characteristics of Discipleship

Now that we understand what the Disciple learns, which is charity, we consider some of the key attributes that characterize this learning process. Speaking of His true Disciples, the Lord stated, "By their fruits ye shall know them" (Matthew 7:20). What are the fruits of discipleship? What were the qualities of Lehi, Enos, Alma the Younger, and Paul that distinguished their times of discipleship from their moments of egoism, Pharisaism, and nihilism? What attributes should we focus on so we can be filled with God's love more regularly and for longer periods of time? There are surely many characteristics that mark discipleship and prepare us to receive God's love. We focus on four attributes that we feel are worth special emphasis:

1) Being humble, which entails recognizing our dependency on God and being submissive to Him
2) Being yoked to Christ
3) Having our hearts transformed
4) Seeing through Christ's eyes

Although one or two of these may be more salient at different times of discipleship, they really belong together and tend to occur together, perhaps even following each other in sequence. That is, humility inclines us to submit and to accept Christ's yoke. As we are yoked to Christ, we experience a mighty change of heart, and we come to see others as Christ sees them. This is not a necessary pattern, but it is one that often characterizes discipleship.

Humility

And if men come unto me I will show unto them their weakness.
I give unto men weakness that they may be humble; and my
grace is sufficient for all men that humble themselves before me;
for if they humble themselves before me, and have faith in me,
then will I make weak things become strong unto them.
—ETHER 12:27

The first characteristic of discipleship is humility. In order to receive charity, the Disciple must first become humble. Humility has two parts. The first part of humility, which will be addressed in this section, is to *recognize* our dependence on Christ for all that we are and all that we do and all that we have. Paul taught the Colossians about our dependence upon Christ, "For by him were all things created, that are in heaven, and that are in earth, visible and invisible, whether they be thrones, or dominions, or principalities, or powers: all things were created by him, and for him: and he is before all things, and by him all things consist" (Colossians 1:16–17).

In His revelation to the Prophet Joseph Smith, the Lord Himself testifies that He is "the light which is in all things, which giveth life to all things, which is the law by which all things are governed, even the power of God who sitteth upon his throne, who is in the bosom of eternity, who is in the midst of all things" (D&C 88:13).

The Disciple acknowledges and appreciates the light of Christ as a necessary condition for every aspect of our being. The light is in us and through us and gives life to us, as it does all things, and without it we could not exist. Thus, the characteristics, activities, and talents of the Disciple cannot be understood apart from Christ and cannot come from the Disciple alone, as if the Disciple were somehow a self-contained entity. Instead, the Disciple's humility depends on Christ's humility, the Disciple's kindness depends on Christ's kindness, and the Disciple's goodness depends on Christ's goodness. Even our capacity for faith in Christ depends upon Christ.

This recognition of our complete dependency upon Christ for all things is the only way we can truly be humble. If we allow ourselves to think of our faith, love, and even our very breath as being in some way independent of Christ, then we inevitably give ourselves some of the credit for our accomplishments and by so doing open the door to the artifices of pride and vanity. We also risk losing the favor of the Lord. Recall that "in nothing doth man offend God, or against none is his wrath kindled, save those who confess not his hand in all things, and obey not his commandments" (D&C 59:21). We cannot receive or keep hold of the love of God if we have offended God. For this reason, genuinely recognizing God's hand in all things, or being properly humble, is the first step toward discipleship.

The Disciple's dependence on Christ clearly contrasts with the Pharisee's notion of independence. Like many of you, we have attended Sunday School and priesthood or Relief Society meetings in which the teacher draws a bar graph on the board or a path with chasms that require bridges to be crossed. At the top of the bar graph or at the end of the path the teacher writes the word "salvation." The instructor then divides up the workload required to achieve salvation into two parts—Christ's part and our part—and designates that distinction by a line on the bar graph or by the steps and bridges on the path. The questions usually asked at this point are something like "What is our part?" "What do each of us have to do to gain salvation?" and "What is Christ's part?" "What does He do for us to gain salvation?" People then proceed to divide up the tasks. Christ conquered physical and spiritual death for us, but we have to keep the commandments and live worthily to do our part.

We take no issue with Christ's part. He alone has trodden the winepress. He raised Himself from the dead. He suffered for our sins alone in the Garden of Gethsemane. But what about our part? Is it really our own? In doing our part are we somehow acting without Christ? How do we reconcile such notions of independence with the scriptures we quoted at the start of this section? Can we be humble and claim independence from Christ at the same time? Doctrine and Covenants 93:30 states that all truth is independent in that sphere in which God has placed it, to act for itself. Doesn't that show our independence, even from Christ? Only if we ignore the sphere in which God has placed us.

God has placed us in a physical world, with physical bodies and in homes with particular parents in particular cultural and geographic locations and temporal eras. We are not independent of these things, nor do they cause us to act, but they do constrain our choices. For example, I[4] would love to slam dunk a basketball, just as I would love to fly through the air like Superman, but these are not genuine possibilities for me given the constraints of my body and the physical world I inhabit. I would love to travel the world and speak fluently the language of every country I visit, but the constraints of my home country and language education limit my fluency possibilities. It is true that I can study more languages and increase my polyglottal fluency, just as I can lose weight, workout, and increase my vertical jump, but there will still be constraints on my agency. I will continue to live in a sphere of limited possibilities for action and I will not be completely independent of everything.

The sphere of our existence in which God has placed us includes spiritual constraints as well. We have spirit bodies. We live with the consequences of the Fall; we have been separated from God's presence and experience the feeling of the void. We are constrained by God's laws of justice and mercy and by the blessings of the Atonement, which require repentance and forgiveness. We are filled with the light of Christ which gives us breath and life. We are enticed by the Spirit to do good and by the adversary to do evil. We are constrained by the agency of others and must deal with the consequences of their actions. The list goes on. None of these things act upon us to make us behave in a determined way, but we are not independent of them either. Each of these constraints limit possibilities, just as they open up choices for us that would not otherwise be available.

This sphere of constraints may be at the heart of the commandment not to judge others unrighteously. We don't know their constraints. We don't know the limitations on their agency. No one is without agency, to be sure, but neither is our agency the same as any other person's, given our different constraints. Only our Creator and Redeemer, who knows each of us and our circumstances completely, can be our judge. Only He knows the unique limitations of our bodies, spirits, environments, and so on. He alone knows for what we can and can't be held accountable. So it is that He alone stands at the gate and hires no servant there to do the work of judgment. Judgment is His alone.

None of us would ever want Christ, our true judge, to judge us as if our constraints don't matter, as if our bodies, spirits, minds, and environment are irrelevant and we are capable of being just like Him. If He judged our agency according to His agency, we would have to be sinless and capable of saving ourselves from physical and spiritual death. These things are, of course, impossible for us. We are not begotten of the Father in the flesh and we were not the first-born in the premortal existence. We have a different set of constraints than Christ. It would be unjust to hold us to His same accountability. Thank goodness, He knows each of our individual constraints and only holds us accountable for what each of us can truly choose.

Thank goodness for His compassion toward us in our limitations and weaknesses. Thank goodness that He throws His arms around us as prodigal sons and daughters each time we repent and come unto Him. No, we would never want Christ to ignore the sphere in which God has placed us and to judge us as if our constraints don't matter.

Remember that at the height of His suffering in the Garden, when all He had asked was that His disciples would tarry and watch with Him for one hour, He returned to them after initiating His Atonement, perhaps looking for some support and companionship in His darkest of hours, and He found them all sleeping. He was suffering for the sins of all humankind, and all they had to do was watch with Him for one hour, and they all fell asleep. At that moment He could have embraced the darkness around Him and turned it into righteous rage. He was fully justified in judging them and berating them. Instead, Christ saw them as they were: His sheep, prone to getting lost, prone to fatigue, and prone to distraction. He acknowledges their constraints and chooses compassion over anger, telling them "the spirit indeed is willing, but the flesh is weak" (Matthew 26:41). He knows His disciples have weaknesses. He knows He has given them—and all of us—weaknesses so that we might become humble.

We should each be so grateful that Christ knows our individual weaknesses and constraints and takes them into account in His judgment of us; that is, He takes them into account if we do not judge others unrighteously. If we judge unrighteously, we have an undesirable fate awaiting us. If we judge others as if their constraints don't matter, as if they should be the same in how they live their lives and live the gospel as we are, then guess how we will be judged? With that same judgment with which we have judged them! (See Matthew 7:2.) If we have judged someone according to our standard as their self-appointed judge, then Christ will judge us according to His standard as our divinely appointed judge. If we have judged as if there are no constraints, then Christ will judge us as if our constraints don't matter as well. We will have to suffer an unfair judgment just as we have meted out unfair judgments to others. This is one reason why humility is such an important protection against unrighteous judgment. By remembering that we depend on Christ for all things, we acknowledge that our judgments can only be righteous judgments through Him. As we will discuss, righteous judgment is only possible if we see others through Christ's eyes and only judge them as He would have us judge them. Only if our judgment is Christ's judgment can it be truly righteous.

As our discussion of judgment illustrates, our dependency on Christ does not cancel our agency; it expands and enables it. Our agency is a gift He has given us (see Moses 7:32). He provides the opposition that is necessary for us to exercise our will. He provides the light of Christ to help us discern right from wrong. He created the sphere that provides the constraints that allow us to choose liberty and eternal life or captivity and the devil. And He provides the breath in our lungs and the strength in our muscles that allow us to actualize that choice. So, it is that our agency in this sphere of existence depends wholly upon Christ, who does not compel us in some deterministic way, but who does not leave us alone to fend completely for ourselves either. Instead, He invites and entices us unto Him and because of His grace, His enabling power, we have the capacity to act for ourselves and to take His hand and become more than we could ever become by ourselves. In this sense, recognizing our dependency on Christ ought not be viewed as a negation of our freedom, but as that which liberates us to love and do good as true disciples of Christ.

Submissiveness

"The submission of one's will is really the only uniquely personal thing we have to place on God's altar."—ELDER NEAL A. MAXWELL[5]

The second part of humility is submissiveness. Disciples not only recognize their dependency on Christ for all things, they also surrender their will to God. Though closely related, recognizing our dependency on the Lord and surrendering our will to His are not the same thing. Children are fully aware that they depend on their parents for almost everything—food, shelter, clothing, and more—but that awareness of dependency often has little or no correlation with their submissiveness, especially when they become teenagers. Similarly, we can exercise our agency to resist the very God who gave us our agency. We can even completely rebel against Him, as did the adversary, even while being fully aware that we owe Him our very being and capacity to choose to rebel against Him. Satan knew full well who God was and knew that, as His spirit child, he owed his existence to His Father. Yet he chose to use the very agency his Father gave him to rebel against Him, as did a third of God's spirit children. Unlike the adversary, the Disciple not only acknowledges his or her dependency on God, but also submits him- or herself to God's will. This is true humility.

When Disciples read, "By grace we are saved, after all we can do" (2 Nephi 25:23), they understand the second "we" to be each of us and Christ together, because the "all we can do" already includes Christ's enabling power. As we stated before, there is no independent self that does all the work it can do alone and then turns to Christ for grace and mercy to make up the difference. Grace and mercy have been there all along. As Elder Neal A. Maxwell's quote at the beginning of this section makes clear, the only part of the "all we can do" that is really our own is the submission of our will to His. The rest we do together with Him or He has already done for us. What a different understanding of this scripture a Disciple has than the exemplars of the other quadrants. The Pharisee, like the Chinese acrobat trying to keep the plates all spinning, is running around trying to do everything and do it all alone. The Nihilists despair because they fail so often and so badly to pull themselves up by their bootstraps and do all they are supposed to. And the Egoist does only that part of what he or she can do that makes him or her feel good. In each case they have missed the mark. They don't realize that the only thing they have that is their own that they can truly give to God is their will.

The Pharisee and the Nihilist in us may say, "But that is not enough! There are so many commandments and practices and ordinances that must be followed and performed. There is much more we must do to achieve salvation than simple submission." The Pharisee and/or Nihilist in us ignores the Lord's promise that "my grace is sufficient for all men that humble themselves before me" (Ether 12:27). That is just too easy for them. They demand more. In fact, as the example of the rich young ruler who approached Jesus illustrates, submission to God's will may be the hardest thing of all. Recall that the rich young ruler came to Jesus asking, "What shall I do to inherit eternal life?" Jesus replied that he should keep the commandments and the man stated that he did, even from his youth until that moment. Then the Savior said, "Yet lackest thou one thing: sell all that thou hast, and distribute unto the poor, and thou shalt have treasure in heaven: and come, follow me. And when he heard this, he was very sorrowful: for he was very rich. And when Jesus saw that he was very sorrowful, he said, How hardly shall they that have riches enter into the kingdom of God!" (Luke 18:22–24).

We often read this as a warning to the rich, but it is really a warning to all of us. It warns us that whatever it is that keeps us from submitting to God's will, no matter how many other commandments we may keep, it is that thing that will make it very hard for us to enter God's kingdom. Any one of us can stand up in church and tell others about all the commandments we keep; we hear it all the time: "I go to the temple every morning"; "I never raise my voice to my children"; "I have always paid a full tithe"; "Our family watches no television on the Sabbath"; and so on. But the Lord looketh upon the heart, and as He did with the rich young ruler, He sees the one thing we yet lack. He sees where our stubbornness lies. He knows what it is that will make us sorry if we have to give it up, and it is that thing He wants, because it is there that our submissiveness is truly tested. Remember that the sacrifice the Lord requires of us is a broken heart and a contrite spirit (see 3 Nephi 9:20; D&C 59:8), which only comes from our total submission to Him, and our total submission to Him is truly evident when we give up whatever it is that is most difficult for us to give up. Only then, He tells us, can we inherit eternal life.

Rather than asserting individual righteousness, the Disciple submits to Christ's righteousness. Rather than asserting his or her own humility, the Disciple submits to Christ's humility. As King Benjamin taught, the criterion of our righteousness and humility is submission, not the assertion of independent action: "The natural man . . . becometh a saint through the atonement of Christ the Lord, and becometh as a child, *submissive,* meek, humble, patient, full of love, willing to *submit* to all things which the Lord seeth fit to inflict upon him, even as a child doth *submit* to his father" (Mosiah 3:19; emphasis added). We adopt a passivity in relation to Christ's will and then allow His will to activate and energize our actions in the world.

The prophet Nephi was a great example of this childlike

submissiveness, both in relation to his Father in Heaven and to his earthly father, Lehi. Unlike his stubborn and unyielding brothers, Nephi, when something difficult was asked of him, prayed to the Lord and his heart was softened. As a result, he was willing to submit to whatever the Lord or his father would have him do. Elder Jay E. Jensen has written, "Beginning with Lehi's son Nephi, we see the qualities children have that we should seek to emulate. Nephi, 'being exceedingly young, nevertheless being large in stature, . . . I did cry unto the Lord; and behold he did visit me, and *did soften my heart* that I *did believe* all the words which had been spoken by my father' (1 Ne. 2:16; emphasis added). Few, if any, spiritual talents exceed that of a soft heart and the talent to believe, for they include the qualities of teachableness and submissiveness, two prominent characteristics of little children. Nephi, an example of righteousness, never lost those divine attributes."[6]

We may reason that it would be much easier to submit if the Lord would just tell us *why* we are being asked to do so and then show us how everything will work out. Even if it is true that everything will work out, it doesn't matter. The Lord doesn't want us to submit because something is necessarily logical or because we can see how things will work out if we do as He asks. Such things are not a test of our faith; it is faith our Savior most desires. Recall that when Christ was with the Nephites after His Resurrection, He said, "blessed are ye if ye shall believe in me and be baptized, after that ye have seen me and know that I am. And again, more blessed are they who shall believe in your words" (3 Nephi 12:1–2). Those who "believe on" the testimonies of those who are witnesses of Christ are "more blessed" because their submission to the will of the Lord stems from a heart softened by faith *without* the sure knowledge that being a direct witness gives.

Ultimately, our submissiveness to Christ's will is an emulation of Christ's submissiveness to His Father's will. Elder Robert C. Oaks writes, "The greatest of all examples of submissiveness is that of the Savior in Gethsemane as He prayed, 'O my Father, if it be possible, let this cup pass from me.' He went on to signal the depths of His character, love, and submissiveness as He declared, 'Nevertheless not as I will, but as thou wilt' (Matthew 26:39). Everything about His life reflects His childlike submissiveness to the will of His Father."[7]

Submission contrasts with the lie because if we are submissive, we do not try to aggrandize ourselves in any way, even by the assertion of our independence. Instead, as did our great example, Jesus Christ, we minimize ourselves. We try to get our own wills out of the way so Christ can guide our life.

The perfection or completion of our humility, then, is accomplished in the submission of our will to Christ. On this point, we believe a fuller rendition of the quotation from Elder Neal A. Maxwell that began this section is in order: "It is a hard doctrine, but it is true. The many other things we give to God, however nice that may be of us, are actually things He has already given us, and He has loaned them to us. But when we begin to submit ourselves by letting our wills be swallowed up in God's will, then we are really giving something to Him. And that hard doctrine lies at the center of discipleship. There is a part of us that is ultimately sovereign, the mind and heart, where we really do decide which way to go and what to do. And when we submit to His will, then we've really given Him the one final thing He asks of us. And the other things are not very, very important. It is the only possession we have that we can give, and there is no lessening of our agency as a result. Instead, what we see is a flowering of our talents and more and more surges of joy. Submission to Him is the only form of submission that is completely safe."[8]

Yoked to Christ

Look up, my soul; be not cast down.
Keep not thine eyes upon the ground.
Break off the shackles of the earth.
Receive, my soul, the spirit's birth.
And now as I go forth again
To mingle with my fellowmen,
Stay thou nearby, my steps to guide,
That I may in thy love abide.

—Joseph H. Dean[9]

As we recognize our dependence on Christ and submit our wills to Him, we become yoked to Christ. A yoke is a frame or bar with two U-shaped pieces that encircle the necks of a pair of oxen (or other beasts of burden—including humans) to carry or pull a heavy load. The yoke balances the heavy load and makes it easier to manage. This yoke metaphor turns our attention toward work. As we mentioned before, humility involves passivity in relation to Christ. We yield to Him, and His work becomes our work. We take His yoke upon us and become active servants, enabled by His grace to do all the works He has commanded us to do. Like Alma the Younger, we are energized by the love of God and can labor without ceasing to help others. We are reminded of our beloved General Authorities, who have an incredible workload to bear and do it with vigor regardless of their age. Surely the prophet and apostles of today, like Paul of old, would proclaim, "I can do all things through Christ which strengtheneth me" (Philippians 4:13).

The term "yoked" has also been used in the scriptures as a metaphor for servitude or bondage (Jeremiah 28:2; Alma 44:2). When we become yoked with Christ, we follow Him, take His name upon us, and give complete servitude to Him. Paul regularly refers to himself as a prisoner of Christ to illustrate Christ's complete Lordship over him (see Ephesians 3:1; Philemon 1:1, 9). We are so used to thinking of these terms negatively that they often don't sit well with our individualistic conception of freedom as independence. In our minds, "prison," "bondage," and "servitude" imply severe restrictions on our freedom. Why would Paul, Jeremiah, and Alma use these terms? It is one of the great and marvelous paradoxes of Christian faith that being a servant or prisoner to Christ is the most liberating thing in the world. How can it be that we have more freedom as we are yoked to Christ? We have already mentioned His grace that makes weakness strength, increases our agency, and enables our actions. But there is more to the paradox than that.

Remember that each of us experiences a feeling of the void because of our separation from our Heavenly Father. If we fill the void with the resources God has provided, our feeling will diminish and we will be liberated from our concern with the void and with the artifices that Satan uses to tempt us. We will be free to think of others, free to do good, free of these powerful constraints that limit our agency. The Egoist, Pharisee, and Nihilist have much less freedom than the Disciple because the individualistic freedoms they pursue (or, in the Nihilist's case, consistently fail to achieve)—such as pleasure, pride, and esteem from others—only increase the void in them, leaving them feeling emptier, more selfish, and more caught up in a void-enlarging tragedy from which it is difficult to escape.

In Lehi's vision, for example, it may seem like the people in the great and spacious building are having a grand old time while they point their fingers and mock those who depend on the rod of iron, but they are acting out a bold-faced charade. They are not free. They are trapped in the building, trapped in the void, and have all but given up their agency. Some holding to the rod don't realize that. They feel ashamed that they need the rod of iron for assistance, so they let it go, asserting their own freedom, and trying to make it on their own. They end up lost, traveling down crooked and unclear paths. Only those who are Christ's prisoner, yoked to Him in servitude, keep hold of the rod and know the love of God. Only they are truly free, and they will grow freer still as they continue to depend on Him. Nothing could be more liberating or more illustrative of discipleship than taking Christ's yoke upon us.

In Matthew 11:28–30, we read Christ's tender invitation to take His yoke upon us: "Come unto me, all ye that labour and are heavy laden, and I will give you rest. Take my yoke upon you, and learn of me; for I am meek and lowly in heart: and ye shall find rest unto your souls. For my yoke is easy, and my burden is light." This is one of the most comforting verses in all of scripture. There are many features of this touching invitation that warrant attention, but we will focus on just a few key points.

First, Christ tells us that He is "meek and lowly in heart." Though He has every right to do so, He does not aggrandize Himself or approach us from an elevated or superior position. Rather, in the same manner in which He lived His life, He comes to us as the abased one, with no "beauty that we should desire him" (Isaiah 53:2). Though He is a God in every sense of the word, He willingly condescended below us all that He might be the least of all. This is His power and His influence. There is no trace of the lie in Him. He is not interested in appearing special to others. He is fully secure in His relationship with His Father and is filled with His Father's love and light. Thus, He is not concerned with Himself, but only with us. So it is that He is perfectly humble, like a lamb without blemish; it is that humility and meekness that makes Him accessible to us and makes us love

Him all the more. Because He is meek and lowly of heart, our Savior meets us and entreats us at our level, not from His. He meets us right there where we need to be met, where we suffer and labor and are heavy-laden with burdens. He offers us His yoke at that level so that we can work side by side with Him and carry His burden together. What love, compassion, and kindness the Savior must have for us, that He would lower Himself to our level so we can work alongside Him in His great cause of serving and loving others.

It is also important to note that the Savior does not say, "Come unto me and I will take away all your burdens." He promises only that we will receive rest unto our souls because His yoke is easy and His burden is light. How can we be burdened and work so hard pulling a yoke and yet receive rest for our souls? Consider the example of the people of Alma who suffered under the unrighteous dominion and terrible persecution of Amulon and his children. Ultimately, Amulon took the people of Alma into bondage and forced them to complete difficult tasks under the watch of punishing taskmasters. Their afflictions became so severe that they cried to the Lord in their suffering for aid, first vocally, and then only in their hearts because Amulon forbade their public prayer. In response, the Lord promised them deliverance would come eventually, but He did not immediately rescue them. Instead, He promised them, "I will also ease the burdens which are put upon your shoulders, that even you cannot feel them upon your backs, even while you are in bondage; and this will I do that ye may stand as witnesses for me hereafter, and that ye may know of a surety that I, the Lord God, do visit my people in their afflictions" (Mosiah 24:14).

Because of their great faith and humility, the people became yoked to the Lord in their afflictions and discovered that "the burdens which were laid upon Alma and his brethren were made light; yea, the Lord did strengthen them that they could bear up their burdens with ease, and they did submit cheerfully and with patience to all the will of the Lord" (Mosiah 24:15). Instead of removing their adversity, the Lord strengthened the people of Alma so their tasks were easy to bear. Put more precisely, because the people were yoked to Christ, they had His strength to help them carry the load. Because the Lord did not remove their burdens, but showed them that work with Him is easy and provides spiritual rest for their souls, they learned to be even more submissive to Him. In fact, they became downright cheerful about giving their wills over to the Lord.

Through being yoked to Christ, we learn firsthand to walk as He walks, to think as He thinks, and to be as He is. On this point, Elder Neal A. Maxwell wrote, "He who bore the atoning yoke has asked us to 'take my yoke upon you, and learn of me' (Matt. 11:29). So the taking of Jesus' yoke upon us constitutes serious discipleship. There is no greater calling, no greater challenge, and no greater source of joy—both proximate joy and ultimate joy—than that which is found in the process of discipleship."[10] Elder Maxwell continues, "Shouldering the yoke of discipleship greatly enhances both our adoration and knowledge of Jesus, because then we experience, firsthand, through our parallel but smaller-scaled experiences, a small but instructive portion of what the Savior experienced. In this precious process, the more we do what Jesus did—allow our wills to be 'swallowed up in the will of the Father'—the more we will learn of Jesus (Mosiah 15:7). This emulation directly enhances our adoration of Jesus."[11] Being yoked to Christ is truly liberating and constitutes a powerful manifestation of the love of God that we give back to Him—and to others—as we labor with the Lord in His vineyard.

Transformation

"One of the principal purposes of our mortal existence is to be spiritually changed and transformed through the Atonement of Jesus Christ."—ELDER DAVID A. BEDNAR[12]

Once we are yoked to Christ, we experience ourselves changing. As the people of Alma illustrate, we become stronger and more cheerful, even in adversity. Ultimately, we become new creatures in Christ, born again of the Spirit, and we experience a mighty change of heart. We are purified in the refiner's fire, wherein we have submitted to Christ and taken His burdens upon us. As Elder Joseph B. Wirthlin described it, "The gospel of Jesus Christ is a gospel of transformation. It takes us as men and women of the earth and refines us into men and women for the eternities."[13] As men and women for the eternities, we become filled with God's love—and there is no feeling of the void in us.

The scriptures tell us that when a person experiences this transformation, they are "changed from their carnal and fallen state, to a state of righteousness" (Mosiah 27:25). They are "awakened . . . out of a deep sleep, . . . illuminated by the light of the everlasting word" (Alma 5:7), and have "humbled themselves and put their trust in the true and living God" (Alma 5:13). King Benjamin's people experienced precisely this transformation after hearing their king's spirit-filled words. "And they all cried with one voice, saying: Yea, we believe all the words which thou hast spoken unto us; and also, we know of their surety and truth, because of the Spirit of the Lord Omnipotent, which has wrought a mighty a change in us, or in our hearts, that we have no more disposition to do evil, but to do good continually" (Mosiah 5:2).

Each of us has experienced moments like these, even if only sporadically—moments where the Spirit is so strong that we want nothing more than to do good continually, and our desire for sin disappears. In such moments, God is not so far away as our separation from Him would seem to imply and our will is now in harmony with His will. We feel true joy; our memories change, our goals change. Our prejudices fall away from us and lay at our feet. We love more easily and even feel a desire to forgive our enemies. We just feel good. Elder Keith K. Hilbig has said, "For each individual, experiencing a mighty change of heart is manifested by feelings of joy and love, both of which eliminate the prior pain of disobedience (see Alma 36:20–21). How kind is our Heavenly Father! How encompassing is His Son's Atonement!"[14]

These good feelings are not the Disciple's goal. Disciples don't become humble and submissive and work hard with Christ so He will give them this wonderful joy. Joy and happiness are the natural effects of a total commitment to Him. Disciples' transformation and the good feelings that accompany it ensue from their desire to be Christ's servants. Their good feelings are not pursued, such that Christ becomes the means to their end. If that were the case, then those good feelings would be prioritized over Him, and Disciples would fall prey to the subtle instrumental egoism we have previously discussed. No, Disciples' eye must be single to His glory, and then, if their eye is single to Him and to no other master, they will be filled with His light, and that light will transform them. Feelings of joy and happiness will attend their transformation to be sure, but will do so as attendant properties of being filled with the love of God, not as the end goal themselves.

When we are blessed to have these moments, when our eye is single to Him and our wills align, we remember, if only briefly, the great intimacy we shared with our Father in Heaven when we lived with Him. We catch a glimpse of the precious parent/child relationship we have. We feel close to Him.

We may not always have transformative experiences as Disciples, but that should not discourage us, because these experiences will come, and when they do we will realize we would go through it all again to have those precious moments when our Father in Heaven bestows His grace and love upon us. When we are humble and submissive and yoke ourselves to Christ, we certainly place ourselves in the right position to have transformative moments of intimacy with our God, and that is all we can do. The rest is up to the will and grace of God.

We would also do well to learn that transformations are rarely "once-and-for-all" events. We learn from Elder Keith K. Hilbig that "the scriptures offer accounts of people who were born again in a remarkable manner, such as Paul (see Acts 9:1–20) and Alma the Younger (see Mosiah 27:8–37). However, for most people in biblical and Book of Mormon times, as well as today, this change of heart is not a singular event but rather a private and gradual process."[15] Elder Bruce R. McConkie taught: "Except in . . . unusual circumstances, as with Alma (Mosiah 27), spiritual rebirth is a process. It does not occur instantaneously. It comes to pass by degrees. Repentant persons become alive to one spiritual reality after another, until they are wholly alive in Christ and are qualified to dwell in his presence forever."[16] This mighty change of heart is a process that takes humility and submissiveness that must be learned, re-learned, and practiced over and over again. And, as we have learned from Elder Hilbig and Elder McConkie, it also takes time.

Because transformation is rarely something that happens once and for all, we cannot expect that we will never sin again. It is true that when we have a transformative experience, we feel no desire to sin, and that is good and right. It clarifies our focus and shows us the goal we should strive for—total transformation. But purification takes time. We will still be tempted by the adversary and will fall back into the Pharisee, Egoist, and Nihilist quadrants, and that is okay too, because if we humble ourselves again, we are on our way to another transformative experience.

Let us not forget that each of us has a conversion *story,* not a conversion punctuation mark. Our conversion story ought to read like a novel, with different characters and venues and experiences that are told across chapters and are interwoven with plots and subplots. There should be many events, both past and present, which make up our conversion story. There should also be a number of future events and experiences yet to be added to the story. The story of Peter's conversion provides a powerful illustration. Recall that the Lord commanded Peter: "When thou art converted, strengthen thy brethren" (Luke 22:32). But when was Peter converted? The Lord gave him this commandment after Peter had witnessed and personally experienced several miracles, visitations, and Spirit-filled teachings. Were these just precursors to his conversion? Was his conversion to be a punctuation mark on a certain day in the future, or the full story of his life? The answer to these questions depends on our understanding of the word *when* in the Lord's command. On one hand, "when" could refer to a future point in time when a total transformation would take place that constitutes true and lasting conversion. On the other hand, "when" could mean "at the time" as in "[at the time] thou art converted, strengthen thy brethren." We are reminded here of the scripture in the Doctrine and Covenants which reads, "If ye receive not the Spirit ye shall not teach" (D&C 42:14). At those times when we have the Spirit with us, we can teach. At those times we do not have the Spirit, we cannot. Similarly, it could be that at the time that Peter is transformed and is a true disciple of Christ, he can strengthen his brethren, but at those times that he is not transformed, he cannot.

With these questions and possible answers in mind, let us consider Peter's conversion story, as retold by Elder Joseph B. Wirthlin:

"Imagine for a moment that you are Peter. Three years ago a holy stranger invited you to set aside your fishing boat and nets, your means of support for yourself and your family, and then asked you to follow Him. You did so without hesitation, and for three years you have continued to follow and to love and support and sustain Him. You have seen Him confound the wise, comfort the weary and the afflicted, heal the sick, and raise the dead to life. You have seen Him conquer evil spirits, calm the troubled seas, and for a few minutes, at least, you even walked on the water toward Him. You were at His side when Moses and Elias appeared to Him; you saw Him transfigured before your very eyes. You have committed your entire life to Him. And now He questions you by instructing you to strengthen your brethren 'when thou art converted.'

"Peter was surprised. He assured the Lord, 'I am ready to go with thee, both into prison, and to death.' (Luke 22:33.) But Jesus knew and understood. He was not condemning Peter for a lack of conviction; Peter demonstrated his conviction during the Lord's arrest. Rather, the Savior was telling Peter what he needed to do when his testimony became more secure."[17]

Through Peter's experiences, we can see that his conversion story was a process and not a onetime event. As we do, he fell out of the Disciple quadrant at times and spent some time in the other ways of responding to the truth and the lie before reentering the Disciple quadrant through humility, submission, and yoking himself to Christ. He surely worked hard to spend more time in the Disciple quadrant each time he arrived, but then would fall out again. Eventually he would remain there, which is what he seems to have done after receiving the gift of the Holy Ghost on the Day of Pentecost. Perhaps both meanings of the word "when" are applicable to Peter's conversion. Perhaps his conversion was a process that culminated in total transformation, and if so, that is the model of transformation we should follow.

As joyous as our personal transformation experiences are, in our experience nothing can compare to witnessing the transformation of others. I[18] had the privilege of serving my mission in Austria, which at the time had taken in thousands of refugees from Eastern European countries. There were missionaries in my mission who taught refugees almost exclusively. In one area of my mission, we worked primarily with some of these wonderful people. We would take a long train ride up into the beautiful mountains of upper Austria until we arrived at the little town of Puchenstuben. It was one of the most beautiful places I had ever been. The Austrian government had placed about one hundred refugees in the ski lodges of Puchenstuben during the off-season, which is where we would teach them.

At our first teaching appointment, there must have been forty people gathered in the main room of the lodge from Russia, Ukraine, Bulgaria, and Romania. It was the largest group I ever taught. The next time, the numbers had diminished by about half and continued to dwindle. In the end, there were two men, a Bulgarian and a Ukrainian, who stuck with it and continued to meet with us. My companion and I felt a special kinship with them both and looked forward to our visits. The Ukrainian, Alexei, had a terrible smoking habit and really wanted to quit, but he was having a hard time. We asked him if he was praying for help from God and he responded that he didn't know if there was a God. He had been raised in a communist country where atheism was taught in the schools and in his home. He was taught there was no God and had lived according to those teachings all his life until he met us. He wondered if his atheist upbringing was correct or if what we had taught him was true. We promised him that if he sincerely prayed and asked God if He was there that God would confirm His existence to Alexei. Alexei, who was always very earnest, said he would think more about it and make a decision about what to do.

The next time we were able to get to Puchenstuben, Alexei was waiting for us at the door of the lodge. He said, "I have been waiting every day for your arrival. I believe I am ready to ask God if He exists, and I need you to come with me to pray." We had expected that he would pray on his own when he was ready, but he felt it was very important that we pray with him. Suddenly it occurred to me that my word was on the line, and I would have to be there when Alexei tested it. Alexei decided to walk down a trail along the mountainside to find a place to pray. As we walked with him, I prayed as fervently as I ever had and pleaded with Heavenly Father to please answer this good man's sincere prayer. He was trying to do all the things we had asked: to be humble, teachable, and good. His desires were sincere. I couldn't think of anyone more deserving of an answer to prayer. I felt so much love and hope for him.

After walking for about fifteen minutes, Alexei stopped and said he would like to pray there where we stood. He closed his eyes and we closed our eyes. He prayed silently as did we, three men all praying as sincerely as they could for one man who had lived his whole life without a knowledge of his divine inheritance, without an awareness of his Father's love, without knowing the source of the void in his heart that signaled a desire and yearning for something he had been looking for but didn't know what it was. I remember the words of my own prayer: *Please let him know you are there. Please let him feel your love. Help him to recognize that you are his Father and that you are reaching out to him. Please, please, please.*

Then I felt Alexei's hand on my shoulder. I opened my eyes and looked at him. He said a word to me in Russian that I didn't understand, and I said, "Alexei, what does that word mean?" Tears began to form in his eyes and he said, "It means I have succeeded." It was the most overwhelming spiritual experience of my life to that point, even more overwhelming than my own answers to prayers. This man, this humble disciple of Christ, had his heart touched by His Father. His face lit up, the tears flowed down his cheeks, and the largest smile came across his face. The three of us embraced on that mountainside. We were all transformed and converted, Alexei for the first time, and the two of us once again. I could hardly walk, I was so filled with gratitude. I fell to my knees for a few moments to give thanks for the wonderful, wonderful grace God bestowed upon us as we willingly sought Him together that day. It was a moment none of us would ever forget.

Months later, after Alexei had been baptized and received the gift of the Holy Ghost and the priesthood, and after I had been transferred, Alexei was moved to another town. He would send me letters, such precious letters, to tell me about his life. He was moved to a town where he was far away from any congregation of the Church. He had to work long shifts of manual labor, sometimes twelve hours long. He was getting worn out and feeling down. Although he was exhausted and just wanted to go to bed, he would get out his Book of Mormon and read it and say a prayer, and that special feeling that he felt that day on the mountainside would come back. He knew that no matter where he was or how hard things got, he had a Heavenly Father who loved him. All Alexei had to do was read His words or say a prayer and his heart would be transformed again.

Seeing with the Eyes of the Savior

"As ye have therefore received Christ Jesus the Lord, so walk ye in him."—Colossians 2:6

Alma described the natural consequence of our transformation: "And now behold, I ask of you, my brethren of the church, have ye spiritually been born of God? Have ye received his image in your countenances? Have ye experienced this mighty change in your hearts?" (Alma 5:14). Because the Disciple is centered in and transformed by Christ, the Disciple's countenance and way of seeing the world is changed. The Disciple comes to see others with new eyes, with Christ's eyes. Because Christ's eyes are always focused on His work (the immortality and eternal life of others), Disciples are concerned not with their own exaltation, but are wholly committed to facilitating the exaltation of others. This quality of seeing through Christ's eyes is a unique characteristic of discipleship.

As we described in the first chapter, we live in a culture of "special," where the focus is always turned inward on the self. Psychologists have conducted research, for example, where they have participants attach a time-diary to their belts. A time-diary has a beeper that goes off at random times during the day. Whenever the beeper goes off, the participant writes down whatever they are thinking at that moment. After a period of several days or weeks, the researchers collect the time-diaries and analyze the entries. With few exceptions, the majority of the entries people record are thoughts about themselves.

This probably comes as no surprise to most of us. We do live in an individualistic society and we are taught that it is the self that matters. The Egoist, Pharisee, and Nihilist are all concerned with themselves, just in different ways. The Pharisee wants to exalt him- or herself above others. The Egoist wants to satisfy the self. And the Nihilist is focused on the inadequacy of the self. Is it any surprise, then, that when we are in these quadrants and we think about exaltation, we think of our own exaltation and not the exaltation of others? Indeed, the ultimate manifestation of being special would be to receive personal exaltation.

If, at the end of the day, it is our individual exaltation that matters most, what does that say about the exaltation of others? It says it is every man or woman for him- or herself. It says other people are ultimately only of value insofar as they facilitate my individual exaltation. If they hinder it, I should avoid them and leave them to themselves. If they help it to occur, I should use them to get me there, until they no longer help, and then I should find someone else who will help me get there. Such ideas conjure the image of a person throwing people to the side, ignoring those who are struggling, and stepping over those in need to gain their own personal exaltation—the sort of person personified in the Book of Mormon anti-Christ Korihor, who preached that "every man fared in this life according to the management of the creature; therefore every man prospered according to his genius, and that every man conquered according to his strength; and whatsoever a man did was no crime" (Alma 30:17). Seems pretty selfish, doesn't it?

Now imagine an individual cheering others on, helping them, supporting them, forgiving them, and helping them lift their gaze to their Savior. These are the true disciples, actively engaged in the exaltation of others, with little concern for themselves. Disciples have truly lost themselves in the service of others. As Elder Robert D. Hales put it, "As true disciples, our primary concern must be others' welfare, not personal vindication."[19] Imagine what would have happened if Eve had partaken of the fruit, brought it to Adam, and

Adam said, "Sorry, lady. You're on your own. That's your sin and your problem and I want nothing to do with it." What if Christ had decided to focus on His own exaltation? He is a God. He lived a perfect life. He could have achieved exaltation without having to agree to the plan and suffer for our sins. What about our Heavenly Father? He is already an exalted being. He doesn't need us at all. Why then, do God the Father and Jesus Christ do all that they do for us? What is their motivation? It is love—nothing more and nothing less than pure and abiding love. That must be our motivation also if we are to be true Disciples.

To have Christ's image in your countenance means in part to see others as Christ sees them. If we look with His eyes, we see the suffering of others and we are filled with compassion. We see the Pharisee consumed with self-righteousness, the Egoist gaining pleasure but enlarging the void, the Nihilist isolated and feeling excluded from the Atonement, and our hearts go out to them and we seek to lift them up and to give them hope. According to Arthur Henry King, discipleship means "losing the self-concern of the struggle within ourselves, and looking outward to be concerned with others and their struggles."[20]

The Catholic monk Thomas Merton described an experience in which he suddenly and unexpectedly became filled with the love of God. It changed his vision of others. He writes:

"I was suddenly overwhelmed with the realization that I loved all those people, that they were mine and I theirs, that we could not be alien to one another even though we were total strangers. . . .

"Then it was as if I suddenly saw the secret beauty of their hearts, the depths of their hearts where neither sin nor desire nor self-knowledge can reach, the core of their reality, the person that each one is in God's eyes. If only they could see themselves as they really *are.* If only we could see each other that way all the time. There would be no more war, no more hatred, no more cruelty, no more greed."[21]

In 2011, I[22] had a very powerful experience with seeing others through Christ's eyes. A close friend of mine had been unfaithful to his spouse, who discovered the infidelity. When I heard the news, it came as a complete shock. Knowing their relationship, it was something I would have never expected. As a close friend, I was saddened by the news, but I was also very angry. My emotions were all over the place. In one moment, I wanted to go find him and do physical harm to him and in the next moment I wanted to go see how he was doing and give him a hug. I leaned more towards anger because of the pain and suffering that his actions had caused his wife and children. A few hours after I heard the news I had a strong impression to visit my friend and to make sure that he wasn't going to hurt himself and leave his kids without a father. During that visit I was cold to him. I was still very upset about what had happened. I wondered how he could do something like this to his family and be so selfish. He sat, mostly looking at the ground, too ashamed to look me in the eye. I recounted his responsibilities to his children and then I got up and walked out of the house without looking at him, still feeling sad and angry for what he had done.

The next evening I visited him again, but this time I went with a mutual friend. As we walked up to the house, I felt sick to my stomach. I was still feeling very strong emotions about what had happened. We knocked on the door and were met by our friend who hung his head in shame and asked us why we were there. We asked to come in and we sat down to talk. It was then that my friend who came along with me began to talk in a very merciful way about repentance and forgiveness, letting our friend know that, even though he didn't feel like it at all, he was a child of a loving Heavenly Father. As I sat there listening to what my friend was saying, it began to humble me greatly because the night before I had sat in the very same place, speaking in a very cold and justice-seeking way.

As I heard the friend who had accompanied me talk of the Atonement, my eyes started to well up. I began to see a man who had made terrible choices but who also deserved the mercy of his Savior. I thought of the woman caught in adultery in the scriptures and how Christ saw her as a child of God and forgave her, unlike the Pharisees who saw her as bad, deserving of death, and unloved by God. I felt awful about my Pharisaical judgment of my friend, knowing that I myself was not—am not—sinless before God. At the end of the conversation that night, my departure was very different than the night before. Instead of shunning my friend and walking past him, we embraced and cried together. For me, as hard as it was, it was one of the most powerful experiences of being able to see another individual as Christ would.

After I left, I wanted that feeling to stay with me forever, but I will admit that I did return to my anger and disappointment for my friend. However, just seeing him as Christ did for a brief moment made me realize that I can have that charity for him again. As I continue to work on my own forgiveness and my love for God and others, my goal is to again see him through Christ's eyes. As I go through this process, I can learn to identify the obstacles that keep me from seeing my friend as Christ would, such as getting caught up in pride like the Pharisee and selfishness like the Egoist. As I am vigilant of my own tendencies toward these false ways of responding to the truth and the lie, I can recognize my dependency on Christ to overcome these tendencies, and I can submit to His will and work alongside Him toward developing the characteristics of the Disciple discussed previously in this chapter.

One of the ways we can develop the attribute of discipleship, the attribute of seeing others through Christ's eyes, is to develop a kind of empathy. We say "a kind of empathy" because secular forms of empathy differ from the theistic empathy we have in mind. A secular form of empathy is typically defined as putting ourselves in the place of another. Essentially, we project ourselves into their experience and try to imagine what it is like to be the other person. Of course, you can never fully imagine what it is like to be them, or be sure your empathy is accurate, because it is still you who is having the experience and your experience is informed by all of your constraints, not theirs. Our purpose is not to denigrate this approach to empathy. It can be a powerful therapeutic tool and has brought many people comfort to know that others are trying to feel their emotions genuinely and sensitively.

However, the empathy we have in mind is different, because it is facilitated by the Spirit. It is true that none of us have the same constraints and our experiences are different, so any projection of ourselves into another person's perspective will inevitably fall short. However, when we are filled with the love of Christ and are His Disciples, the Spirit helps us to see the other person as Christ sees them. Christ's perspective is greater than and different from any projections we may attempt, but it is also greater than the perspective of the person with whom we empathize. Christ knows us better than we know ourselves. He sees constraints upon our agency that we don't know about. He also sees us as we lived before this life, as spirit children of our Heavenly Father, and He sees all that awaits us in the hereafter. So, when the Disciple is given the gift to see others as Christ sees them, the Disciple sees them with a heavenly perspective, with a deeper and fuller awareness of who they are than they have of themselves. This is Godly empathy and it is the reason why Thomas Merton said that if we could see others as God sees them, "we would fall down and worship each other."[23]

It often surprises people when I[24] tell them that I felt the Spirit most strongly as a bishop in disciplinary councils. They imagine such events to be awful and painful and sad. There is much of that, to be sure, but there is so much more. Perhaps these events are so spiritual because the Atonement is directly at work in the repentance process and nothing brings the Spirit like the Atonement. But there is another reason why they were so spiritual for me. Like many church leaders in this position, I put a great deal of spiritual preparation into these councils, including fasting and prayer. I did this because the responsibility of being a common judge in Israel is a massive burden and I would not want to make any decision that was counter to God's will, given what is at stake. So I would do everything in my power to see the person as Christ sees them, and each time the Lord's grace was bestowed upon me and my counselors in a miraculous way that made that possible.

It was truly an incredible experience as I looked at them with eyes that were not my own. I could feel their sincerity, when it was there. I could sense their struggles and appreciate the limitations on their agency. I could detect their intentions and their willingness to submit to the Lord. I could also detect what decision was needed to help them fully embrace the Atonement in genuine repentance and help them be fully forgiven. But that is not all. I could also sense the hurt they had caused others and the obligations they had to them and to the Lord to make restitution. I could see the balance of justice and mercy and what God required of them to make things right.

On a few occasions, the person disagreed with the decision.

Sometimes they thought it was too harsh; sometimes they were sure they deserved worse. This confirmed to me that they did not know themselves as well as God knew them. He alone knew exactly what they needed to do to gain the full power of the Atonement in their life, and He granted me the ability for a brief time to see and know that so I could best help the person repent. There have been few times where I have seen as clearly and known as confidently what God sees in His children and what He wants for them, and I have never felt His love more strongly than I felt it for these suffering souls. The Disciple's goal must not just be empathy, but Godly empathy if we are to do His will.

Recognizing our dependence on Christ, becoming submissive, taking upon us His yoke, becoming transformed, and seeing others through Christ's eyes brings us one step closer to being as He is. It brings us one step closer to actualizing the great power He has given His Disciples to act on His behalf. Those who have received God's power to bind in heaven what is bound on earth are unique but powerful examples of discipleship. The prophet Nephi in the book of Helaman, for example, was blessed with the Lord's sealing power because he would ask nothing of God that could be contrary to His will. So perfectly aligned was Nephi's will to God's that God gave him His complete trust and power. There truly was no difference between what Nephi would do and what God Himself would do if He were present. This is the full realization of discipleship—a son or daughter who does nothing but that which the Father would do. When a Disciple realizes this perfection—that is, the completion of our will with God's—nothing is impossible. As the Lord says, "If ye shall say unto this temple it shall be rent in twain, it shall be done. If ye shall say unto this mountain, Be thou cast down and become smooth, it shall be done. And behold, if ye shall say that God shall smite this people, it shall come to pass" (Helaman 10:8–10). Filled with God's love and power, a Disciple becomes a powerful force for good in the world, seeking only to help others and to do God's will.

CHAPTER 8

The Fluidity of Quadrants

"To every thing there is a season and a time to every purpose un-der the heaven."—ECCLESIASTES 3:1

Now that we have reviewed the four exemplars of responding to the truth and the lie, we should reemphasize that no one is uniquely suited to or necessarily situated always in one quadrant. Instead, we live in a dynamic relationship to the truth and the lie, such that within any given time period we are likely to move among several of the quadrants multiple times. Our movements among the quadrants may become habitual or we may reside in one quadrant more often than others, but we are not consigned to any one quadrant. They are not like personality traits or dispositions.

Sometimes, our movement into or out of a quadrant may be pre-cipitated by a significant life event. At other times, the behavior of others may incline us toward a given response to the truth and the lie. There are many things that can influence our movement among the quadrants, and for some of us it can feel like our shifting and chang-ing response to the truth and the lie is out of our control. It seems as if on some days we just wake up with a nihilistic view of the world or, for whatever reason, we find ourselves feeling especially judgmental or deserving of selfish pleasure. And at other times we are filled with an unusually high level of love for others.

Psychologists have known for a long time that people are not particularly skilled at self-awareness; there is much about us that is unconscious. We have a hard enough time identifying and describing our feelings, let alone understanding where they come from and what triggers them. Our focus tends to be exterior, out there in the world where we have to make a living, raise children, negotiate relationships, and take care of ourselves. There is so much to pay attention to in the world that can either harm us, help us, or be influenced by us that we rarely take the time for introspection about ourselves and our motives and desires. Consequently, it should not surprise us to find out that we are not keenly aware of our location in the quadrants and the causes of our movements among the quadrants. We lack the training and discipline required for that kind of sensitivity.

Our purpose in this chapter is to provide some practical guidelines to help readers better identify their movement through the quadrants. Specifically, we suggest a four-step process that will help focus your awareness on the ways in which you respond to the truth and the lie. The first step is to use a form of the hindsight bias mentioned in chapter 4 by looking back at your actions during a specific period of time and evaluating them through the lens of the quadrants. After you develop some skill at hindsight evaluation, we encourage you to practice a form of mindfulness through which you can become better aware of your present manner of responding to the truth and the lie. The third step involves learning to let go of your attachment to a given quadrant. Finally, we encourage vigilance toward the triggers that move you out of or into quadrants, for good or ill. Throughout our discussion of this four-step process, we use a number of examples

	Accept the Truth	Deny the Truth

Accept the Lie	*Pharisee Exemplar*
	
	• Lifted up in self-righteous pride
	• Shut up heaven against themselves and others
	• Usurp God's judgment for themselves
	• Evidence of Pharisaism:
	  ◦ *"Special"*
	  ◦ *More righteous*
	  ◦ *Perfectionists*
		Egoist Exemplar
		
		• Pursues self-gratification as the ultimate end
		• The subtlety of selfishness: Often we do not notice the subtle ways in which the self has displaced God as the master we serve
		• Manifestations of egoism:
		  ◦ *Hedonism*
		  ◦ *Vanity*
		  ◦ *Greed*

Deny the Lie	*Disciple Exemplar*
	
	• Filled with a love of God and all people
	• Charity: The Disciple partakes of God's love through the Atonement and immediately desires to share God's love with others
	• Characteristics of discipleship:
	  ◦ *Humility*
	  ◦ *Submissiveness*
	  ◦ *Yoked to Christ*
	  ◦ *Transformation*
	  ◦ *Seeing with the eyes of the Savior*
		Nihilist Exemplar
		
		• Hopeless and self-deprecating
		• Doubts about worth: Sometimes we feel unworthy and undeserving of God's love and mercy
		• Alienation: When we feel cursed or unworthy we tend to withdraw from God and others
		• Common sources of nihilism:
		  ◦ *Sin and perfection*
		  ◦ *Addiction and pleasure*
		  ◦ *Abuse and shame*
		  ◦ *Adversity and abandonment*

of our own movement through the quadrants, as well as other, better-known exemplars.

Hindsight Evaluation

"With the benefit of historical hindsight we can all see things which we would wish had been done differently or not at all."
—Queen Elizabeth II[1]

We begin with what will probably be the easiest method of examining our movement through the quadrants: Hindsight Evaluation. You may recall that hindsight bias occurs when we make a judgment about others after an event has passed, treating them as if they should have known then what we know now. Given our knowledge of the outcome, we act as if we would have behaved differently if we were in their shoes. For example, we think we would have behaved differently if we were the wicked Nephites that Samuel the Lamanite warned about the signs of the coming Christ. We make that judgment with the benefit of knowing what happened following Samuel's prophecies. We know how it all turned out, and that insight biases us in how we judge the Nephites of that time who did not have the clear knowledge about what was going to happen that we have now.

This bias represents the negative side of hindsight, but there is also a positive side. The positive side of hindsight is manifest when we can better understand ourselves by looking back on our own actions with the benefit of the insight we have gained after the fact. Often, we can see more clearly how things happened and why we acted the way we did after an event is over than we could have in the moment when we were caught up in the event and focused on managing it. How many of us have looked back on an argument we had with our spouse and thought, "You idiot, why did you say that? You know that just pushes her buttons and causes her to get defensive. What were you thinking?" This kind of hindsight evaluation often lies at the heart of regret. Regret could be defined as looking back on what we did, realizing all the bad choices we made at the time, and wishing we had behaved differently. Our regret is only exacerbated by our belief that we should have known then what we know now about the outcomes of our actions.

Rather than getting bogged down with the "would've, should've, could've" thoughts of regret that hindsight evaluation can often engender, we could focus on what can be learned from our mistakes and what might be changed so things go better the next time. We could even use hindsight to evaluate our successes, to identify what we did right to bring about a desired outcome. We can look back on our work on a project, for example, and identify our good decisions and actions. We might think, "I didn't know how it would turn out at the time, but now I can see what a good idea that was. It really ended up tying everything together and it came out great." Looking back on where we have been and examining how it all led up to a successful outcome can become an important guide going forward.

The purpose of hindsight evaluation, with respect to the quadrants, is to look back on an event or period of time that we have experienced in the past and identify our movement among the quadrants in a way we probably could not have done at the time. Often, it is only after the fact that we are able to see clearly the ways in which we accepted or denied the truth and the lie. We can see the mistakes we made or temptations we fell prey to that shifted us out of the Disciple quadrant into one of the other quadrants, or we may recognize the manner in which we took advantage of the resources God has provided us to fill our feeling of the void with the love of God. The events we evaluate using this hindsight technique may have occurred as long ago as our childhood or during a critical time in our life, or they may be recent events that are fresh in our mind. The key, at least initially, is to identify those events that will manifest your place in and movement among the quadrants in ways that are obvious and may help you identify habits and patterns.

An example that clearly manifests some of my[2] habits of moving through the quadrants in predictable ways took place at a session of general conference I attended at the Conference Center with my parents when I was visiting them in Utah. At the end of the session, the congregation all stood and spontaneously sang, "We Thank Thee, O God, for a Prophet."[3] The Spirit became very strong as President Hinckley stood and waved his cane to the crowd. I felt a confirmation that he was God's prophet. I felt his love and the Lord's love for all of us at the same time. Tears filled my eyes as I expressed my gratitude in song. I was humbled to be a child of God and to be there at that time. I felt transformed and I wanted to do good continually.

As we left the Conference Center, I didn't speak to my parents because I wanted to hold on to the special feeling I had. We got in the car and I just sat there in the glow of this special moment. As soon as we started driving, my mother began to ask me questions about the conference and other things. I tried not to get distracted and only gave short one-word answers so as not to disrupt the wonderful feeling I was having. Everything she was talking about seemed mundane and superfluous by comparison. I wanted to stay in the glow of the Spirit; I didn't want her to pull me out of my elevated state. But her questions kept coming and before long they started to bother me. Why wasn't she basking in the glow as I was? Couldn't she tell how powerful this experience had been? Didn't she appreciate the need to hold on to it for as long as possible? Even if she wasn't able to feel the Spirit as strongly as I was, she could at least leave me alone in my clearly elevated spiritual state. After all, I didn't get to go to conference as often as she did. This was a special opportunity for me. Why couldn't she just leave me alone for a little while? How insensitive.

Her "mundane" questions and comments continued and then I couldn't feel the Spirit anymore. It was gone. *Thanks a lot, Mom,* I thought. *You just ruined my spiritual experience.* Then it occurred to me that I was being mad at the very person who took me to the conference so I could have the experience, someone who only wanted happiness for me and had dedicated much of her life toward that end. And there I was being angry with her again, just as I had been many times in the past. Had I not heard anything that was said in conference? What kind of person am I if I can't even think kind thoughts about my mother after having such a profound spiritual experience? How could I slip so quickly into selfish pride and meanness? I didn't deserve the experience and I certainly didn't learn the lesson I should have from the Spirit. Maybe there's something wrong with me. Maybe I can't put feelings into action. Maybe I'm not a good son or a good child of God. Maybe I should repent. Maybe Christ will forgive me for this as He has for so many things. Maybe I can learn from this and love more fully and feel the Spirit again. And so it went for me—as it does for all of us as we shift from quadrant to quadrant, sometimes as rapidly as I did in this example, and sometimes in longer-lasting and even more habitual ways.

Although that event took place several years ago, I recall it easily now and I can clearly see my movement through the quadrants. I can see how I came into the Disciple quadrant as we sang to the prophet of God. I can also see how I unfortunately and quickly moved into the Egoist quadrant where I wanted to hold onto the good feelings for myself because they were so pleasant, and I didn't want anyone to ruin them for me. They were mine to enjoy and bask in. Just as quickly as I moved into the Egoist quadrant I moved out of it into the Pharisee quadrant where I found myself judging my mother as being less spiritual than I was. I saw her as seemingly unaffected by the Spirit, whereas I was fully transformed.

For a moment, I lifted myself above my mother as if I was more spiritual than she was. Then came the guilt and shame as I shifted into the Nihilist quadrant and saw myself as a bad son, both in terms of my being a son to my mother and to my God. I must be the worst of the worst, I thought. But then I took hold of the thought of repentance and the mercy of the Lord and I started back toward the Disciple quadrant. I couldn't see this all that clearly at the time, though I surely felt the emotions commensurate with each way of responding to the truth and the lie, but looking back at the event with the framework of the quadrants as a guide, it is obvious to me what I was doing and how I allowed myself to do it. I can see my pattern, and I have a better sense of what I can do to have a similar experience turn out differently next time.

Mindfulness

> *"One must be conscious of his movements and acts so that nothing of what goes on in him escapes his attention."*
> —SPENCER J. PALMER[4]

Mindfulness comes from a long tradition of developing a practice of mental discipline most famously demonstrated by Eastern religious traditions, but also emphasized by various strains of the Christian contemplative tradition. Speaking of the meditation required to achieve mindfulness, the prophet David O. McKay said, "I think we pay too little attention to the value of meditation, a principle of devotion. . . . Meditation is the language of the soul. . . . Meditation is a form of prayer. . . . Meditation is one of the most secret, most sacred doors through which we pass into the presence of the Lord."[5]

Recently, psychotherapists have included mindfulness practices in therapy to address a number of cognitive issues that can disrupt normal functioning, such as obsessive thinking. In its simplest form, mindfulness is nonjudgmental awareness of the thoughts that come into our minds. We all experience thoughts coming to mind as we are engaged in a task, a conversation, or just sitting quietly by ourselves. Typically, we judge these thoughts to be good or bad, wanted or unwanted. Sometimes, we indulge the thoughts more than we should or we might get distracted by our thoughts, as in daydreaming. We may chastise ourselves for having distasteful or self-defeating thoughts and at other times we try to keep unwanted thoughts out of our minds altogether. For many of us, our thoughts seem chaotic and unbridled and we wish we could just turn our minds off.

Mindfulness is an approach to thinking that does not try to control our thoughts, at least not as we typically try to control our thoughts, such as by stopping them or keeping them on task. Mindfulness is a method of observing our thoughts and recognizing them for what they are without judging them as good or bad, wanted or unwanted. They are just thoughts, no more, no less. They do not make you a demon or a saint—that has more to do with what we do with our thoughts after they arise. To be mindful is to notice the thoughts that emerge in our mind as we might notice the faces of people as they walk by us in a crowded hall. We see each face and acknowledge that each person is a person, but with so many faces passing by, we don't have the time, ability, or motivation to judge what kind of person each one passing by us is. We may notice that each face has different features, including shape, skin color, expressions, attractiveness, and so forth, but we are not inclined to become attached to those features and judge them as good or bad. We just notice each passing face as it presents itself to us, without thinking much more about it.

With regard to the fluidity of the quadrants, mindfulness is the practice of being aware of our present response to the truth and the lie or our movements among the quadrants. At this level of examination it is not necessary to judge the goodness or badness of our current position in the quadrants or to try and move ourselves into another quadrant such as the Disciple quadrant. Instead, the goal is to become more clearly aware of our immediate way of living in response to the truth and the lie without judgment. Thus, there are two tasks involved in mindfulness about the quadrants. First, we practice identifying our immediate position in and among them, and second, we practice not judging our current response to the truth and the lie. How is this two-fold task accomplished? We recommend two approaches.

The first approach is done through a simple meditation exercise. In order to practice this meditative form of mindfulness, it is important to find a quiet space where you can be alone for several minutes. If you have a private office at work or a quiet room at home, find a place where you can sit comfortably. Close your eyes and focus on your breathing. Notice your breaths. Are they short or long? Are they deep or shallow? Put one hand on your chest and one hand on your belly and notice whether you are breathing mostly from your chest or from your diaphragm. After paying attention to your breathing for a few minutes, turn your focus to your body. Notice where you are sore or tense. Identify places where you feel pressure or discomfort. Don't try and do anything about it at this point, just become more aware of the places on your body where you are tense or relaxed.

Now, pay attention to your feelings. What, if any, emotions are arising in you? Are you happy? Sad? Annoyed? Self-conscious? Again, don't fight the emotions or try to identify their causes. Just notice what emotions you have and how they feel as they emerge. Now, notice your thoughts. What ideas are coming to your mind? Are they ideas about yourself, others, this task you are performing? Are they random thoughts? Don't concern yourself with what these thoughts might mean or tell you about yourself at this point. Just identify them for what they are. As you notice the thoughts and feelings you are having, pay attention to whether any of them are indicative of your response to the truth and the lie. If not, don't try and force thoughts or feelings into the quadrants. If they fit in a quadrant, identify them accordingly. If not, then let the thought go and examine the next thought. Thoughts befitting a given response to the truth and the lie may not come every time. If so, you can try the practice again another time and see if the thoughts and feelings come then.

If you do notice thoughts or feelings that are relevant to the quadrants, just notice them emerging and identify their location in the quadrants. Are these thoughts Egoistic? Do you feel better than others? Do you feel inadequate? Perhaps the thought emerges that you are not doing this exercise properly and you are never good at these kinds of things. If so, identify that feeling and think about where it fits in the quadrants—for example, in the Nihilist quadrant. Perhaps the thought comes to your mind that this is a stupid task that is only needed by people who are weak and lack the mental discipline you have cultivated. If so, notice that thought and the feelings attached to it and consider where it might belong in the quadrants—perhaps in the Pharisee quadrant.

We can't identify all the types of thoughts and feelings that might emerge for you, and we can't tell you where they belong in terms of the quadrants. That is your task, and it is one that requires practice, so be patient with yourself. Be particularly mindful not to judge the thoughts you are having. Like those faces passing by you in the hallway, all thoughts and feelings have different features. Some seem unkind or mean. Others appear sad or self-deprecating. Still others seem haughty and rude. And some feel wonderful and happy. Don't dwell on these features, good or bad. Notice them, but don't get attached to them. Perhaps you had a rude thought come to your mind. So what? Recognize it and place it in the appropriate quadrant and then move on to the next thought, which surely will come. At this point, you are only a thought inspector. Your job is to identify the thought and make sure it goes to its proper quadrant. That is all.

The second method of mindfulness takes place while we are engaged in life activities. This form of mindfulness is not a meditative practice, though it does require self-awareness. The example of a therapist helps illustrate what we mean. Therapists are often trained to be of two minds. One mind is described as *presence*. "Presence" means being right there with the client, listening attentively, empathizing with their experience and feeling as fully as possible their emotions and understanding as completely as possible their thoughts. You are present in the moment with the client and they know they have your attention. The therapist's other mind is referred to as *reflection*. "Reflection" involves identifying areas where the client may need to do more work, thinking about what technique might be applied for the given issue, and reflecting on the theoretical concepts which help the therapist frame his or her understanding of the client's symptoms, diagnosis, and presenting problems. Therapists have to learn to be of two minds at, or nearly at, the same time with their clients. If they are too present to the client, they won't be thinking about how to best help the client and therapy won't progress. If they are too reflective, the client won't feel listened to and therapy won't progress. They have to be both present and reflective, which is no easy task.

We want to encourage you to practice being present and reflective as you engage in your everyday activities. For example, as you are talking to a fellow church member in the hall on Sunday, practice both listening to and empathizing with the member, but also practice reflection on the thoughts and feelings you are having as you participate in the conversation. Are you feeling annoyed by this person or are you excited to talk with him or her? Do you have thoughts of comparison to this person? Do you feel better or worse than him or her? Do you feel an overwhelming love for the person as he or she talks about a recent event he or she went through, or are you looking for the exit and thinking, *Too much information?* Can you notice, in the moment of the conversation, while still being focused on the conversation and present to the other person, where you are in the quadrants and/or how you are moving among them? Can you be immediately mindful of your thoughts and feelings in context? Can you see what things are happening in the conversation that are triggering your movement in and out of the quadrants?

Here again, the purpose of this mindfulness practice, in context, is not to stop your thoughts or to change them. At this point, you are focused on observing them as they arise, and doing so without judging them and without losing your presence to the person. You are having a learning experience. You are learning how you think and feel and how those thoughts and feelings manifest your response to the truth and the lie with certain people and during certain activities. You can do it while you are playing basketball, writing a paper, taking a walk, or e-mailing a colleague. As you do it you will notice patterns that attend certain kinds of activities or interactions with certain people. With some people, you may notice thoughts of inferiority emerging habitually. With other people you almost always have feelings of love arise.

A little reflection can go a long way in teaching us our habitual ways of responding to the truth and the lie. Just don't let it get in the way of being present to the person or activity you are engaged in or you might miss out on an important experience. Try and find the balance of your two minds. And, most importantly, be patient with yourself as you participate in this practice.

Letting Go

"A thought is harmless unless we believe it. It's not our thoughts, but the attachment *to our thoughts, that causes suffering."*
—Byron Katie[6]

As we become more proficient with our practice of mindfulness we will gain some perspective on our thoughts and feelings. We come to realize that there are different ways of relating to our thoughts and feelings. We can be more or less attached to their content. We can judge them to be good or bad or identify them without judgment. We can observe them coming into our mind and leaving without acting on them. Or, we can let our thoughts and feelings affect us and motivate us to action. We can examine them or just let them be.

As we practice mindfulness we see that we can gain some control over our thoughts and feelings or we can let them control us. We can learn which thoughts and feelings attract or repel us the most. We can see which thoughts and feelings recur most often. We can notice whether our thoughts focus on ourselves or others. We can identify times when there is relatively little or no thought or feeling and our minds are somewhat empty. There is a great deal we can learn about our mind and how it works and how we can use it in a variety of different ways. We will leave most of that work to the Buddhist monks and Hindu yogis who spend their lives interrogating the workings of the mind. Our interest, for the purposes of this book, focuses on just a few practices in relation to our thoughts and feelings from which we can learn.

One practice that is usually easier said than done is learning to let thoughts and feelings go. By this we mean learning not to get attached to a given thought or feeling. In our work with addicts, we have found that there are certain thoughts and feelings that emerge in their minds that they dwell on and empower so much that the thought can form an obsession, which often can only be resolved by acting on it. The alcoholic who is working on his or her sobriety may happen to drive by a bar and the image of a favorite drink pops into his or her mind. Once there, it is very easy for the alcoholic to imagine him- or herself taking that drink in his or her hands. He or she can imagine its smell and its taste and the satisfying feeling of letting go of life's worries that it brings.

The alcoholic may tell him- or herself that this is just fantasy and indulging a little imagination can't hurt. He or she hasn't really done anything wrong, after all, such as actually going to the bar and having a drink. It just feels good to fantasize a little. No harm, no foul. But it is a slippery slope from thought to action and eventually fantasy leads to genuine temptation and soon the alcoholic finds him- or herself driving by that bar more regularly, even going out of his or her way at times to drive past it.

These thoughts gain more and more power and influence and become harder to resist. They recur all the time and push other important thoughts away, like thoughts of the bad consequences that follow from drinking and thoughts of shame and guilt that arise after getting drunk, and so on. Then rationalizations come in. "One little drink won't hurt. I can handle that without a problem. I just want the taste of it. I'm not going to get drunk off of one little drink." We know how the story ends. One drink turns into two, two to four, and so on.

This story is so familiar that it has become a sad cliché. Whether it is an alcoholic driving by a bar, a drug addict running into her old dealer, or a person addicted to pornography who sees a beautiful woman on the cover of a magazine at the grocery store, relapses often begin with a fleeting thought that is dwelt on, then entertained and empowered. The fact is that at the level of thoughts popping into our heads, addicts and non-addicts are not very different. We all have random thoughts come into our mind. Some of them are strange and unexpected. Some may frighten us, like when we are driving along and we think, *I could just turn this steering wheel ever so slightly and drive this car into an oncoming truck.* It's just a crazy thought that comes and goes. We don't typically dwell on it or give it another thought. A person who has never had a drink could have the thought, *I wonder what alcohol tastes like?* come to mind, or *I wonder what it feels like to get high.* In a given day, all sorts of ideas come along, from *I could just kill that person* to *I'm never talking to him again* or outlandish thoughts like *I wish I could fly like Superman* and *I wonder what it would feel like to be a butterfly.* From the mundane to the fantastical, the sublime to the grotesque, thoughts and feelings of all types are a part of mental life.

The issue, as we have discussed, isn't in the arrival of a thought. The issue is in our treatment of it. When a thought emerges, do we bring it into our mind, offer it a room, make up its bed, and give it a place to stay? Or do we acknowledge its presence, greet it at the door, and send it on its way? It is at that choice point that our agency is engaged. We may not have much control over which thoughts and feelings arrive at the door of our mind, but we do make the choice about how we treat the thoughts that emerge (within our own individual constraints, of course). Given our habits, predilections, addictions, and other constraints, some thoughts are harder to turn away at the door than others, but we do have the choice. How can we empower our agency so that we are not at the mercy of those thoughts that tempt us most?

One approach would be to divert our energy and resources away from trying to control which thoughts arrive at our doorstep and point them toward what we *do* with the thoughts when they arrive. It is very hard to stop a thought from coming into our mind. Try not to think of a pink banana right now. Don't let the thought in. Keep it out of your head. And don't think of a pink monkey riding a unicycle on a tightrope with a purple polka-dot umbrella in one hand and that pink banana in the other. Don't do it. Don't you dare let that thought into your mind. It is hard not to think of it, isn't it? The image seems to arrive in our minds the moment we read the description of it, whether we want it to or not. In fact, the harder we try not to think of it, the more the image sticks around.

Now, instead of trying not to think of the pink monkey holding the pink banana on the unicycle on the tightrope with the umbrella, allow the image to come into your mind, identify it for what it is—a funny image—and let it go from your mind. Release it and let the next thought come. Perhaps, the next thought is the monkey again. It is a funny image and you may want to look at it again in your mind's eye. That is fine. Let it come to mind, see it for what it is, and let it go again. Other thoughts will come along as well and they too can be identified and let go. The key is to continue the practice of nonjudgmental awareness that you learned in the mindfulness section but to add to it the practice of letting go.

Let the thought come and then let it go. If it comes back, let it come again and let it go again. It's just a thought, after all. It has no inherent power or influence beyond that which you give to it, no matter what the thought is. So open the door and greet it when it comes knocking. Acknowledge its presence, thank it for visiting, and then send it on its way. If it comes back, do the same thing again. If we try to resist the thought instead, if we don't open the door and acknowledge it for what it is, just another thought, it will keep knocking. It knows we are inside and it is going to keep knocking, growing more persistent and eager to get in. Don't give it that power. Open the door, see it for what it is, and let it go. Don't empower it by trying not to think about it, and once you do open the door, don't indulge the thought, dwell on it, and let it take up occupancy in your mind. Acknowledge it as just a thought with no greater power than any other thought, and release it. Set it free. Let it dissipate as it naturally will if we treat it in a nonjudgmental, observational way.

What does any of this have to do with the truth and the lie and the quadrants? As we become more proficient in identifying our place in the quadrants at different times and with different people, we will become aware of our habits and the pattern of thinking that leads us into egoism, Pharisaism, and nihilism. We may decide that we are going to fight the thoughts that lead us to those quadrants and try not to think them anymore. We may try and attach ourselves to discipleship because we know it is the best quadrant to be in and so we try to only have thoughts and feelings commensurate with discipleship. Although this may seem like a good and reasonable method to increase our discipleship, we may find that this practice works against our goal.

The paradox is that if we try not to think egoistic, Pharisaical, or nihilistic thoughts, we have to think of them to know which thoughts we don't want to think of, which leaves us having egoistic, Pharisaical, or nihilistic thoughts—seemingly against our will. Moreover, our efforts to resist these thoughts can empower them and give them undue influence over us, as they push aside other thoughts and knock on the door of our consciousness even harder. This approach can become a self-defeating cycle that only increasingly works against us as we try harder to enact it. As an alternative, we could practice the method of mindfulness and let those thoughts go. When a selfish thought comes to mind, we can identify it as being egoistic, but we don't have to get upset about it or otherwise judge and empower it. Instead, we can recognize it as one of the many thoughts we have, no more or less important or characteristic of us than any other thought, and having disempowered it, we can let it go. Then we can do likewise with the next thought that comes along, and so on. The key is to learn to let thoughts come and go.

Once you have developed the skill of letting thoughts go, you can slowly begin to learn to dwell on and empower thoughts selectively. That is, when a loving thought or feeling toward God or other people comes to your mind, you can selectively indulge that thought for a little longer than other thoughts before you release it. The next time it comes along you can hold on to it even longer, letting it fill your whole soul and following whatever actions it inclines you toward. This is the process of *cultivation*. Through it we learn to cultivate thoughts of the Spirit while weeding out the noise of other thoughts by letting them go. We first learn to let go generally and then selectively, choosing to hold on to the thoughts that are noble and good and empowering them to make us instruments in God's hands.

Recall from my[7] general conference experience that we cannot force spiritual feelings and thoughts to stay in our minds and hearts. If we try to compel them to stay, we risk damaging and destroying them. Spiritual thoughts are like a delicate butterfly. If we are fortunate enough that a butterfly lands on our shoulder, we must enjoy it for as long as it abides with us, but if we try to make sure it stays on our shoulder, we will handle it in a way that damages its delicate construction and we may destroy it. Instead, we must learn to be grateful for its visitation, soak in the beauty and wonder of the experience, and then let it go when it is ready to leave, with thanks in our heart that the event took place at all. Our experiences with the Spirit are delicate as well. We should receive them with gratitude when they occur, when the Spirit dwells in our hearts or enlightens our mind. We ought to soak in the beauty and awe of the experience, but when the feeling begins to dissipate and other thoughts begin to knock at our door, we cannot force the Spirit to remain. We must let Him go and look forward to His next visitation, which, if we have received Him in love and gratitude, will likely be sooner and more often than we think.

Vigilance

"Watch and pray, that ye enter not into temptation."
—MATTHEW 26:41

As we begin to cultivate the thoughts and feelings of a true disciple of Christ by being mindful and learning to let go, we will find that our time in the Disciple quadrant increases incrementally in our lives. We find that, when we don't try to make ourselves into Disciples by sheer will, but instead receive Spirit-filled thoughts and feelings with gratitude and awe whenever they arrive, they seem to arrive more often and dwell with us longer. We learn to recognize what kinds of activities we engage in are more conducive to the arrival of Spirit-filled thoughts and feelings, and we willingly engage in those activities so that we can create a space for the opportunity for these noble and good thoughts and feelings to arrive and dwell in us more regularly. Sometimes they do come and sometimes they don't, but that doesn't deter us or upset us. We continue to participate in these good activities to give ourselves the opportunity for the Spirit to attend our thoughts and feelings, knowing that the Spirit, like the butterfly, will come to us in His own time.

Our cultivation process also reveals to us the activities we participate in that seem to facilitate the arrival of other, less-desirable thoughts and feelings, such as feelings of superiority, inferiority, selfishness, vanity, or pride. When we participate in these activities, we see that the thoughts and feelings of discipleship don't knock on the door very often, but the loud knocking of Pharisaism, egoism, and nihilism echoes in our head. Under these circumstances, it can be difficult to practice nonjudgmental awareness and letting go. We get frustrated with ourselves for having unsavory thoughts and find it difficult to let them go. At some point, they seem to break down the door of our mind and force themselves in.

For example, people who struggle with pornography addiction may find that being alone in their house on the computer is an activity that facilitates the arrival of sexual thoughts more than other kinds of thoughts, because in the past they looked at pornography primarily on their computer. These thoughts keep coming to the door of their mind and knocking loudly, and even if the person has become skilled at letting them go, when the thoughts do not relent but come one after the other, the person's capacity to release them from his or her mind can weaken, and thoughts sneak in behind the person's defenses and end up dwelling in his or her mind. Once that happens, the thoughts are easily indulged and empowered and become powerful temptations that push all other thoughts out of the mind, including the Spirit.

Although we have used a specific example to illustrate this point, we want to be clear that it is not our purpose in this section to delineate a list of prescribed and proscribed activities. We do not need to do that, because if you will practice hindsight evaluation, mindfulness, and letting go as we have described them, you will learn to discern for yourselves which kinds of activities facilitate the arrival of thoughts and feelings that are more or less characteristic of discipleship. You will learn the circumstances that facilitate noble and good thoughts and feelings and distinguish them from the situations and contexts that prompt less desirable thoughts to come to mind. Your ability to discern the situations, activities, and social contexts that bring to mind more (or less) Spirit-filled thinking and feeling will be a far greater and more important compass through the quadrants than any list of dos and don'ts we might provide, which cannot help but be inadequate to the variety of unique contexts you will find yourself in. Thus, our final step in this fourfold process of attending to and learning from our movement through the quadrants is *vigilance.*

The scriptures are rife with references to watchmen on the tower. Whenever the people of Israel would establish a settlement or a community, they would quickly erect a tower so watchmen could look out across the land to see if there were any threats on the horizon. From their elevated position, they had the best view of their entire surroundings and could warn the people of an impending threat from any direction. The men selected as watchmen had to be extremely dependable and vigilant. If they were to fall asleep or get distracted, the settlement could be overrun before the people had a chance to defend themselves or escape.

As we strive to create a settlement in the quadrant of discipleship, we too will need to develop a vigilant and constant watch for those activities and situations that foster the arrival of thoughts from the quadrants of Pharisaism, egoism, and nihilism. We need to train ourselves to see these thoughts approach long before they arrive at our doorstep, where they may overwhelm us, force out Spirit-filled thoughts, and occupy our mind. Much of this training can be done on our own through the practices we have described in which we learn how to discern the triggers that shift us out of the Disciple quadrant or move us deeper into one of the other quadrants.

The pornography addict, for example, needs to watch for those things that make viewing pornography a powerful temptation. Some triggers may be obvious, like being home alone with the computer, or watching a television show with racy content, or even women's magazines at the grocery store. Exposure to any one of these things can prompt thoughts of a sexual nature to come to mind more frequently. But there are less obvious triggers as well, some of which may not be immediately intuitive. For example, for many people, the secrecy of viewing pornography—its forbiddenness—can provide nonsexual arousal that triggers pornography viewing and becomes combined with sexual arousal to form a very strong temptation. It can be thrilling to try and figure out the password your spouse has put on the computer or to find a novel way to access pornography. Sneaking forbidden pornography into the house past the watchful eye of a parent or spouse can make the experience all the more tantalizing. These subtle and indirect triggers must also be discerned, and careful watch must be kept over our thoughts and feelings lest they find their way into our minds and dwell there.

We can also be aided in our discernment by others. My[8] wife has helped me learn a number of my triggers toward unwanted thoughts or actions that I don't see very clearly on my own, and she has helped me to become more vigilant toward them. This is a funny example, but my wife has learned that I get fussy when I am hungry. Often I'll come home from a particularly busy or challenging day where I have neglected to eat for several hours, and I am not in a good mood. My wife can immediately sense my mood, and she knows its cause. Before she asks me how my day went or engages me in any way, she will sit me down at the table and put a plate of food in front of me and tell me to eat. Meanwhile, I'm thinking, *I don't want to eat right now. I'm upset about my day and I want to process it with you. I want to talk.*

My wife will not oblige me until I eat something, so I do, and sure enough, as I start to eat and fill my stomach, my mood starts to change and I begin to forget what it was that bothered me so much in the first place. She can see it happening as well. In her wisdom, she knows that we will have a very different conversation after I eat than we would have had before I ate. It has gotten to the point now where I will come home and start into my tirade and I will look at her, looking at me with a knowing look, and I will say, "I should probably eat something, shouldn't I?" and I will go fix myself something. I have learned that an empty stomach can be a trigger for less-desirable thoughts and feelings, and I owe my wife for that. Thank goodness we are not the only watchperson on our tower.

It will take time, effort, and the aid of others, but with practice we can become sensitive to many of the triggers that send undesirable thoughts our way. Once we know what they are, we can learn to avoid them. We can stay far away from them. We can give ourselves more time in the discipleship quadrant and share the love of God that we receive there with others. This is one reason why prophets are so impressive to us. They can stay in that discipleship quadrant so much longer than the rest of us. Sure, they have their triggers and they too move among the other quadrants to some extent, but not as often as we do. They are disciplined and have cultivated a sensitivity to the Spirit. They are also well aware of the things that would draw the Spirit away and are hypervigilant to those distractions. They put themselves in the right kinds of situations and engage in activities that keep spiritual thoughts and feelings coming to their mind in abundance.

We do not mention the example of prophets to create upward social comparison and make us all feel inferior. Our taking the example that way would be a sure sign that we are in the Nihilist quadrant. Instead, we share the example of prophets to illustrate what can be accomplished by those who discipline themselves through Christ's enabling power. Regardless of where we are in the process, we can start now to cultivate discipleship and increase our vigilance so we may spend just a little more time in that quadrant than before. It doesn't matter if you have failed to practice mindfulness or letting thoughts and feelings go in the past. You can start, wherever you are now, on the path to increased time in the Disciple quadrant. Pray for divine assistance, let others help you see your triggers, and learn to discern the activities and circumstances that help or hinder spiritual thoughts and feelings. Remember, you are a son or daughter of a divine King who loves you and is constantly seeking to lift you up. He will not let you fail. He will empower your discipleship and fill your soul with light and love.

Because we all inevitably move among all the quadrants, we should be able to relate to anyone in any quadrant at any time. If we cannot relate we are probably not being honest with ourselves about our own Pharisaism, nihilism, egoism, or even discipleship. For example, we have surely learned of a person's selfish sin or arrogant misdeed and have allowed ourselves to react with shock or anger. We may see them as repulsive or even disgusting. We may find ourselves saying, "I would never do that" or "I have never been tempted like that" or "How could someone do something like that and call themselves a member of the Church?" When that occurs, the person is blocking their own admission that they too have spent time in that quadrant; perhaps not as much time as the person they are judging and perhaps not through the same set of sins or challenges, but they too have been there. When we deny our own participation in one of the quadrants, we are living the lie which tells us we are better than that person. This creates a hierarchy between us and that person where we stand above them and they stand below. We think, *I don't have that problem and one ought not have that problem, so they must be deficient where I am complete.*

Christ has shown us a different path. In His suffering and atoning sacrifice, the Savior of the world, an almighty God, condescended below all things. He allowed Himself to experience the angry pride of the Pharisee, the Egoist's self-interested pursuit of gratification, the Nihilist's self-loathing and despair, and the compassion and humility of the Disciple. He did not deny Himself these experiences in order that He could fully succor each of us in our suffering and our sinfulness: "Jesus' perfect empathy was ensured when, along with His Atonement for our sins, He took upon Himself our sicknesses, sorrows, griefs, and infirmities and came to know these 'according to the flesh' (Alma 7:11–12). He did this in order that He might be filled with perfect, personal mercy and empathy and thereby know how to succor us in our infirmities. He thus fully comprehends human suffering. Truly Christ 'descended below all things, in that He comprehended all things' (D&C 88:6)."[9]

Christ meets us where we are. He comes to us "meek and lowly of heart" (Matthew 11:29). Recall that when Christ faced the woman caught in adultery, unlike the Pharisees who stood over her with their fingers pointed down at her, He stooped down to write in the sand, to meet her eyes with His and to offer His hand of forgiveness to lift her up. When He washed the disciples' feet, He knelt beneath them. The greatest of us all made Himself the least of all, for our sakes, because He loves us and knows how best to help us. If we are to follow Him and be His disciples, should we not do likewise? Indeed, we should and we must.

How can parents reach out to their child who is suffering through a bout of hopelessness if they cannot acknowledge their own times of despair? How can a wife help her husband with his pornography habit if she cannot recognize how hard it is for her to stop gossiping? We cannot forget that "all we like sheep have gone astray" (Isaiah 53:6), and there is not one of us who is pure before our Lord. But even if we *were* pure and holy like our Savior, we would still lower ourselves to our fallen brothers and sisters because it is only in that way that we can help them be yoked to Christ and lifted up by Him.

Our movement through the quadrants, like Christ's, facilitates our discipleship because it helps us serve others from a place of love, compassion, and understanding. It levels the playing field among us because we all spend at least some time in each of these quadrants. None of us is or should pretend to be above anyone else.

CHAPTER 9

The Path to Discipleship

———+>•<+———

"[The Atonement] is the most important single thing that has ever occurred in the entire history of created things; it is the rock foundation upon which the gospel and all other things rest. Indeed, all 'things which pertain to our religion are only appendages to it,' the Prophet said."—ELDER BRUCE R. MCCONKIE[1]

In the simplest terms, the Atonement of Jesus Christ is the path to discipleship. In Elder Neal A. Maxwell's *Ensign* article entitled "King Benjamin's Manual of Discipleship," he states, "Benjamin's speech reveals the nature of divine discipleship as it can be displayed only by one who has become a saint through the atoning blood of Christ."[2] With respect to the quadrants, a specific emphasis on the Atonement is required in each case. Pharisees need to recognize that they are sinners who depend on the Atonement to be whole just as much as anyone. Egoists have to turn away from the vain pleasures of the world, acknowledge their dependency on the Savior for true happiness, and repent of their sins. Nihilists must acknowledge that the Atonement can and does reach them, and they must accept the forgiveness of their Heavenly Father. Disciples must watch always lest they fall prey to the temptation to disregard the Atonement after the manner of the other three quadrants. The best way for the Disciple to do this, and for each of us to move from the other quadrants into the Disciple quadrant and stay there longer, is to continually repent and forgive.

The Atonement, when fully embraced, will purify our motives and remove any trace of the lie from our lives. We embrace the Atonement only through genuine repentance and sincere forgiveness, which cannot be motivated by selfishness, but must be based on love. The highest and purest motive for any of our actions is charity, the pure love of Christ. As Elder Jeffrey R. Holland describes it:

"True love blooms when we care more about another person than we care about ourselves. That is Christ's great atoning example for us, and it ought to be more evident in the kindness we show, the respect we give, and the selflessness and courtesy we employ in our personal relationships.

"In all that Christ was, He was not ever envious or inflated, never consumed with His own needs. He did not once, not ever, seek His own advantage at the expense of someone else. He delighted in the happiness of others, the happiness He could bring them. He was forever kind."[3]

One of the best ways to get in touch with our capacity for Christlike selfless love is in parenting. Before I[4] became a parent, people would often tell me that when I had a child I would develop a certain type of love not found anywhere else. Before my wife and I had our first child, a son, I questioned this love and had no understanding of it. After his birth, I began to feel a truly selfless love, a love I had not previously known. Now I can feel a complete willingness to sacrifice for him and a great desire to love him unconditionally. I want to give up anything for his well-being. My motives become pure and selfless in this relationship because I care more about his happiness than I do my own.

The musician Brandon Flowers puts these feelings I experienced with the birth of my son into words beautifully in his *I Am a Mormon* video, stating, "It's like there's a chamber in your heart that you don't know exists that opens up when you have a baby . . . overflowing with that love that I didn't know was there before."[5] As we feel this love for our children, we can begin to catch a glimpse of the pure love that our Heavenly Father has for us and that He desires us to have for others.

Repentance

We are often taught that our desire to repent begins with the feeling that we have done something wrong. We are told that we have to recognize that we have committed a sin and that recognition often takes the form of guilt. We feel badly about what we have done and to be rid of that bad feeling, we must properly and fully repent. When we repent, the bad feeling leaves and we feel better. This is one approach to repentance, one that the Lord accepts and for which He blesses us with forgiveness and relief from guilt. However, it is not the only or best motive for repentance. In fact, it could be seen as a more selfishly motivated form of repentance. It is selfish in the sense that I feel badly when I break a commandment, and to alleviate my bad feelings, I repent. At a motivational level, this form of repentance really has little to do with the people we have wronged or even with the God we have wronged. Yes, we have to go to the person we have wronged and make amends and we have to make amends with God as well, but if we are motivated to do so primarily by the desire to be rid of our feelings of guilt and shame, it is basically a selfish repentance process.

To become disciples of Christ, His true followers, we want to be motivated by the same motivations that Christ had. Christ's motivation for His actions could not have been guilt because He committed no sin. He did no wrong to any person or to God, so He had none of the bad feelings we have when we break a commandment. Then, we might ask, what motivated His actions? Why did He go into the Garden of Gethsemane and willingly atone for all of our sins when He was sinless Himself? It could not have been to alleviate His bad feelings; He had no bad feelings to alleviate. There were only our bad feelings that needed alleviating. So it is that He atoned not for Himself, but for us, to help *us* find peace and comfort, to alleviate *our* guilt and shame. If we are to truly emulate His example, we too must learn to repent for the sake of others, to help them feel the love of God that we feel, to help them come closer to their Savior. Our motives for our actions—including our repentance—must also be selfless. If we can move from the motivation of selfish guilt reduction to the motivation of charity because of the love of God that we feel, we will truly be on the path to discipleship.

When we recognize that Disciple repentance stems not from self-centered guilt but from other-centered love, we begin to understand the words of King Lamoni's father when he exclaimed, "I will give away all my sins to know thee" (Alma 22:18). His desire to repent originated from his strong yearning to know God. After hearing the words of the Lord's missionaries, Lamoni's father, like my[6] friend Alexei, yearned for the love of his Father in Heaven and it was *that* desire, not guilt or shame, which made him willing to give up anything that stood in the way of that relationship, including his sins. What if our desire for our Heavenly Father's love and our yearning for an intimate relationship with Him inspired us to repent, not guilt or shame? What would be different about us? At the very least, we would spend less time focused on ourselves and *our* feelings and more time focused on our Heavenly Father and others. We would operate from a void-diminished rather than a void-enlarged motivation. We would look outward to others and seek their well-being because our concerns with ourselves and our feelings about ourselves would not occupy our thoughts. We would act from a base of love, not one of guilt and fear.

I[7] had a shift toward the motive of love on my mission. As a new missionary, I often thought to myself, *I don't want to lose the things that make me who I am. I don't want to become a stereotypical missionary.* So, to stay true to myself, I kept some of my pre-mission idiosyncrasies. I rolled the short sleeves of my white shirt up to show off the muscles I had worked to develop before my mission. I kept an Elvis poster on the wall of my apartment to remind me of my greaser self-image and my "coolness." I displayed a picture of my girlfriend and secretly prayed that her dates would go badly and that she wouldn't fall in love. I worried that I would miss the really good movies that would come out while I was gone, and I missed my car, my friends, and all the things back home. My thoughts and even my prayers were still back home in California, not there in Austria. I didn't want to lose myself or my life. I felt a little bad about indulging these non-mission distractions, and I knew I should probably repent for them, but I was caught up in selfish pride.

As my mission went along, I started to get to know those I served among better. I visited them in their homes and taught them about the gospel. I started to care about them and I began to desire their well-being. As I got closer to them and more invested in them, I found myself strongly desiring that they might feel the Spirit and find the truth. I wasn't conscious of it at first, but the content of my prayers started to change from a focus on what *I* needed or wanted to sincere pleading with the Lord that He would help those people whom I was starting to love feel His love. My thoughts changed as well. I thought about those I served throughout the day and prayed for them both morning and night. In those prayers, I found myself promising the Lord that I would give up anything He asked of me if He would just touch their hearts and let them feel His love. It became clear to me that I hadn't given up whatever He had asked. My sleeves were still rolled up. The poster was still on the wall. I was still holding on to my pre-mission self and trying not to lose my old life.

Because I loved these people so much and wanted them to feel the love of their Heavenly Father, I took down the Elvis poster and the picture of my girlfriend. I unrolled my sleeves. I did anything else I could do to show the Lord that I would give away all my sins for these good people to know Him as I had come to know Him. It wasn't guilt that changed me. It wasn't a fear that my mission president would be disappointed, or even that God was unhappy with my pre-mission attachments. It was love—love for those good people who were genuinely searching for truth and light—that changed my heart, that helped me to lose myself, that led me to repent.

Forgiveness

Much like repentance, forgiveness must be purified of any selfishness through the Atonement. This is even more challenging than repentance because in this case, we are not the sinner. We are the victim of sin. For many, given the severity of the wrongs that have been done to them, forgiveness can feel like an insurmountable requirement. It seems almost absurd to ask someone who has been abused or whose child was killed by a drunk driver to forgive the person responsible for their suffering. How can the Lord ask that of us? Forgiveness of such terrible wrongs would be impossible on our own. Instead, our forgiveness of others depends wholly on the grace of Christ. We can only truly forgive with Him. How is this achieved? How do we yoke ourselves to Christ in forgiving others? How can we be transformed so that we see the sinner who has wronged us through Christ's eyes instead of through the eyes of our anger and hurt?

We do it only by focusing on Christ and not on the sinner. If we focus on the sinner, we will only fan the flames of our anger. We will think of all the reasons why the sinner does not deserve our forgiveness, and we will be logically justified. A focus on the sinner cannot lead to forgiveness because the sinner can do nothing to deserve forgiveness. If Christ decided to forgive based on our deserving it, none of us would be forgiven because we are always unprofitable servants. No, Christ does not forgive us because we deserve it. He forgives us because He loves us. To be His disciples, we too must learn to forgive because of the charity that fills us. True forgiveness is only achieved by focusing on God's love for us. When we focus on God and are filled with His love, forgiveness will ensue, even for the most undeserving of sinners.

When I[8] was a young teenager I was beat up in my Sunday School classroom by a man twice my age. He was furious with me for misbehaving in his wife's class and lost control of his temper, hitting me in the face with his fist, throwing me against the wall, and kicking me in the back. He swore at me and yelled at me that he was going to kill me. I saw the faces of ward members watching all of this unfold through the window of the classroom door and doing nothing about it. One of my friends told me later that he had asked the adult members to do something to help me and they said, "Maybe he deserved it." It was a horrifying experience made worse by the fact that no one helped me.

After getting free of the man's attack by my own efforts, I

immediately felt hurt, embarrassed, and angry. I decided then and there that I was going to get him back for what he did, that I was going to hurt him or kill him. I spent years hating the man and wishing him ill. I couldn't look at him without getting upset. I wanted him to suffer as I did and worse. My anger was only fueled by the absence of any remorse in him for what he did. He never apologized or expressed regret for what he did in any way. On the contrary, he told the bishop that he did want to kill me and that I deserved what I got. This increased my hatred for the man even more. I told myself I would never forgive him for what he had done. He didn't deserve forgiveness, only hate and vengeance. Adding insult to injury were the members who also expressed no remorse for failing to come to my aid. I was left to feel utterly alone in the very community that was supposed to comfort those in need of comfort.

Three years passed. I turned eighteen and began preparing for a full-time mission. As part of that preparation, I had the opportunity to go on a two-week mission in a nearby town with the full-time missionaries serving there. I had pretty much buried my feelings for the man who hurt me three years earlier by that time. I hadn't forgiven him or forgotten what he did in any way, but I had learned to live with my anger and hate. As I began my two-week mission, I could tell there was a difference between the full-time missionaries and me. They had such confidence in their testimonies and such power in their teaching. I felt inferior to them in pretty much every way. I decided I wanted to change, to become more like them, more sure of my testimony. I asked them how they were so sure about the truthfulness of the gospel and so confident in their testimonies. They each told me their conversion stories and how they had read the Book of Mormon and prayed to know that it was true and received confirmation from God that it was.

I realized I hadn't really had a conversion experience. I was active and appeared to be as engaged as any teenager in the ward, but I wasn't really converted. At least I didn't think I was, especially in contrast to these good missionaries. So even though I hadn't read all of the Book of Mormon by that point in my life, I decided to read as much of it as I could in one night and to pray and ask my Heavenly Father if it was true. I stayed up quite late reading and praying for an answer that the Book of Mormon and the Church were true. When the answer didn't come, I read more and prayed again. I repeated the process several times, never receiving any identifiable feeling of an answer at all. Finally, I gave up and went to bed. I figured I hadn't read enough to warrant an answer or I hadn't prayed fervently enough to get an answer. I just hadn't put in the requisite effort to warrant God's response. I decided to keep reading the Book of Mormon until I finished it, hopefully before the start of my own full-time mission, and then to pray for an answer at that time.

A couple days later, we went to teach a man who had been a member of the Church for much of his life but had been excommunicated from the Church several years earlier because of a number of repeated and unrepented sins. I'll call this man John. John was trying to turn his life around and was taking the discussions in an effort to become truly converted and to petition the Church to be rebaptized. When we arrived at his home, I immediately noticed how hard this man had lived. He was a muscle-bound guy with many tattoos, scars, and a missing front tooth, the result of many fights over the years. He had joined the Navy as a young man and was clearly not well educated. Without thinking, I stereotyped him immediately as a "meathead."

Before we got into our discussion, John was eager to tell us a story about being out at sea the week before and getting into an argument with another sailor. The other man wanted to fight, but John told him he didn't want to fight because he was trying to live a better life. This was hard to do because John used to fight at the drop of a hat. The sailor kept taunting John, and finally John agreed to go down a ladder into a more private area of the vessel to work things out. When they got there, the man immediately charged John and tried to hit him. John resisted hitting the man and just restrained him and told him he did not want to fight. He let the man go and he came at him again. John restrained the man again and said, "Look, I'm not going to fight." The man said he understood and wasn't going to attack John again, but as soon as John let him go, he came at John again. This time John let his impatience and old habits get the best of him and he hit the man squarely in the face. He fell down to the ground.

John told us that he felt badly about losing control and taking a big step backward in his efforts to be more spiritual. The sailor eventually regained consciousness and got up. John tried to tell him he was sorry, but the man ignored him and quickly climbed up the ladder to the upper deck. John felt awful and decided he would find him and give him a genuine apology. He slowly climbed up the ladder. When he got to the top deck, the man was waiting there for John with a big claw hammer which he immediately swung at John's head. John moved his head back just in time to avoid the claw of the hammer to his head, though it caught the bill of his baseball cap and knocked it off his head. Several people saw what happened and grabbed the man before he could swing the hammer again. The man was immediately placed in the brig.

John told us he was full of all sorts of emotions and distress. A man had just tried to kill him and he was upset. That evening he couldn't sleep, he told us. He got the feeling that he should read his Book of Mormon, so he reached for it and opened it to a random page. As he told us this part of the story, he took out his Book of Mormon and read the verse aloud that he read that night over and over again: "Behold, I am Jesus Christ, whom the prophets testified shall come into the world. And behold, I am the light and the life of the world; and I have drunk out of that bitter cup which the Father hath given me, and have glorified the Father in taking upon me the sins of the world, in the which I have suffered the will of the Father in all things from the beginning" (3 Nephi 11:10–11).

As he read those verses to us, I started to feel a strong and unexpected emotion come over me. I didn't know exactly what the emotion was but I felt it through my whole body, a kind of energy or undefined physiological arousal. When he read the words, "Behold I am Jesus Christ," it resonated with my whole soul. I could literally feel the truth of the words in my body, like an energy welling up inside of me. I felt the tears start in my eyes. I didn't want them to come and I tried to hold them back. After all, I was supposed to be there for this man, not for me. Also, I knew it would seem strange to everyone if I was the one bawling over this man's experience. So I tried to hold it all in as he continued with his story.

He went on to tell us that when he read those words of the Savior, he realized that his feelings weren't really anger or hate for the man who attacked him. His feeling for the man was love. He knew that Christ's Atonement was real and that it covered this man as much as it covered him, and that it was John's responsibility to love and forgive this man, even if the man had tried to kill him. He then said that he went to the brig to visit the man. He went up to him in his cell and the man swore at him and told him that when he got out he was going to try and kill John again. John told us that despite the vitriol this man displayed, John went up to him and asked him to forgive him for hitting him and told the man that he loved him.

I couldn't handle the feelings any longer. I had the full memory of the man who beat me up three years previously in my mind and all of the hate and anger that I had kept in my heart. I thought, *How is it that this guy, this meathead, who has been excommunicated from the Church, who's lived so hard a life, was able to forgive a man who tried to kill him, and I can't forgive the man who beat me up three years ago?* I was overwhelmed by emotion and couldn't stop myself from crying openly. I knew that the answer to my prayer from the night before was right in front of me, exemplified by John, a man I had mistakenly stereotyped. I knew I needed to forgive the man who beat me. I needed to accept the Savior's words in 3 Nephi—that He did atone for all of our sins, including the sins of the man I hated, and that I had to accept that Atonement and forgive this man with all my heart.

John and the missionaries looked at me crying and asked if everything was okay. I told them that three years previously a man had beat me up during the break after Sunday School and said he wanted to kill me, and I had not forgiven him. I harbored only hatred for him. And here was John loving and forgiving a man who tried to kill him on the same day it happened. I was so much worse than John, even though I wasn't excommunicated, and I needed to repent of my unwillingness to forgive and of my hate. I left John's house that day knowing that I received the answer to my prayer. I knew there is a resurrected Christ who atoned for all of us. I knew the Book of Mormon was a true witness of Christ, and I knew that I must repent and forgive because Christ had atoned for all of our sins.

The first Sunday after my two-week mission concluded, the bishop asked me to give a report about my missionary experience in sacrament meeting. I knew what I had to do. I stood up and briefly shared the story of John, and then I looked out into the congregation and found the face of the man who had beat me three years previously. I stated that I had been holding a grudge for three years against a man who hurt me very badly and that I had hated him. I looked right at him as I spoke and asked him to please forgive me for my anger and hate and I told him that I was sorry. He showed no change in his demeanor at all and seemed completely unaffected by my apology, but I was free. The anger was gone, the hatred dissipated, and in that moment I was a disciple of Christ, full of His love and grateful for His mercy.

As wonderful as it is to experience this gift of forgiveness, it often doesn't last. We will inevitably shift out of the Disciple quadrant at some point and when we do, those feelings of anger and resentment are bound to come back, even if to a lesser degree than before. This may surprise and dismay us because we thought we had forgiven the sinner, and yet here we are, angry and needing to forgive again. This idea that forgiveness should be a once-and-for-all act is an unfortunate stereotype about forgiveness. On the contrary, forgiveness, like repentance, is rarely a one-time activity. It must be repeated on a regular basis. Recall that when Peter approached Christ to inquire about forgiveness he received an unexpected response: "Then came Peter to him, and said, Lord, how oft shall my brother sin against me, and I forgive him? till seven times? Jesus saith unto him, I say not unto thee, Until seven times: but, Until seventy times seven" (Matthew 18:21–22).

In this spirit of seventy-times-seven forgiveness, we would recommend that at least once a week, when we renew our covenant of baptism with the sacrament, that we couple our prayers of repentance with prayers of forgiveness. If done correctly, partaking of the sacrament is an act that places us in the Disciple quadrant and fills us with the love of God, which makes possible our genuine repentance and sincere forgiveness. As disciples of Christ we don't repent and forgive because we feel bad. We repent and forgive because we feel good. We are filled with a love for others and our God and we want nothing to stand in the way of those special relationships, including our sin or our unwillingness to forgive, even when we have to forgive those who have wronged us in some of the most hurtful and heinous ways. The pure love of Christ fills us with a desire to make repentance and forgiveness regular activities in our life, and with time and repetition we will eventually be able to fully and ultimately forgive as God commands, just as we can ultimately forsake the sins we must repent for each week.

When it comes to forgiving others, we must do as Christ commanded and forgive all people. We cannot put ourselves in Christ's position to decide who deserves forgiveness and who does not. This is easy to do when we are focused on the sin. We focus on how wrong the offender's act was, how it crossed a line and cannot ever be made right. We resist the Atonement on another's behalf just as the Nihilist resists the Atonement on his or her own behalf. All of us can imagine that if someone cut us off on the highway that we would feel angry and unforgiving, but if we found out that the person was on the way to the hospital to be with a dying spouse we would easily forgive them and the forgiveness would be justified in our eyes. However, if they cut us off just to get farther along in traffic, then our forgiveness is not justified and we remain angry. We feel justified in not forgiving the person and stay focused on the violation, the sin. Essentially we put ourselves in the position of deciding who deserves forgiveness and who does not, based on the severity of the potential sin and our ability to decide if it is reasonable and justifiable.

But that is not our prerogative. That is the Lord's responsibility and His alone. Our obligation is to forgive everyone, not whomever we pick and choose. It is not our place to decide another's fate, and how dare we make ourselves into Christ? The Nihilist does this to himself when he decides he is undeserving of the Atonement. The Pharisee does this to others when she stands in judgment over those around her. In fact, when we choose not to forgive ourselves or others, we elevate ourselves to the Savior's position, pretending we have the right to mete out judgment and forgiveness, as if we had performed the Atonement ourselves. Could anything be more illustrative of accepting the lie than this? Can any other false notion of being special even approximate this hubris?

The miracle of forgiveness that is possible through the love of God is no more remarkably manifest than by those who have suffered most severely and forgiven their persecutors. Consider, for example, a prayer written on a piece of paper and later found in a pocket of a child's tattered clothing. The child was found dead at Ravensbrück, one of the largest concentration camps in northern Germany during World War II. Ravensbrück was a camp where over 90,000 women and children were murdered by the Nazis. Surely, there was no justification for forgiveness in this most dire and despicable of conditions. Despite all this, the prayer reads:

"O Lord, remember not only the men and women of good will, but also those of ill will. But do not remember all of the suffering they have inflicted upon us: Instead remember the fruits we have borne because of this suffering, our fellowship, our loyalty to one another, our humility, our courage, our generosity, the greatness of heart that has grown from this trouble. When our persecutors come to be judged by you, let all of these fruits that we have borne be their forgiveness."[9]

Grace

An important purpose of Christ's Atonement is to free us from concern with the impossible demands of the law so we can live from a motivation of love instead of guilt, fear, reward, or duty. More than any other act, the Atonement illustrates the grace of our Heavenly Father, which enables our pure motivation in love. Without God's enabling power, the creation is for naught, our coming to this world has no purpose but to condemn us to a life of misery and ultimately death, and we would have no chance to return to our Father in Heaven and experience the full joy of having the void filled by the one Being who can truly do so. Every aspect of the Atonement should fill us with such joy and gratitude that we happily do His will and follow His example because we love Him.

Consider the superlative demonstration of grace that is the Resurrection, which brings to pass the immortality of all people. What an incredible gift this is and what unconditional grace and mercy is displayed by it! Yet for those whose pursuit of being special is grounded in being superior to others, this gift is really nothing special at all. After all, if it is given to everyone, righteous and unrighteous, rich and poor, thief and martyr alike, then how special is it really? It does nothing to separate the chosen from the unchosen and does not reward those who deserve it or punish those who do not. Thus Pharisees in particular are disinclined to fully appreciate the wonder of this gracious gift. They focus instead on exaltation, which they believe is given only to those few deserving it by virtue of their superior righteousness. This is a truly "special" achievement of the truly pure in heart. When looked at in this way, it is also a lie.

Rather than downplay the significance of the Resurrection and the gift of immortality because it is not "special" in this Pharisaical way, the Disciple celebrates the abundance of love and grace manifest by this greatest of gifts and is humbled to receive it. Filled with a deep and abiding gratitude for the gift of immortality, the disciple fully and joyfully accepts his or her dependency on God's grace and mercy and seeks to follow Christ's example and live a good and loving life as an expression of thanks to the God who provided this sacrifice so all may live. Thus, if we accept the truth and reject the lie we will respond to God's grace as manifest by the Resurrection and the gift of immortality with immense gratitude. We will be grateful that we have been saved from physical death and rejoice that this gift is given to all His children.

If we truly appreciate the grace of the Resurrection we will not be like the laborers in the Lord's vineyard who were hired in the morning and received a penny for their day's labor and were angry with their Lord for paying the same amount to laborers who were hired in the evening and worked far fewer hours (see Matthew 20:1–16). We will just be grateful that God condescended to sacrifice for us at all. We won't compare ourselves to others because we have all already received far more from our Lord than we could ever deserve. We all live in an overabundance of grace, and it should be our gratitude for this overabundance that motivates all else we do.

I[10] have learned a great deal about this response of gratitude from my Southern Baptist friends. Not long ago I described my experience with people in the southern United States to a colleague, having lived in Georgia for nine years. He asked me why I thought people there were so nice and friendly and relaxed. Why did life seem easier and less stressful? Even students at the university where I taught seemed okay with not getting an A in every class. How is it that they are so easygoing?

My answer to his question came to me more quickly and clearly than I expected. I explained that the people there were, for the most part, raised in a Christian culture in which they were taught that they were saved by the grace of God and that their confession of faith in Christ was sufficient to warrant that salvation. Because they truly believe they are saved by grace, they are freed from the concern of having to live up to every commandment and gospel principle with perfection. They believe they can be saved, even as flawed and imperfect people, and they are grateful for that. As a result, they are not typically guilt ridden about coming up short before God. They don't obsess over getting everything right and performing every jot and tittle of the law.

They acknowledge themselves and others as sinners before God—and that's okay. They don't act out of guilt because they believe their salvation is already secured. Instead, they accept the Lord's saving grace with thanks and joy. Because they do not fear damnation, they are free to act out of other motives than fear or guilt. They don't have to act for the sake of rewards either, because they already believe they are saved in heaven. Thus, they are free to choose other motives beyond heavenly hedonism. This is not to say that they are free from hedonism and selfishness, but their acceptance of grace does facilitate their service toward others, their kindness toward others, and their general hospitality, which comes from a different place than guilt or from seeking heaven.

I[11] was sitting in a church meeting not long ago where the relationship of grace and works was being discussed. As often happens when this topic is discussed, a member raised his hand and said, "Those Baptists think it is so easy. They think all they have to do is believe in God and they are saved. They don't realize all the important work we have to do on our part to earn exaltation." Knowing I had lived in Georgia, the teacher of the class asked me if that was true of my experience. I replied that I have lived with and befriended many Baptists, and I have witnessed many of them do a lot of good and hard work. Some of them go to church meeting several days a week. They go out and visit people in their homes and share their faith publicly. They pray regularly and pay generous offerings to their church. They go on missions all around the world at their own cost and try to help the sick and the poor. They do all these things believing that they have already been saved by grace. Why would they do that? They don't believe they are going to be more or less saved if they do these things. Their place in heaven is already secure. They have nothing to gain or lose, so why do they do it? From my experience, I would have to answer that it is because they are grateful to God for all their blessings, including the blessing of salvation.

We believe the debate over grace and works is based on a false dichotomy which pretends as if those who believe we are saved by grace don't do anything and those who believe we are saved by works think they have to do it all on their own. This makes no sense to us. On the contrary, it appears to us that when we truly accept the grace of the Savior, manifest in the many wonderful gifts He has given us, from the creation of the world to our own breath to the gift of immortality through the resurrection of the dead, we are so filled with the love of God that, like Lehi, Alma the Younger, and so many other prophets, we cannot help but want to do His will, share His gospel, and help others partake of the love we feel. We desire to keep the commandments, not because it will alleviate guilt or bring us closer to a heavenly reward, but because we want to do anything that such a gracious and giving God would ask of us. We want nothing but to thank Him and to please Him, and so we do His works with love and joy.

How would the Pharisee, Egoist, and Nihilist live differently if he or she focused on the incredible love and grace manifest in Christ's free gift of resurrection? How might his or her relationship to the commandments and to God differ if he or she lived the commandments because of gratitude and love for the Savior rather than to achieve a higher standard of righteousness than others? How might the Pharisee, Egoist, and Nihilist relate differently to other people if they recognized that God loves all His children equally and provides His grace to all of them? How would God feel toward His children who live the commandments and do good to others because it is right and good rather than because they believe it will get them a mansion in His highest kingdom? Once we live from love and grace, we are liberated to do the right thing for no other reason than because it is good and right. To illustrate this all-important point, consider the following parable:

The Parable of the King and the Righteous Man

There once lived a beloved and good king who ruled his kingdom in wisdom and order. Early in his reign he instituted a number of laws designed to maintain peace and facilitate happiness and righteous living among his people. Years had passed and he wanted to see how his people were faring with the laws. Indeed, he wanted to see if he could find a village in his kingdom and perhaps also an individual who was exceedingly righteous among all others.

The first village he visited had taken the king's laws very seriously, so seriously that the village leaders instituted very severe punishments for violations of the laws, including imprisonment, loss of property, and indentured servitude. The village leaders were considered the most righteous people in the village and sat in judgment on any violators of the law. When the king visited and inquired as to who might be the most righteous of the villagers they directed him to the chief village elder, an extremely pious man who lived every law the king instituted to the letter. When the king asked him why he lived the law so perfectly, the chief elder answered that if he didn't live the law with exactitude he would lose his position of leadership, he would lose face with his peers, he would be punished and lose his property and freedom, and most importantly he would lose the king's favor. Moreover, the loss of confidence in him might lead the village to lose confidence in the laws and fall into chaos.

"That sounds like quite a burden to bear," responded the king. "You have to be so mindful of everything you do and of what you could lose if you err. You must be exhausted with worry."

"To be honest, if I may, good king," the man replied. "It is a difficult path and I often do feel weighed down by the heaviness of the law. However, there is some solace in the knowledge that if I keep the law I won't have to feel the guilt that would come from letting you down, or the village, or myself. I don't think I could live with that."

"But are you happy?" the king replied. "Is your life filled with joy? You keep the law with the utmost diligence and you are therefore righteous indeed, but if all it does is keep you from feeling badly, then the purpose of the laws has clearly not been realized in you or this village. My only desire was to create laws that would facilitate the happiness of my people. Can you say that the laws have done that for you?" The man dared not respond for fear of displeasing the king. His silence was answer enough and the king took his leave.

The second village the king visited also took the king's laws very seriously—so much so that the village held an annual contest to see which of the villagers could live most obediently to the laws for the year. The winner would receive the finest hut in the village, an honored place on the village council, a special monument in the village square honoring the winner's accomplishment, and a year's supply of food and servants to wait on his or her every need. It turned out that the current winner had won the contest for the last ten years in a row and was deemed the all-time most righteous person in the village.

When the king met the man and asked him why he lived the law so perfectly the man exclaimed that it was easy to do so when the rewards were so great. "If I do a good deed for my neighbor each day as the law requires, then I move one step closer to the prize," the man exclaimed. If I do two or three good deeds daily, I virtually guarantee the win, and what a win it is. I receive the admiration of everyone in the village and all of my needs are met for the following year. I love your laws. They've really made me somebody in this village, somebody people respect and look up to."

"But with so many of my laws focused on loving and serving your neighbor don't you feel badly about helping them only so you can have the prize?" asked the king. "Don't you also feel badly about eating their food and having them serve you simply because you won a contest?"

"That's the beauty of this contest," the man quickly retorted. "It's a win-win scenario. I do a whole heap of good deeds for them all year long and win the prize of them doing good deeds for me in return. I scratch their backs and they scratch mine. Everybody wins."

"But, what if you had no chance of winning the prize?" inquired the king. "Would you keep doing all those extra good deeds? Would the villagers continue to share so much of their food and service with you?"

"Absolutely not," the man replied. "There would be no incentive to do so any longer. That's why I have to keep winning."

"So in the end, the contest is more about getting the rewards than the service itself?" the king asked.

"I don't like to put it in those terms," said the man, "but you're probably right." The king knew that he was and thanked the man and the village and took his leave.

The king visited many more villages. He found that some villages lived the law because they hoped the king would hear of their obedience and righteousness and perhaps reward them with a reduction in their taxes or a larger supply of grain. Others hoped the king would notice them individually and reward them with a position on the king's court. Still, others kept the minimal requirements of the law; just enough so as not to be noticed and perhaps punished by the king for their less than perfect diligence.

The king journeyed farther and farther across the land until he came to the farthest boundary of his kingdom, a village so remote that the king didn't know it existed at all. The villagers weren't aware they belonged to the king's kingdom either. They didn't even know there was a king and they were unaware of any laws they should obey. The king had no reason to expect that any person in the village lived according to the laws. He fully expected there to be chaos. Still, he was committed to his task.

When the king arrived in the village he asked the villagers he came across who, if anyone, was considered the most righteous person in the village. They didn't quite know what the king meant or what he was asking for, but they all agreed on the person who they thought lived the best kind of life in the village. This man was known for his honesty, his generosity, and his kindness. He would give a person the shirt off his back if they asked for it, and do so with a smile. He helped others without complaint or expectation. He treated people gently, even when they didn't deserve it. He held no grudges and if he thought he might have wronged another he immediately went to the person to ask forgiveness and make it right. He listened to others more than he spoke and never acted annoyed or put out, even when they rambled on and on.

After hearing of all these things and more the king knew he had to find this man and find out why he lived this way. After all, the man was living exactly the form of life the king wanted for his people and that the laws were designed to facilitate. Yet the people of the village had no idea of the laws, the king, or the kingdom. How could this man be living this way? Perhaps the man had travelled outside of the village and had come into contact with the laws somehow? The king had to find out. After searching and searching he finally found the man, repairing his neighbor's roof, and asked him if he might talk to him.

The man came down from the roof and the king immediately asked him one simple question: "Why are you living this way?" When the king asked this of the man, the man appeared confused, as if he didn't understand the question. He answered that he never really asked himself why. He just did it. He loved the people of the village and he cared about their well-being. He wanted to do his part to help them. It never occurred to him that he needed a reason. It was simply the right thing to do.

"And you have never heard of me or my laws?" the king inquired.

"No sir," came the response. "I don't mean any disrespect, but I don't know who you are and I don't know of any laws."

The king's eyes began to tear up. He had searched for so long and traveled so far to find the most righteous man in his kingdom, a man that lived his laws most perfectly, only to find that the most righteous man was a man who did not live for the laws or for the king at all. He knew nothing of such things. Indeed, he sought no reward, no freedom from guilt. He didn't scheme to win the king's favor or avoid his punishment. He sought only his neighbors' well-being. He sought only to do what was right. He was not compelled in any way. He made a free choice to be good for goodness' sake. He was clearly the most righteous man in all the land.

"Are you happy?" asked the king. Again, the man seemed confused by the king's question.

"I never really thought much about it," replied the man, "but yes, I suppose I am."

The king knew it was true. It was obvious that the man and the entire village shared a common peace and joy that the king had always wanted for his people. Now, if he could just figure out how to get all of his people to choose good living for the right reasons, like this man did. The king thanked the man for his time and took his leave.

When the king returned to his castle he called a meeting of all the people in the land to let them know what his journey had revealed. People came from all around, hoping to hear that their village and the person in their village who was deemed most righteous would be acknowledged as the most righteous village and person in the kingdom. The chief elder from the first village was there. He acted as if he wasn't invested in the acknowledgment, but secretly he knew he would lose face with his village and might lose his privileged position if he wasn't chosen. The man from the second village was there hoping to receive the special recognition and great reward the king would surely bestow upon the person achieving such a high honor. All the other villages were there also hoping to be honored. The man from the last village was not there at all, nor were his fellow villagers. They still didn't know there was a king or any kingdom to which they belonged, so they had no reason to attend.

The king took his place on the highest wall of the castle where his voice could reach all the people gathered there and he addressed his people, "I have traveled far and wide throughout my entire kingdom to find the most righteous village and perhaps the most righteous person in the land, and I am here to report that I found just such a village and just such a person. But my heart is troubled, for this village and this person know nothing of me and my kingdom or of my laws.

They do not have all the protection and services I have provided you. They have never come to my castle and communed with me. They are not as blessed as you are with the abundance of wealth and resources that I have provided you. Yet without all of these things, they live my laws. They do good to one another. They are kind and gentle and selfless. They are quick to repent and to forgive. Indeed, they live my laws exactly as I have always desired that my people would, yet they know nothing of the laws or of me."

The people gasped in amazement and could not understand how this village could live this way and why they would freely choose to live this way. "What did they get out of it?" some wondered. Knowing their thoughts, the king stated, "These people do none of these things because they expect a reward from me or because they fear a punishment from me. They don't even know I'm their king. They do these things because they love one another and because it is the right thing to do. It is as simple as that.

"Now, I ask you my people, with all that you have been given, with my laws, my resources, my gifts, and my abundance, how much more should you be keeping my laws because you love me, you love each other, and because it is right? You know me, many of you personally, and you know of my desires for you to be good and kind, and yet many of you keep my laws because you fear my punishment or you want to set yourselves above others to be noticed by me. Some of you keep my laws in the hopes of rewards or special treatment, even as you exploit one another to accomplish these goals. What excuse do you have, knowing me as your king and knowing my desires for you to love one another and to do good because of that love? Who do you think is more deserving of my recognition and my kingdom? Who should I bring into my castle to be with me, those who know me and who know better, but do it not, or those who know nothing of me or my laws, but live as I would have them live, in love and goodness? I think you know my answer and now you know who is the most righteous in the kingdom." The king stepped down from the wall and left his people to ponder on what he said.

The true King, our Heavenly Father, knows exactly how to help all of His people live for the right reasons. He has given us every means to do so. We are His children and He has provided a way for us to have joy and return to Him. But this way is not just a set of laws to be followed for the reward of exaltation or to avoid the punishment of falling short of celestial glory. It is a frame of mind and a state of the heart. Remember that the Lord requires of us a broken heart and a contrite spirit. His Atonement provides for exactly that. First of all, it overcomes physical death, and for that we should all be so grateful and joyful that we want nothing more than to do good continually and to love our neighbors and help them. The gift of the Resurrection alone should be enough to break our hearts and make our spirits contrite, but God does not stop there. He has also overcome spiritual death, and that too should fill our hearts with joy and gratitude, purify our motives, and lead us to do good and uplift others continually.

Chapter 10

Conclusion

"Think of the purest, most all-consuming love you can imagine. Now multiply that love by an infinite amount—that is the measure of God's love for you."—President Dieter F. Uchtdorf[1]

We began this book with a description of contemporary Western culture as one that is more focused on displaying the special qualities, abilities, and accomplishments of individuals than ever before. We have also discussed several possible sources of this desire to be special. One of the chief sources is the lie whispered to us by the adversary, which tells us that each of us is a uniquely gifted individual who stands above others as a superior being. Imagine what life would be like if the lie was true and was the only source of this special feeling. We would always be caught up in comparing ourselves with others and trying to outdo each other, which can only lead to some form of superiority or inferiority complex, or more often than not some combination of the two.

If the lie was true, everything about our lives would be competitive and self-interested. Parents would be constantly trying to one-up their own children just as spouses would compete for greater superiority over each other. It would be a world of pride and arrogance, vanity and greed, self-righteousness and disregard for others. There would be no charity or compassion, no altruism or self-sacrifice. Even if selflessness was possible, we would be constantly trying to be more compassionate and altruistic than others, taking pride in our goodness and nobility, which would only undo the true meaning and intention of such feelings and actions. Godly motives and feelings simply could not exist in the world of the lie.

A world governed solely by the lie would be very similar to the world of the Nephites at the end of the Book of Mormon or the world of the wicked people at the time of Noah. Their hearts became so focused on the treasures and accomplishments of this world that they lost any concern for the things of the next world, the things of God's world. They became so shortsighted that they could only see their position relative to their competitors. They became obsessed with getting ahead of others in their accumulation of material wealth, fame, or beauty.

For these people, there was no time or reason to raise their gaze up to the heavens. They were too busy looking at those around them and comparing themselves to them. We know how their stories turned out. Their hearts grew cold and hard. They became obsessed with themselves and disregarded their Heavenly Father. They lived the lie completely, and as a result, they became beyond feeling, beyond repentance, beyond coming back to their God. They destroyed themselves inside first and then they were completely wiped off the face of the earth from the outside. They became everything the adversary wanted. They became his slaves, constantly seeking gratification in the artifices of wealth, fame, power, and sex. Caught in an inescapable void-enlarging tragedy, they became completely lost and beyond hope.

While it is true that we can live as if there is only the lie and we can become obsessed with comparing ourselves with others, the lie is not the only source of our special feelings. In fact, the lie can only ever be a false source of our special feelings that is provided by the adversary who desires to enslave us. The truth is that there is another source of our special feelings, a true source that pertains to all of us and provides the proper understanding of our true nature. We are children of a God, a divine King who loves His children with a love only a God can provide. We feel special because of our divine birthright. We feel special because we experienced this pure love of God when we were with Him prior to coming to this world, and we feel special because the resources God has provided us offer us the opportunity to feel that love again.

In the end, this is the most important message of this book: You are a son or a daughter of a King, and that King, your Heavenly Father, loves you so fully and completely that you are truly special indeed. You need only to raise your gaze to the heavens and accept His love and then the feeling of the void you experience as a consequence of this temporary separation from your Father will be filled with love and light. Recall the words of the Savior regarding the need to lift our gaze to the heavens. He said, "The light of the body is the eye: therefore when thine eye is single, thy whole body also is full of light. . . . If thy whole body therefore be full of light, having no part dark, the whole shall be full of light, as when the bright shining of a candle doth give thee light" (Luke 11:34, 36). Following this all-important teaching of the Savior, we conclude this book with the commandment from our Heavenly Father to us: "Look and live" (Alma 33:19).

God's Love for Us

With all the challenges human beings have with feeling, expressing, and sharing genuine love with each other, it should not surprise us that we have a hard time imagining the full measure of God's love for His children. Some of us have grown up in homes where our parents rarely, if ever, told us they loved us. Others have grown up without one or more of their parents living with them, and are left wondering if they were loved by that absent parent at all. Even in homes with parents who do express their love for their children there can be messages of love mixed with disapproval and disappointment. As we get older and experiment with loving others, we can experience rejection and deceit and develop feelings of distrust for the love expressed by others. In short, loving and being loved by each other, as important as these things are to us, are not easily achieved or trusted. As a result, we can transfer our feelings of mistrust, fear, and hesitation about love to our relationship with our Heavenly Father.

Though our concerns with love may be understandable in light of our challenges with loving and being loved by other people, any transference of our imperfect ideas about love to the love God has for us is a grievous mistake. God's love for us is unwavering and infinite. It cannot be diminished or distorted, no matter what we do. Our Heavenly Father's love is eternal and boundless. If we could comprehend the magnificence of His absolute and pure love for us, we would realize that we are much harder on ourselves than He is. We would see just how badly we underestimate the grace and mercy He provides us. We would recognize that our flawed perceptions about love have led us to believe that God's love has to be earned and that our Heavenly Father will love us less if we fall short of perfection or become steeped in sin. These are our limited human views, not His. Our love may be restricted in these ways because we are constrained by our human context and personal experiences, but God's love knows no earthly or human bounds because it is heavenly and divine.

Instead of leaning on our own mistaken understanding, let us accept President Dieter F. Uchtdorf's words concerning God's love for us. He said: "I believe that He doesn't care one bit if we live in a castle or a cottage, if we are handsome or homely, if we are famous or forgotten. Though we are incomplete, God loves us completely. Though we are imperfect, He loves us perfectly. Though we may feel lost and without compass, God's love encompasses us completely.

"He loves us because He is filled with an infinite measure of holy, pure, and indescribable love. We are important to God not because of our résumé but because we are His children. He loves every one of us, even those who are flawed, rejected, awkward, sorrowful, or broken. God's love is so great that He loves even the proud, the selfish, the arrogant, and the wicked.

"What this means is that, regardless of our current state, there is hope for us. No matter our distress, no matter our sorrow, no matter our mistakes, our infinitely compassionate Heavenly Father desires that we draw near to Him so that He can draw near to us."[2]

We can spend so much time examining all the reasons why we think God should not love us that we fail to appreciate that He cares deeply and fully for each one of us, no matter what. Even those people who are notorious for their wickedness and rebellion against God are infinitely beloved by Him. Recall that in the book of Moses in the Pearl of Great Price, Enoch was blessed to have a conversation with God. As part of that conversation, God and Enoch discussed the wickedness of the people at the time of the flood. These people were so evil that there was no hope for them. God brought the purging waters of the flood to wipe them out because there was no hope that they would repent. As their discussion of the flood ensued, Enoch noted with surprise that God was weeping for these people. As do many of us, Enoch seemed to think that God is so great and powerful, so sovereign and self-sustaining, that He is not emotionally affected by the actions of His children. If they choose to misuse the agency He has given them, that's their problem, right?

On the contrary, God shows Enoch that He is deeply invested in each and every one of His children. He who notices the falling of a sparrow certainly notices and weeps over the physical and spiritual deaths of His children. Few verses of scripture are more touching than God's response to Enoch's inquiry, "How is it that thou canst weep, seeing thou art holy, and from all eternity to all eternity?" (Moses 7:29). Simply, but profoundly, the Lord replies with tears in His eyes, "Behold these thy brethren; they are the workmanship of mine own hands" (Moses 7:32). As we are, the people at the time of the flood are His children. He created them and He loves them and weeps over them and their suffering, regardless of how they choose to live their lives. May each of us be taught, as was Enoch, that our Heavenly Father doesn't seek to punish us and He is not indifferent to our suffering. He loves each of us fully and intimately and reaches out to us with that love to lift us up and redeem us as often as we are willing to look up to him and believe.

This is a key message we have discussed throughout this book: It doesn't matter where you find yourself in terms of the quadrants and it doesn't matter how long you have been there. Right now, at this very moment, you can raise your gaze and look upon Him whose love is beyond comprehension, and be lifted and strengthened and healed. It is the adversary who tells you that you have gone too far down the dark path or that you could never keep all of the commandments, so why not just give up. His lie focuses you on yourself. God's truth focuses you on Him and His pure love for you.

This focus on God reminds us of the children of Israel who were visited by fiery serpents because they murmured against God and His prophet Moses. They focused on themselves and their suffering and complained, as they had so many times before. To humble them, the Lord sent the serpents among them and many of the people were bitten and died. Eventually, the people were humbled and cried to their God and to Moses for help. The Lord commanded Moses to make a serpent of brass and to place it on a pole. The only thing the people had to do was look upon the brazen serpent and they would be healed. They needed simply to raise their gaze, to look beyond their suffering, both the suffering of the venom and the suffering of their lives since leaving Egypt. They simply had to look at the serpent and they would be well.

Surprisingly, for many of these sick Israelites the task was too easy and they would not look upon the serpent. As Nephi described it, "The labor which they had to perform was to look; and because of the simpleness of the way, or the easiness of it, there were many who perished" (1 Nephi 17:41). We can also find the way to discipleship too easy. We may have become convinced that Heavenly Father is a strict and demanding taskmaster who withholds His love and blessings from those who don't live righteously. We think we have to follow all of the commandments all of the time for Him to be pleased with us. We think we have to be aware of and repent for all of our sins, both those of commission and omission. We have to be sure to forgive everyone immediately and fully. We have to fulfill our callings without complaint and to the highest level of diligence. We have to be parents who do no wrong or we have to be children who never disobey. We have to pay a full tithing and keep the Sabbath day holy all of our lives, and go to all our church meetings with a cheerful demeanor, and so on and so on. Like the children of Israel, we think we know better. It can't be that easy. The path to God has to be hard; if we don't do all we have been commanded, we aren't going to receive exaltation in the celestial kingdom.

The Why and the How

Much of this sentiment is true. We do need to keep the commandments and we do need saving ordinances. We do need to labor all of our lives to build God's kingdom and we must repent and forgive always. All of that is work, and hard work at that. But we should not confuse the *why* of what we do with the *how*. The political scientist Kiersten Renwick Monroe wrote a wonderful book titled *The Heart of Altruism* in which she records her interviews of people who risked their own lives and the lives of their families, even their own children, to rescue Jews in the occupied countries of Europe during World War II. In her interviews with these amazing people, she found several recurring themes. First of all, none of these people thought what they did was extraordinary. They believed anyone would have done it. Of course, we know that is not true. There were many people who stood by and did nothing and others who perpetrated the horrific acts of the Holocaust, but there were relatively few rescuers.[3]

The other theme that speaks more directly to our topic here is that, almost without exception, the rescuers never deliberated about whether they would help the Jews when the opportunity presented itself. They just helped. When a Jewish family arrived at their door or approached them on the street for help, even when they were complete strangers, the rescuer did not mull it over. Their decision to help was simple and yes, even easy. They took the responsibility to aid the family without question or doubt. They did deliberate a great deal about how to best hide them and get them food and keep them safe from being discovered, but the question of whether or not to help never entered their minds. They just did it because it was the right thing to do.

This is what we mean by not confusing the *why* with the *how* of our work. Yes, there is much thought that must go into *how* we serve others and do our part to build up the kingdom of God. We must deliberate about how we can best keep the commandments, repent, and forgive in the different circumstances and contexts of our lives. But the question of *why* we do all of these things should not be a question at all. We should do these things for the same reason Christ did all that He did for us: because of our Heavenly Father's love which is in us. We should do these things because we are filled with gratitude for Christ's grace and redemption and because we look up to Him with a faith and hope that needs no deliberation, but only thanksgiving.

Too often we think we have to get our lives in order and then we'll be worthy and prepared for His love, so we focus on all the things we have to do, as if we could do them without Him in the first place. We think we have to first keep the commandments and then He will extend His hand to us to lift us up. We think we have to first repent fully and forsake all sin and then we will be worthy of His love. We think we have to earn His grace and love, even though King Benjamin has already taught us that no matter what we do we would still be unprofitable servants.

No, like the Israelites who were bitten and were sick, it was precisely then and there in their suffering that they had brought upon themselves, a suffering that was fully justified and deserved, that they were to look up and be healed. They did not have to get themselves healed first and then look up. They were commanded to look up in their sinful and suffering state immediately, and so are we. We understand why this seems too easy and too simple. The rational mind tells us that you don't get something for nothing in this world. You have to do something to deserve or earn what you want and only then do you receive the gift. This is how we treat each other in much of our interactions, so it is understandable that we would apply this reasoning to our God. However, it is a mistake to do so.

We did not earn the great blessing of resurrection. We could not earn it as fallen and sinful as we are. We certainly did not deserve the atoning sacrifice for sin that Jesus willingly offered in the Garden of Gethsemane. These gifts were given freely in love by a being whose love, like His peace, surpasses all understanding. He does not do what He does for us because we deserve it. He does it because He loves us, as undeserving as we are. We need not and cannot comprehend with our limited minds and hearts why a God, so holy and so pure, so far above and beyond us in every way, would abase Himself for our sakes and suffer for us all. All we can do is give thanks that He did it. All we can do is praise and worship God and love Him even more for His sacrifice. Instead of trying to figure it all out, we need only look and live. We need only receive His gifts and then as we receive them we will be filled with such gratitude and such love that we will want nothing more than to do His will and to help others also receive His gifts.

How can we learn to disentangle the why from the how, so we too can appreciate the simplicity of receiving God's love? Perhaps one of the first things we can do is learn to understand that discipleship is not achieved by trying not to be a Pharisee, Egoist, or Nihilist, just like love isn't achieved by trying not to hate, faith isn't achieved by trying not to doubt, and hope isn't achieved by trying not to despair. Discipleship, as we have discussed in previous chapters, is not about trying at all. It is about yielding, submitting, and giving one's self over to God.

Don't Try to Not Do Something Bad. Do Something Good.

"Darkness cannot drive out darkness; only light can do that. Hate cannot drive out hate; only love can do that."—Martin Luther King Jr.[4]

Imagine what would happen if we tried to be a Disciple by trying not to be a Pharisee. We could easily become Pharisaical about not being Pharisaical, counting all the times we have slipped into Pharisaical behavior and keeping track of it and trying to reduce the number. We might compare our number to others' numbers and participate in downward social comparison. In short, we become fixated on not being a Pharisee rather than focused on Christ.

We don't become a Disciple by trying not to be something else. When we do that we end up becoming beholden to the thing we want to be rid of. By doing so we give it a power over us. It's like trying not to think of that pink monkey on the unicycle on the tightrope with the pink banana. When someone asks us not to think of it, the image just pops into our heads.

When we work with addicts we never tell them to try and not think of alcohol, drugs, or pornography. We know that will only strengthen the thought in their mind and increase its tempting power. It is like sitting in front of a big, beautiful piece of chocolate cake and staring at it and trying not to eat it. Such an exercise borders on cruel and unusual punishment! The tempting power of trying not to think of something you want, reminds me[5] of an experience I had when I was younger. When I was about ten years old, I found a box of Ding Dongs hidden back in the back of the freezer. I knew I was not allowed to eat them. Ding Dongs were a special treat and had to be distributed by Mom. They couldn't just be taken.

I remember thinking, *I am not going to eat those Ding Dongs. They are not mine and it would be wrong to steal them.* I tried to put the thought of them out of my mind. I tried to act as if I never saw them. I tried to engage in other activities to distract myself. But all I could think about was that box of Ding Dongs and the foil-covered chocolate pucks inside. I tried harder to get the thought out of my mind, but the thought grew even stronger: their chocolate goodness, the crème filling. I wanted them more than I ever wanted a Ding Dong before. (Just writing about them now makes my mouth water again.) Those Ding Dongs occupied all my thoughts now. Then came the rationalizations: "Mom probably forgot they were even in there. I'm sure she was going to give me one eventually anyway. I can just have mine now. There's like twelve of them in there. One won't be missed."

Eventually, I gave in. I stole one of those tasty Ding Dongs out of the freezer and I ate it. Even frozen, it was delicious. It was the best Ding Dong I ever ate. I expected to be satisfied and to move on, but the Ding Dong tasted so good that I couldn't stop thinking about having another one. It didn't take long before I gave into temptation again and ate another one. Over the next few days, I consumed the whole box. I did have moments of resolve where I went several hours without indulging my desires. I even took some pride in the strength of my resistance. But inevitably, my obsession with those Ding Dongs got the better of me and I went back to the freezer again and again and indulged my appetite. After I ate them all I felt tremendous guilt.

What had I done? I was only going to have one and now I've eaten the whole box. What is wrong with me? Where is my self-control? What is Mom going to do to me? I remember getting in big trouble for eating all those Ding Dongs. I remember the disappointment on my mom's face and the upset it caused my siblings who had practiced self-control. But as bad as it sounds, I also remember going back to that freezer a week or two later to see if a new box of Ding Dongs or Zingers might be found there. They were just so good!

Like any of us who become addicted to something, I became caught up in temptation, and the more I tried not to think about the thing that tempted me, the more energy I put into it and the more it became an obsession to me.

Perhaps the most striking example of the debilitating effects of trying not to think about something is found in people who suffer from severe symptoms of obsessive-compulsive disorder (OCD). Let us introduce you to a young mother named Andrea. Prior to the birth of her son, Andrea struggled with moderate symptoms of OCD, particularly focused on germs, but she was able to manage them for the most part. However, when she had her first child, her OCD went into overdrive. She became obsessed with protecting her son from anything that might infect him. She couldn't touch the mail because people had licked the envelopes shut. She couldn't go for walks with her son in a stroller because she might push the stroller over a cigarette butt or a piece of trash and infect it. She couldn't take her eyes off of her son when she stopped her car at an intersection because someone might sneak up, open the car door, and infect her son in some way.

Andrea would set up traps in her house whenever she would leave so she could detect any intruders who might have infected the house while she was away. In one half-hour period she typically washes her hands an average of twenty-two times. Her hands would become so dry and cracked that she could not make a fist without her skin tearing and bleeding. She didn't want to obsess over germs infecting her son. In fact, she tried hard not to. She tried to push the thoughts out of her mind. However, the more she tried, the stronger the thoughts became until the only coping mechanism she could practice was to engage in compulsive behaviors, like washing her hands over and over again, to ameliorate her obsession. But these compulsive behaviors were hindering her ability to parent her child. It seemed that the more she tried not to be germophobic, the stronger her obsession with cleanliness became. She was caught in a vicious cycle and needed help.

Interestingly, part of the therapeutic treatment she eventually received involved her exposing herself to germs, the very things she feared the most. At first blush, this seems counterintuitive. Wouldn't this increase her obsessive thinking about cleanliness and her compulsive coping rituals? Wouldn't this send her over the edge? Actually, and surprisingly, it did not, at least not after a while. In one example of exposure, her therapist asked her to get the mail and bring it in the house and open it, which is something Andrea had not done for over a year. Although Andrea experienced a great deal of anxiety, with the assistance of her therapist, she was able to do it.

She even got up the courage to take an opened envelope and wipe it vigorously all over the couch, "infecting" the couch and herself. She then worked up the strength to put her son on the "infected" couch. As she exposed herself and her son to her fears she did experience strong anxiety, but it didn't last long or stay as strong as she expected once she allowed herself to do the very thing she feared. Eventually, her obsessions, which focused on trying to avoid germs, were counteracted by her exposing herself and her son to germs and seeing for herself that everyone was okay. It wasn't the end of the world that she envisioned. She can now get the mail, take walks with her son and even pick up leaves. She doesn't wash her hands every few minutes and she genuinely enjoys her son.

In this book we have practiced a mild form of exposure therapy. We have tried to expose you, the reader, to your Pharisaical, egoistic, and nihilistic tendencies. Rather than trying to avoid these ways of responding to the truth and the lie, which only empowers them and puts them at the center of your thinking, we have asked you to acknowledge the time you have spent indulging each quadrant; to accept that you participate in Pharisaical, egoistic, and nihilistic thinking, feeling, and behaviors. We don't want you to try not to be any of these things. We want you to expose yourself to them and to see that having characteristics of each way of being is not the end of the world. They won't infect you and destroy you. In fact, as we have shown, you won't stay in any one quadrant indefinitely. You will move in and out of them as you go through life.

We ask that when you slip into a quadrant—and you will—that you not beat yourself up over it and swear to leave it and never return. Let yourself be exposed to the quadrant by acknowledging that it is part of life to respond to the truth and the lie in each of these ways. The goal is to steadily decrease the time spent in each one, and to increase the time spent in the Disciple quadrant. How does that happen? How do we get there? As we have said, we don't get there by trying not to be in the other quadrants.

You may recall the parable of the Wish-Fulfilling Tree that was introduced in chapter 3. In that chapter, we discussed one message of this Hindu parable, which is that many people find themselves under the wish-fulfilling tree, wishing for things like money, power, fame, and sex, and getting what they want and the opposite too: insecurity, shame, sadness, and despair. The people end up miserable but they don't know how to get out of the cycle. They think they just need to change their wishes, improve them, and they will finally receive what they want without its undesirable opposite. They never succeed and become caught in a void-enlarging tragedy from which there appears to be no escape. But the parable doesn't end there. As the storyteller says, "parables don't end that way."[6]

The parable goes on to tell the story of a crippled boy, who, when he hears about this magic tree that grants wishes, runs along with the other children toward the tree so he can start wishing. But he can't run very well because of his disability and he falls down. All the other children pass him by and take up the space beneath the tree. The boy decides he will wait in a small hut near the tree for his turn to go under the tree and make his wishes. He watches the children making their wishes through the hut's window. He sees them wishing for candy and getting stomachaches. He sees them wishing for toys and getting boredom. He sees them wishing for power, sex, wealth, and fame and getting depressed and unhappy. He sees them try different wishes and get more negative consequences. He sees them suffering and despairing and giving up and wanting to die. He sees them getting reborn and having to go through the process all over again.

And in his observation of all these things, as he marvels at all that is happening to his friends, something happens. As the storyteller tells it, "There was a gush of compassion in his heart for his companions under the tree. And in that gush of compassion, he forgot to wish. He forgot to wish *and the tree couldn't touch him.* He was free."[7] At this point the audience to the parable always wants to understand this gush of compassion better, so inevitably the question is asked: "But how is it possible? What kind of thing is this pure act that you talk about, this non-wishing, gush-of-compassion act?"[8] Because it is something that cannot be explained but only exemplified, the storyteller provides two additional examples of it in response to the question.

First, the storyteller says, "Don't ask me. Ask any mother why she puts the baby on the dry side of the bed at night and puts herself on the wet side, joyfully. Is it because she wants the baby to look after her twenty years later? Could be a very calculated act. Is it instinctive? Could be. Let's ask a psychologist. Is it because she's irrational? Could be. Is it because she gets a Freudian kick out of it? Could be. Ask *her* and she'll say, 'Would you mind not wasting my time? You go to college and find out. Meanwhile, let me look after the baby, please.' She just does it. And the others try to find out what's going on."[9]

The storyteller's second example begins with a question to the audience: "'Does any of you have a rupee note?' (A rupee note is hardly ten cents). Everyone has it and they produce it. He says, 'Now you can do four things with it. One, you give it to charity, you do good to someone, you put your name to it—you do for yourself, too—you'll get heaven. Serves you right—you'll be born again' [for Hindus, heaven is a temporary place for people who will be reborn and given a chance to do better]. 'You can take the rupee note and spend it all on yourself, act as if you live in a vacuum and no one else exists in the world, you'll get hell. Serves you right—you'll be born again, and given another chance to do better. You can do the absurd act. . . . You can take the rupee note, tear it into little bits, and put it into the trash can. It's your life; you're free any time to take it. Or you can do the pure act, too. You can take the rupee note and give it in charity and, like the mother who puts the baby on the dry side of the bed and puts herself on the wet side at night joyfully, like the boy who stood there marveling at the cosmic spectacle of the universe, you, in a gush of compassion, give it; and though you want to add your name to it, you, in that gush of compassion, forget to add your name to it and by doing so you have done the pure act.'

"Ah, but don't *remember* to forget or the tree will get you.'"[10]

The parallel between this parable and the Savior's teaching in Matthew 10:39 is unmistakable: "He that loseth his life for my sake shall find it" (see also D&C 98:13, Matthew 16:25). When we are filled with the love of God and have compassion toward those around us, we will forget our desires and lose ourselves in the service of others. We do not try to make better wishes or try not to wish. We lose the desire to wish at all. We want only to fulfill His wishes, to do His work, and to lift the gaze of those around us. We yield our will to His and our desires to be self-righteous, egoistic, and hopeless are forgotten. Of course, in doing this we cannot harbor a secret desire to find ourselves through losing ourselves. This would make losing ourselves a means to a selfish end. In other words, we would still be wishing. Instead, we must truly give our will over to Christ's. We must allow it to be swallowed up in Him completely. We must truly lose ourselves and forget our own desires if we are to be His disciples.

We won't be able to lose ourselves in His will all of the time. We will fall back into egoism, Pharisaism, and nihilism, but only temporarily. Grace will fall upon us again, and when it does, we need only receive it by lifting our gaze and looking toward the Savior; by accepting His embrace through our participation in the Atonement; by repenting and forgiving; by loving others and losing ourselves in service toward them, we look and live. By latching onto His word, putting our hand in His, and making Him our focus, we look and live. It is by yielding to Him and accepting His love that we enter the Disciple quadrant, not by trying really hard not to be bad. As we take His hand, He will lift us up and out of the ways of living that beset us. Our Pharisaism, egoism, and nihilism will slough off of us, not because we tried to be rid of them, but because when you yoke yourself to Him and His love, sin just falls by the wayside. He purifies you and you no longer have the disposition to do evil. The feeling of the void leaves you as you embrace Him and serve Him and others. Yielding our will to His will is all that is required. When we do that, the rest will take care of itself.

Notes

Introduction

1. Boyd K. Packer, "Little Children," *Ensign,* November 1986, 17.

Chapter 1: The Culture of "Special"

1. Deb Caletti, *The Secret Life of Prince Charming* (New York: Simon & Schuster Books for Young Children, 2009), 321.
2. Darren Reidy, "Five Questions: The World's Greatest Floater," *Men's Journal,* September 2010, 26.
3. See http://www.celeb4aday.com/Home.html; accessed 18 August 2012.
4. See *Narcissism and Machiavellianism in Youth: Implications for the Development of Adaptive and Maladaptive Behavior,* Christopher T. Barry, Patricia K. Kerig, Kurt K. Stellwagen, and Tammy D. Barry, eds. (Washington, DC: American Psychological Association, 2011).
5. Jean M. Twenge and W. Keith Campbell, *The Narcissism Epidemic* (New York: Free Press, 2009), 191.
6. Ibid.
7. Andrew Kohut, et al., *How Young People View Their Lives, Futures and Politics: A Portrait of "Generation Next"* (Washington, DC: Pew Research Center, 2006), 12.
8. See http://www.time.com/time/magazine/article/0,9171,1570810,00 .html; accessed 5 September 2012.

9. *Diagnostic and Statistical Manual of Mental Disorders, Fourth Edition, Text Revision* (Arlington, VA: American Psychiatric Association, 2000), 717.

10. Radiohead, "Creep (BBC Radio 1 Evening Session)," *Pablo Honey (Collector's Edition),* audio CD (Los Angeles: Capitol Records, 1993).

11. Twenge and Campbell, *Narcissism Epidemic,* 16.

12. Ibid.

13. Drew Pinsky and S. Mark Young, *The Mirror Effect: How Celebrity Narcissism Is Seducing America* (New York: HarperCollins, 2009), 107.

14. George Lucas, *Star Wars: Episode III—Revenge of the Sith,* directed by George Lucas, DVD (Los Angeles: 20th Century Fox, 2005).

15. Andy Wachowski and Larry Wachowski, *The Matrix,* directed by Andy and Larry Wachowski, DVD (Los Angeles: Warner Home Video, 1999).

16. J. K. Rowling, *Harry Potter and the Sorcerer's Stone* (New York: Scholastic, 1998); *Harry Potter and the Chamber of Secrets* (New York: Scholastic, 1999); *Harry Potter and the Prisoner of Azkaban* (New York: Scholastic, 1999); *Harry Potter and the Goblet of Fire* (New York: Scholastic, 2000); *Harry Potter and the Order of the Phoenix* (New York: Scholastic, 2003); *Harry Potter and the Half-Blood Prince* (New York: Scholastic, 2005); *Harry Potter and the Deathly Hallows* (New York: Scholastic, 2007).

17. Stephenie Meyer, *Twilight* (New York: Little, Brown and Co., 2005); *New Moon* (New York: Little, Brown and Co., 2006); *Eclipse* (New York: Little, Brown and Co., 2007); *Breaking Dawn* (New York: Little, Brown and Co., 2008).

18. J. R. R. Tolkien, *The Fellowship of the Ring; The Two Towers;* and *The Return of the King;* 2nd edition(Boston: Houghton Mifflin, 1982).

19. For this and subsequent first-person reminiscences, we will cite the name of the author in an endnote; the speaker in this reminiscence is Jeffrey Reber.

20. Jeffrey Reber.

21. See Daniel L. Wann, Michael A. Hamlet, Tony M. Wilson, and Joan A.

Hodges, "Basking in Reflected Glory, Cutting Off Reflected Failure, and Cutting Off Future Failure: The Importance of Group Identification," in *Social Behavior and Personality* 23(4), 1995: 377–88.

22. Steven Moody.

23. Jeffrey Reber.

24. Pinsky and Young, *Mirror Effect*, 6.

25. Jean M. Twenge, *Generation Me: Why Today's Young Americans Are More Confident, Assertive, Entitled—and More Miserable Than Ever Before* (New York: Free Press, 2006), 88.

26. Pinsky and Young, *Mirror Effect*, 73–74.

27. Ibid., 82.

28. See Chris Arlens, "Twitter: A 'Gateway Drug to Full-Blown Media Narcissism'?" *Social Times,* 28 February 2009; available at http://socialtimes.com/twitter-a-gateway-drug-to-full-blown-media-narcissism_b49523; accessed 5 September 2012.

29. Walter Schwabe, "Twitter is a narcissism machine!" 18 April 2009, *fusedlogic.com;* available at http://www.fusedlogic.com/twitter-is-a-narcissism-machine-1288/; accessed 5 September 2012.

30. See http://twitter.com/ConanOBrien/status/10041591698; accessed 4 September 2012.

31. See http://www.examiner.com/article/conan-o-brien-s-twitter-move-gives-sarah-killen-a-wedding; accessed 4 September 2012.

32. See Laura E. Buffardi and W. Keith Campbell, "Narcissism and Social Networking Web Sites," in *Personality and Social Psychology Bulletin,* 3 July 2008; available at http://psp.sagepub.com/cgi/content/abstract/34/10/1303; accessed 5 September 2012.

33. Pinsky and Young, *Mirror Effect,* 79; emphasis in original.

34. John Lahr, *The Guardian,* 2 August 1989.

35. Philip Cushman, "Why the Self Is Empty: Toward a Historically Situated Psychology," in *American Psychologist* 45(5), May 1990:599.

36. Ibid., 604.

37. Jeffrey Reber.

38. Frank C. Richardson, "Psychotherapy and Modern Dilemmas," in

Critical Thinking about Psychology: Hidden Assumptions and Plausible Alternatives, Brent D. Slife, Jeffrey S. Reber, and Frank C. Richardson, eds. (Washington, DC: American Psychological Association, 2005), 21.

39. Ibid.

Chapter 2: The Truth

1. *Discourses of Brigham Young,* sel. John A. Widtsoe (Salt Lake City: Deseret Book, 1954), 50.

2. George Q. Cannon, *Gospel Truth,* sel. Jerreld L. Newquist, 2 vols. in one (Salt Lake City: Deseret Book, 1987), 103.

3. Boyd K. Packer, "Why Stay Morally Clean," *Ensign,* July 1972, 111.

4. Robert L. Simpson, in Conference Report, April 1970, 89; or *Improvement Era,* June 1970, 83.

5. Packer, "Why Stay Morally Clean," 111.

6. Matthew O. Richardson, "Three Principles of Marriage," *Ensign,* April 2005, 21.

7. Beth Azar, "A Reason to Believe," *Monitor on Psychology* 41(11), December 2010:53.

8. Neal A. Maxwell, "Patience," *Ensign,* October 1980, 28.

9. Jeffrey Reber.

10. Steven Moody.

11. Arthur Henry King, "Atonement: The Only Wholeness," *Ensign,* April 1975, 12; emphasis in original.

12. Victoria Anderson, "Filling the Void," *Ensign,* March 2006, 56.

13. Jennifer L. Thwaites, "Walking in Newness of Life," *Ensign,* January 1999, 47.

14. Barbara Szabo, in "The Power to Change," *Ensign,* January 1995, 10.

15. Name withheld, in ibid., 15–16.

16. Jeffrey R. Holland, "None Were with Him," *Ensign,* May 2009, 87–88.

17. Holland, "The Hands of the Fathers," *Ensign,* May 1999, 15, citing David Blankenhorn, *Fatherless America: Confronting Our Most Urgent Social Problem* (New York: Basic Books, 1995), 1.

18. See Judith S. Wallerstein and Joan B. Kelly, *Surviving the Breakup* (New York: Basic Books, 1996).

19. See National Center for Fathering, "The Consequences of Father-lessness"; available at http://www.fathers.com/content/index.php?option=com_content&task=view&id=391; accessed 20 August 2012.

20. M. Stern, J. E. Northman, and M. R. Van Slyck, "Father Absence and Adolescent Problem Behaviors: Alcohol Consumption, Drug Use, and Sexual Activity," in *Adolescence* 19 (74), 1984, 301–12.

21. See Dewey G. Cornell, Elissa P. Benedek, and David M. Benedek, "Characteristics of Adolescents Charged with Homicide: Review of 72 Cases," in *Behavioral Science and the Law* 5(1), 1987: 11–23.

22. R. A. Knight and R. A. Prentky, "The Developmental Adaptation and Adult Antecedents of Racist Subtypes," in *Criminal Justice and Behavior* 14 (4), 1987: 403–26.

23. See Paul L. Adams, Judith R. Milner, and Nancy A. Schrepf, *Fatherless Children* (New York: John Wiley & Sons, 1984).

24. Cynthia C. Harper and Sara S. McLanahan, "Father Absence and Youth Incarceration," in *Journal of Research on Adolescence* 14(3), 2004: 369–97.

25. Steven Moody.

26. Thomas S. Monson, "Your Patriarchal Blessing: A Liahona of Light," *Ensign,* November 1986, 65.

27. Robert D. Hales, "How Will Our Children Remember Us?" *Ensign,* November 1993, 9.

28. Charles Didier, "The Church: A Community of Saints," *Ensign,* April 2006, 48.

29. Jeffrey Reber.

30. Joseph Fielding Smith, "Eternal Keys and the Right to Preside," *Ensign,* July 1972, 88.

31. Maxwell, "Patience," 28.

Chapter 3: The Lie

1. The lie can afflict us both individually and collectively. Many couples believe theirs is a unique love in the world, unlike any other, stronger than any challenge, and chosen by God. Some couples take pride in this belief and assume a superiority to weaker, less special pairs. We may also believe that we have been born into a chosen family unlike those weaker, less worthy families in the world, probably because of our special premortal valiance and the closeness we shared before this life. Indeed, some talk as if there are special friendships, special wards and stakes, special countries ("the promised land") and special worlds (of all the worlds in God's universe, he sent Christ to this one), and so forth. Clearly, the false notion of special can be applied at many levels. We focus on the individual level here because individualism is so pervasive in our culture.

2. C. S. Lewis, *Mere Christianity* (New York: HarperCollins, 2001), 49.

3. Dieter F. Uchtdorf, "Pride and the Priesthood," *Ensign,* November 2010, 56.

4. Hugh Nibley, "A Strange Thing in the Land: The Return of the Book of Enoch, Part 8," *Ensign,* December 1976, 74.

5. Pradip Bhattacharya, "The Wish-Fulfilling Tree," available at http://www.beliefnet.com/Faiths/Hinduism/2000/08/The-Wish-Fulfilling-Tree.aspx; accessed 5 September 2012.

6. Purushottam Lal, "The Hindu Experience: An Examination of Folklore and Sacred Texts," in *Literature of Belief: Sacred Scripture and Religious Experience,* Neal E. Lambert, ed. (Provo, UT: Brigham Young University Religious Studies Center, 1981), 105.

7. Ibid., 104.

8. Nic Sheff, quoted in "Addiction: Life on the Edge," *CNN Presents,* 16 April 2009; transcript available at http://transcripts.cnn.com/TRANSCRIPTS/0904/19/cp.01.html; accessed 5 September 2012.

9. Stephen Diamond, "Is Greed Ever Good? Psychological and Spiritual Perspectives on Selfishness," *PsychologyToday.com,* 5 October 2011; available at http://www.psychologytoday.com/blog/evil-deeds/201110

/is-greed-ever-good-psychological-and-spiritual-perspectives-selfishness; accessed 5 September 2012.

10. M. Russell Ballard, "O That Cunning Plan of the Evil One," *Ensign,* November 2010, 108.

11. Delores Curley, "Eating to Fill a Void?" *Real Advice from a Weight Loss Coach,* March 2007; available at http://www.weight-loss-consultant .com/2007/03/eating-to-fill-void.html; accessed 5 September 2012.

Chapter 4: The Pharisee

1. Bible Dictionary, s.v. "Pharisee," 750.

2. Ibid.

3. By divine design, the law is too strict for any person to earn entry into the kingdom of heaven except Christ. As part of God's plan, our inadequacy before the law shows us our absolute dependency on the Savior's mercy and promotes our full submission to Him (see Chapter 7: The Disciple). The acceptance of the lie blinds Pharisees to this essential truth, keeping them from the tender mercies of their Lord, enlarging their feeling of the void, and giving them no hope for a reunion with their Heavenly Father.

4. In this way the Pharisee shares a common misconception of the truth with the Nihilist that will be addressed in greater detail in chapter 6.

5. Jeffrey Reber.

6. One is reminded of Luther's ninety-five theses concerning the corruption of the Catholic Church.

7. Jeffrey Reber.

8. Jeffrey Reber.

9. Jeffrey Reber.

10. Jeffrey Reber.

11. See Bible Dictionary, s.v. "Grace," 697.

12. Jeffrey Reber.

CHAPTER 5: THE EGOIST

1. Laurence J. Peter, cited in Everett L. Worthington, Jr., *Humility: The Quiet Virtue* (West Conshohocken, PA: Templeton Foundation Press, 2007), 69.

2. Dallin H. Oaks, "Unselfish Service," *Ensign,* May 2009, 95.

3. Elton O'Keeffe, *Egoism & the Crisis in Western Values* (London: Online Originals, 2011); available at http://www.onlineoriginals.com/showitem .asp?itemID=135; accessed 5 September 2012.

4. See Daniel Batson, "Addressing the Altruism Question Experimentally," in *Altruism and Altruistic Love: Science, Philosophy, and Religion in Dialogue* (Oxford: Oxford University Press, 2002), 89–106.

5. Steven Moody.

6. See Batson, "Addressing the Altruism Question," 89–106.

7. Viktor L. Frankl, *Man's Search for Meaning* (Boston: Beacon Press, 2006), 16–17.

8. C. S. Lewis, *Surprised by Joy: The Shape of My Early Life* (New York: Harcourt, Brace and Company, 1955), 164.

9. Thomas More, *Utopia* (Rockville, MD: Arc Manor, 2008), 69.

10. See Craig Nakken, *The Addictive Personality* (Center City, MN: Hazelden, 1996).

11. Jeffrey R. Holland, "'He Hath Filled the Hungry with Good Things,'" *Ensign,* November 1997, 64.

12. See B. Davidson, "A Test of Equity Theory for Marital Adjustment," in *Social Psychology Quarterly* 47 (1), 1984, 36–42.

13. Jeffrey Reber.

14. We recognize that there are people suffering in marriages of abuse and exploitation. It is not our intention in any way to suggest that suffering and pain are irrelevant in marriage or that leaving a marriage that is abusive is somehow wrong. Our concern here is the egoism that can emerge when individual pain and pleasure are the only criteria of marital well-being.

15. Unfortunately, many of the therapies used to treat these troubled marriages also assume a fundamentally hedonistic motivation in human

beings (see J. Ostenson, "Measuring marriages or measuring individual: An ontological analysis of marital therapy outcome measures," unpublished dissertation [Provo, UT: Brigham Young University, 2011]). Consequently, the hedonistic model of marriage is rarely questioned as to whether it is the best way to understand or treat marriage. Most therapies take it for granted as being true. As a result, many types of therapy treat marital problems by trying to increase received benefits (pleasure) for the dissatisfied partner(s) or by decreasing the dissatisfied partner's contributions (pain) to regain a perceived hedonistic homeostasis in the relationship. These therapies do not consider whether the emphasis on hedonism and perceived equity is itself the problem. Consequently, if efforts to help the dissatisfied partner see the relationship more equitably fail to resolve the dissatisfaction, then there is really nothing left for the hedonistically minded therapist to do to preserve the marriage. Moreover, because the assumption of hedonism is never questioned or challenged in the marital therapy, then divorce will do nothing to solve the problems of hedonism that undergirded the failed marriage, nor will it prepare the ex-spouses for the effects of the hedonistic perspective on their future relationships, including a possible new marriage. Consequently, the same hedonistic issues that plagued the previous marriage will likely arise in any new marriage.

16. Henry B. Eyring, "Prayer," *Ensign*, November 2001, 16.

17. "Line upon Line: Psalm 24:3–4," *New Era*, November 2007, 7.

18. Robert E. Parsons, "I Have a Question," *Ensign*, February 1991, 52.

19. Eyring, "Prayer,"16.

20. Douglas Bassett, "Faces of Worldly Pride in the Book of Mormon," *Ensign*, October 2000, 48.

21. Mahatma Gandhi, cited in *Gandhian Approach to Development and Social Work* (New Delhi, India: Concept Publishing Company, 2005), 131.

22. William R. Bradford, "Selfishness vs. Selflessness," *Ensign*, April 1983, 49.

23. Quinn G. McKay, "All That Glitters Isn't Celestial," *Ensign,* June 1987, 20.

24. Richard Tice, "Greed: When Enough Is Not Enough," *Ensign,* June 1989, 30.

25. Ibid.

26. Dieter F. Uchtdorf, "Pride and the Priesthood," *Ensign,* November 2010, 56.

27. Gordon B. Hinckley, "'Thou Shalt Not Covet,'" *Ensign,* March 1990, 4.

28. John De Graaf, David Wann, and Thomas H. Naylor, *Affluenza: the All-Consuming Epidemic, Second Edition* (San Francisco: Berrett-Koehler Publishers, 2002), 2.

29. Jeffrey Reber.

30. George Santayana, *The Life of Reason* (New York: Charles Scribner's Sons, 1920), 284.

31. F. Burton Howard, "Overcoming the World," *Ensign,* September 1996, 13.

32. Brigham Young, cited in Bryant S. Hinckley, *The Faith of Our Pioneer Fathers* (Salt Lake City: Deseret Book, 1956), 13.

CHAPTER 6: THE NIHILIST

1. Albert Camus, *The Rebel: An Essay on Man in Revolt* (New York: Vintage Books, 1991), 57–58.

2. Naomi Ward Randall, "I Am a Child of God," *Children's Songbook* (Salt Lake City: The Church of Jesus Christ of Latter-day Saints, 1989), 2–3.

3. Chauncey C. Riddle, "Prayer," *Ensign,* March 1975, 15.

4. See Erik H. Erikson, *Childhood and Society, Anniversary Edition* (New York: W. W. Norton and Company, 1986).

5. "The Wise Man and the Foolish Man," *Children's Songbook* (Salt Lake City: The Church of Jesus Christ of Latter-day Saints, 1989), 281.

6. Steven Moody.

7. *Merriam-Webster's Collegiate Dictionary, Eleventh Edition* (Springfield, MA: Merriam-Webster, 2005), s.v. "alienation."

8. Jeffrey Reber.

9. Jeffrey Reber.

10. See Gerald N. Lund, "Salvation: By Grace or by Works?" *Ensign*, April 1981, 17–21.

11. Russell M. Nelson, "Perfection Pending," *Ensign*, November 1995, 86.

12. Jeffrey Reber.

13. Hara Estroff Marano, "Pitfalls of Perfectionism," *Psychology Today*, 1 March 2008; available at http://www.psychologytoday.com/articles /200802/pitfalls-perfectionism; accessed 6 September 2012.

14. Dieter F. Uchtdorf, "Forget Me Not," *Ensign*, November 2011, 120. © by Intellectual Reserve, Inc.; used by permission.

15. Neal A. Maxwell, "'A Brother Offended,'" *Ensign*, May 1982, 38.

16. Craig Nakken, *The Addictive Personality: Understanding the Addictive Process and Compulsive Behavior* (Center City, MN: Hazelden, 1996), 59.

17. Ibid., 59–60.

18. Steven Moody.

19. Richard G. Scott, "To Heal the Shattering Consequences of Abuse," *Ensign*, May 2008, 41. © by Intellectual Reserve, Inc.; used by permission.

20. Jeffrey Reber.

21. See, for example, Martin E. P. Seligman, *Helplessness: On Depression, Development, and Death* (San Francisco: W. H. Freeman, 1975).

Chapter 7: The Disciple

1. Chauncey C. Riddle, "Becoming a Disciple," *Ensign*, September 1974, 81.

2. See http://www.youtube.com/watch?v=-DIETlxquzY; accessed 14 September 2012.

3. Gordon B. Hinckley, Ricks College regional conference, Rexburg, Idaho, 29 October 1995; cited in "Words of the Living Prophet," *Liahona*, December 1996, 8.

4. Jeffrey Reber.

5. Neal A. Maxwell, "'Swallowed Up in the Will of the Father,'" *Ensign*, November 1995, 24.

6. Jay E. Jensen, "Little Children and the Gospel," *Ensign,* January 1999, 33.

7. Robert C. Oaks, "Believe All Things," *Ensign,* July 2005, 33.

8. Maxwell, "Insights from My Life," *Ensign,* August 2000, 9.

9. Joseph H. Dean, "Before Thee, Lord, I Bow My Head," *Hymns of The Church of Jesus Christ of Latter-day Saints* (Salt Lake City: The Church of Jesus Christ of Latter-day Saints, 1985), no. 158.

10. Maxwell, "Becoming a Disciple," *Ensign,* June 1996, 12.

11. Ibid.

12. David A. Bednar, "Ye Must Be Born Again," *Ensign,* May 2007, 19–20.

13. Joseph B. Wirthlin, "The Great Commandment," *Ensign,* November 2007, 30.

14. Keith K. Hilbig, "Experiencing a Change of Heart," *Ensign,* June 2008, 33.

15. Ibid., 32–33.

16. Bruce R. McConkie, *Doctrinal New Testament Commentary,* 3 vols. (Salt Lake City: Bookcraft, 1966–73), 3:401.

17. Wirthlin, "Spiritual Bonfires of Testimony," *Ensign,* November 1992, 34.

18. Jeffrey Reber.

19. Robert D. Hales, "Christian Courage: The Price of Discipleship," *Ensign,* November 2008, 73.

20. Arthur Henry King, "Atonement: The Only Wholeness," *Ensign,* April 1975, 12.

21. Thomas Merton, *Conjectures of a Guilty Bystander* (Garden City, NY: Doubleday, 1966), 153–54, 155.

22. Steven Moody.

23. Merton, *Conjectures of a Guilty Bystander,* 155.

24. Jeffrey Reber.

CHAPTER 8: THE FLUIDITY OF QUADRANTS

1. Queen Elizabeth II, remarks at Irish State Dinner, Dublin Castle, 18 May 2011, cited in Alvin Jackson, *The Two Unions: Ireland, Scotland,*

and the Survival of the United Kingdom, 1707–2007 (Oxford: Oxford University Press, 2012), 182.

2. Jeffrey Reber.

3. William Fowler, "We Thank Thee, O God, for a Prophet," *Hymns of The Church of Jesus Christ of Latter-day Saints* (Salt Lake City: The Church of Jesus Christ of Latter-day Saints, 1985), no. 19.

4. Spencer J. Palmer, "Buddhism," *Ensign,* June 1972, 67.

5. David O. McKay, "Consciousness of God: Supreme Goal of Life," *Improvement Era,* June 1967, 80.

6. Byron Katie, with Stephen Mitchell, *Loving What Is: Four Questions That Can Change Your Life* (New York: Three Rivers Press, 2002), 4.

7. Jeffrey Reber.

8. Jeffrey Reber.

9. Neal A. Maxwell, "Enduring Well," *Ensign,* April 1997, 7.

Chapter 9: The Path to Discipleship

1. Bruce R. McConkie, *Mormon Doctrine,* 2d ed. (Salt Lake City: Bookcraft, 1966), 60.

2. Neal A. Maxwell, "King Benjamin's Manual of Discipleship," *Ensign,* January 1992, 8, 10.

3. Jeffrey R. Holland, "How Do I Love Thee?" *New Era,* October 2003, 6.

4. Steven Moody.

5. See http://mormon.org/brandon;accessed 6 September 2012.

6. Jeffrey Reber.

7. Jeffrey Reber.

8. Jeffrey Reber.

9. Cited in Erwin W. Lutzer, *When You've Been Wronged: Moving from Bitterness to Forgiveness* (Chicago: Moody Publishers, 2007), n.p.

10. Jeffrey Reber.

11. Jeffrey Reber.

CHAPTER 10: CONCLUSION

1. Dieter F. Uchtdorf, "The Love of God," *Ensign,* November 2009, 22.
2. Ibid., 22–23.
3. See Kiersten Renwick Monroe, *The Heart of Altruism* (Princeton: Princeton University Press, 1996).
4. Martin Luther King Jr., *Strength to Love* (Minneapolis: First Fortress Press, 1981), 53.
5. Jeffrey Reber.
6. Purushottam Lal, "The Hindu Experience: An Examination of Folklore and Sacred Texts," in *Literature of Belief: Sacred Scripture and Religious Experience,* Neal E. Lambert, ed. (Provo, UT: Brigham Young University Religious Studies Center, 1981), 104.
7. Ibid., 105.
8. Ibid.
9. Ibid., 105–6.
10. Ibid., 106.

Index

—→➤•◄←—

to comparison, 98–99; due to
perfection, 121–22
Apostles, 24, 33, 119, 143, 150
Atonement: as path to discipleship, ix,
155, 199; purifying power of, ix,
54, 118, 127, 169, 200; preceded
by spiritual death, 31–32; helps fill
the void, 37–38, 119; motivation
for, 84, 197, 202, 234–35;
conditions for receiving blessings
of, 141–42, 200, 204, 225, 243; as
path to discipleship, 155, 199–200,
213–14
Attraction, equity theory of, 88–89.
See also Hedonism
Autonomous self, 20, 21–22, 39
Azar, Beth, 26

Ballard, M. Russell, 46
Baptism, 34, 59, 211
Barrett, Justin, 26
Basking in reflected glory, 13
Bassett, Douglas, 95
Batson, C. Daniel, 83, 86
Bednar, David A., 155
Benjamin, King: on deserving versus
undeserving poor, 66–67; on all
being unprofitable servants, 70,
73, 234; on submissiveness, 147;
speech of, 155, 199
Benson, Ezra Taft, 95
BIRGing. *See* Basking in reflected
glory
Body dysmorphic disorder, 93. *See also*
Vanity
Book of Mormon: on Zoramites, 65;
on wealthy Nephites, 94; lessons
of past in, 102; on transformation,
157; anti-Christ Korihor in, 164; as
true witness of Christ, 209–10
Bradford, William R., 96
Buffardi, Lauren, 17

Cain, 41
Caletti, Deb, 1
Campbell, W. Keith, 4, 5–6, 17
Camus, Albert, 104
Cannon, George Q., 24
Celeb 4 A Day, 3–4
Celebrities: seen as characters they
play, 11; infatuation with, 12; and
self-esteem, 13–14
Charity: as motivator, ix, 200, 202; as
pure love of Christ, 132, 200; as
attribute of discipleship, 134–35,
138, 139, 174
"Chosen one": in movies, 9; in
literature, 9–10; resonance with, 22
Collective culture, 19.
Comparison, social: downward, 98,
99, 236; upward, 98, 100–101; in
quadrants of agency, 105, 196. *See
also* Greed: mistaking wealth for
prosperity
CORFing. *See* Cutting off from
reflected failure
"Creep," 5
Cultivation, of spiritual thoughts, 190,
192
Cushman, Philip, 20, 22
Cutting off from reflected failure, 14

de Graaf, John, 99
Dean, Joseph H., 150
Defense mechanism, 7, 33
Diamond, Stephen, 46
Didier, Charles, 35
Disciple: agency of 50; characteristics
of, 59, 132, 134, 171; definition
of, 132
Discipleship: two-step process of, 132–
36; scripture examples of, 134–35;
and self-love, 136–38; attributes
of, 138–70; humility in, 139–44;
submissiveness in, 145–49; being
yoked to Christ in, 150–54;

for prosperity, 97–98; through comparison, 98–101; replaces spirituality, 102–3
Guilt: and identification, 7; as source of nihilism, 124–28; from addiction, 186; as source of repentance, 201, 202; alleviated by Atonement, 202, 213–14; in discipleship, 216–17

Hales, Robert D., 35, 164
Harper, Cynthia C., 33
Heart of Altruism, The, 233
Hedonism: definition of, 87–88, 174; in marriage, 88–91; of Church members, 92
Helaman, 96, 135
Hilbig, Keith K., 156, 157
Hinckley, Gordon B., 99, 137, 177
Hindsight, in evaluation of quadrants of agency, 175–79
Hindsight bias, 63
Holland, Jeffrey R.: on Christ's Atonement, 31–32; on child-parent separation, 31; on hedonism, 88; on charity, 200
Holy Ghost. *See* Holy Spirit
Holy Spirit: as means to God's love, viii, 43; withdrawal of, viii, 32, 43, 81, 92; companionship of, viii, 34, 114; comfort through, 33–34, 104–5, 120, 125, 130; power of, 34; gift of, 58, 160; voice of, 94; in prosperity, 97; teachings of, 133, 158; influence of, 142, 155; as facilitator of empathy, 168; brought by Atonement, 169; thoughts filled with, 190–91; 191–94
Howard, F. Burton, 102
Humility: of Christ, 77, 147, 152; as attribute of discipleship, 139–44; 174; true form of, 145, 149;

measured by submission, 147; enables transformation, 157, 159

"I Am a Child of God," 105
I Am a Mormon, 201
Identification, 7. *See also* Defense mechanism
Individualistic culture: versus collective culture, 19; limitations of, 20, 21; paradox of, 20–21
Instrumentalization, 85–86, 156. *See also* Egoism: subtlety of
Isaiah, 106, 119
Israel: house of, 56; children of, 63, 193, 231–32, 234

Jacob, 48
Jensen, Jay E., 148
Jeremiah, 23, 151
Jesus Christ: light of, 34, 139, 142, 144; mercy of, 49; resistance to, 54; dependence on, 59, 74, 139–40, 144; law of, 72; power of, 76–77, 114, 145, 196; attributes and character of, 77, 119, 147, 152, 198; divine assistance of, 80; service centered on, 86–87, 163; alienation from, 113–14; completion in, 119; love of, 132, 200, 212; part of, 140; judgment by, 143–44; will of, 147, 149, 243; desires faith, 148; empathy of, 197; grace of, 205, 234; motivation of, 234. *See also* Atonement; Seeing with Savior's eyes; Yoked to Christ, being
Jingjing, Guo, 19
Job, 75, 76, 106, 107, 128
Judas Iscariot, 41

Katie, Byron, 185
Kelly, Joan B., 32
Killen, Sarah, 16–17
King, Arthur Henry, 28, 165

INDEX

Tree of life, Lehi's dream of, 132–34, 151–52

Truth: based on scriptures, vii; about human nature, vii, 23–38, 228; counterfeits for, 44; ways of responding to, 48–51, 174

Twenge, Jean, 4–5, 6, 15

Uchtdorf, Dieter F.: on pride, 40, 98; on perils of perfection, 121; on God's love, 226, 230

US Department of Health and Human Services, 32

Utopia, 87

Van Slyck, M. R., 32

Vanity, 92–95, 174

Vigilance: against pharisaism, 57; against nihilism, 108, 123; with respect to quadrant of agency, 167, 173, 191–96

Void: due to separation from God, vii–viii, 29, 38, 151; enlarged by adversary's lie, viii, 43–47, 48, 134, 227; filled by love of God, viii, 29, 37–38, 43, 47, 132–133, 155, 176, 228; felt by all, 22, 28, 151; significance of, 28–29; experienced by Christ, 31; due to separation

from parent, 32–33; misguided attempts to fill, 46–47, 57, 81, 82, 92; of the abused, 125–26; consequence of filling, 137, 151

Wallerstein, Judith S., 32

Wann, David, 99

"We Thank Thee, O God, for a Prophet," 177

Wirthlin, Joseph B., 155, 159

"Wise Man and the Foolish Man, The," 112

Wish-fulfilling tree, parable of, 44–45, 240–42

Yoked to Christ: as perfection, 119; as attribute of discipleship, 150–54, 174; enables transformation, 155, 157, 159; brings man closer to God, 170; by focusing on Christ, 205

Yorke, Thom, 5

Young, Brigham, 23, 103

Young, S. Mark, 8, 16, 18

Zoramites: poor versus wealthy, 41–42; mistook wealth for blessings, 65, 97; disease of, 95

About the Authors

——⋅►•◄⋅——

Jeffrey S. Reber, PhD, has a doctoral degree from Brigham Young University in psychology with a dual emphasis in social psychology and theoretical/philosophical psychology. He is an associate professor in the department of psychology at Brigham Young University. He has published numerous scholarly articles and book chapters on the relationship between religion and psychology and interpersonal relationships and is coeditor of a textbook on critical thinking about psychology. He is a licensed professional counselor and worked for several years as a part-time counselor with LDS Family Services. He also served for five years as the bishop of the Carrollton Georgia ward.

Steven Moody, MSW, received his bachelor's degree in psychology and social behaviors from the University of California–Irvine. He went on to receive his master's degree in clinical social work from the University of Southern California. At USC, his clinical focus was on working with families, including marital therapy and relationships. Steven worked for three years as a part-time counselor with LDS Family Services and is currently working as a therapist in private practice specializing in both relationships and addictions.